Best Wishes

[illegible] #14

MW00658902

PRAISE FOR
THUNDERMOUTH

"Joe is one of those unforgettable people. He was—and still is—an intense competitor on the ice and quite the off-ice storyteller. I'm sure you'll enjoy reading about his many decades in and around our great sport."

—**Bobby Clarke**, Hockey Hall of Fame center

"Joe and I have been buddies for almost sixty years. We were teammates for almost our entire careers in Boston and Philly. We've had so many great times together, on and off the ice. It's fun to relive some of them. We could do a whole book just on the stuff we got into together. I always appreciated his friendship, his leadership, and his enthusiasm. It's a beautiful thing! Also, he helped me a lot as a goalie. Joe always played the man, and nine times out of ten, I knew where the shot was going, whether it was coming from a left-handed or right-handed shooter. He bailed me out many times over the years. Of course, I bailed him out even more. Just kidding, Joe!"

—**Bernie Parent**, Hockey Hall of Fame goaltender

"When I was chasing my dream to be a Philadelphia Eagle in 1974, Joe Watson had his ultimate dream come true as a key part of the Stanley Cup champion Philadelphia Flyers. *Thundermouth* is a down-to-earth and unpretentious recollection of Joe's trek from the rural mill town of Smithers, British Columbia, to the tough streets of South Philly. Reading his book made me laugh and cry. Joe—along with his brother Jimmy—is still beloved by the tough Philly fans and community after all these years. After reading *Thundermouth*, you will be inspired to take the ultimate risk to make your wildest dream come true!"

—**Vince Papale**, former Philadelphia Eagle, coauthor of *The Last Laugh*, and subject of the feature film *Invincible*

"Joe was one of a kind—a great teammate, friend, and mentor for us young guys making a step into the NHL. He competed hard and was demanding in a *loud* way of us young guys. Our dressing room was never quiet if Joe was around! He had humor and a presence about him. I thank him to this day for helping me with my career. As Joe says in the book, a leader is someone who knows the way, goes the way, and shows the way. He lives by those words."

—Bill Barber, Hockey Hall of Fame left wing

"Besides being the ultimate warrior as a competitor and teammate, two words come to mind when describing Joe: authentic and unfiltered. His book is the same way, minus the legendary handshake. If you survive his grip, you will have just brushed up against a world-class human being."

—Bill Clement, two-time NHL All-Star, Hockey Hall of Fame broadcaster

"I first met Joe Watson when I was a student-athlete at the University of Pennsylvania. The spirit and enthusiasm for his team and teammates was always something I observed. Joe played a simple, honest, unappreciated game, not as a star but rather as a foundation block of a *true* team—a championship team. Joe, as the veteran leader, certainly was the cheerleader for all who wore the orange and black. He could make practice look like fun! Joe's book is a winner, and why not? He's been a winner every day since arriving from Smithers. Thank you for sharing your life's energy with us."

—Paul Stewart, U.S. Hockey Hall of Fame player and referee

THUNDERMOUTH

MASCOT BOOKS
an imprint of Amplify Publishing Group

www.mascotbooks.com

Thundermouth: Memoirs of a Broad Street Bully and NHL Lifer

©2024 Joe Watson. All Rights Reserved. No part of this publication may be reproduced, stored in a retrieval system or transmitted in any form by any means electronic, mechanical, or photocopying, recording or otherwise without the permission of the author.

Second Printing. This Mascot Books edition printed in 2024.

For more information, please contact:
Mascot Books, an imprint of Amplify Publishing Group
620 Herndon Parkway, Suite 220
Herndon, VA 20170
info@amplifypublishing.com

Library of Congress Control Number: 2023914640
CPSIA Code: PRV1223B
ISBN-13: 978-1-63755-950-5
Printed in the United States

In loving memory of my late mother,
Mary Watson:
a wonderful, loving mother,
my first and most devoted fan,
and the number-one supporter of hockey in Smithers.

THUNDERMOUTH

Memoirs of a Broad Street Bully and NHL Lifer

JOE WATSON

MASCOT BOOKS
an imprint of Amplify Publishing Group

"Win today, and we'll walk together forever."

—Coach Fred Shero

CONTENTS

FOREWORD

Although Joe Watson and I only spent one year together as teammates, he had an immediate impact on me as a rookie in the National Hockey League.

His work habits were exemplary, and he was a steady defenseman for us during his time in Boston. He was a player that I assumed would be a Bruin for a long time.

However, Joe ended up heading to Philadelphia as an Expansion Draft pick by the Flyers. Our loss was their gain. Joe would go on to play a significant role on two Stanley Cup championship teams.

I have no doubt that Joe will share his unique view of his time with the Flyers in true "Thundermouth" fashion!

Bobby Orr,
eight-time Norris Trophy winner
and two-time Stanley Cup champion

CHAPTER 1

You Can't Eat Scenery

Did you ever see the movie *Local Hero*? It was set in the fictitious village of Ferness in western Scotland, where little seemed to change from decade to decade.

The main character, named MacIntyre, is an oil-and-gas executive in Houston, Texas. He's been sent by his employer to acquire all the properties in the village, which are to be cleared out to make way for a refinery.

Upon his arrival, "Mac" is amazed that most of the residents of Ferness work multiple jobs, depending on the season and one-off opportunities to make some extra money. The residents, in turn, are surprised to learn that Mac only has one job.

Soon, the village's slower pace of daily life, the slightly eccentric but fundamentally good-hearted residents, and the place's natural beauty win Mac's heart. He becomes increasingly conflicted about the impending demise of the town and its way of life once the acquisition is completed.

Meanwhile, the local residents view Mac's arrival as a gateway to a better life. Privately, they are very eager to sell. They fear that the deal will fall through. Life isn't easy for them. While they currently eke out a living, their ability to continue doing so becomes less and less certain with each passing year.

During his stay in Ferness, Mac befriends a Russian fishing boat captain named Victor. A periodic visitor to the village, where he comes annually both for business and social reasons, Victor himself has grown fond of Ferness and its people.

One night, Mac confides in Victor that he is troubled by the thought of how an oil refinery will ruin the natural beauty of the village's pastoral beachfront and shoreline locales. He also hates the thought of forcing the residents to relocate from their homes. Victor assures him that the people of Ferness are very eager to see Mac succeed in his acquisition effort and tells him not to feel bad about it.

"You can't eat scenery," Victor explains.

When Mac later returns to his apartment in Houston, he tacks up photos of the people he met and the places he saw in Ferness. With Mac missing everyone more than he ever expected to at the beginning of his trip, the final scene of the movie depicts a telephone ringing in the old-fashioned phone booth in the village. The viewer assumes that it's Mac calling.

My hometown of Smithers, British Columbia, is a lot like a real-life Ferness.

Located in the Bulkley Valley in northwestern BC, roughly 750 miles north of Vancouver and 150 miles from the Alaska border, there is breathtaking natural beauty in the region. The spectacular Hudson Bay Mountain peak rises above my hometown. If you love the great outdoors and are into fishing, hunting, skiing, and/or hiking, the region is an ideal location.

When I was growing up, forestry was (and still is) the predominant driver of the Smithers economy—so was farming, often tied to the beef and dairy businesses.

Smithers was founded in 1913 as a railroad town. First Nation settlements in the Valley go back centuries before that. When I grew up in Smithers in the 1940s and 1950s, there were only about 800 people living there. The town has grown since then, but the population was still only 5,351 in 2016.

As with the village of Ferness, when I grew up in Smithers, it was common for people to work multiple jobs to make a living. The town was so small in those days that everyone lived within about three or four blocks of Main Street.

My dad, Joe Watson Sr., was a logger, a farmer, and a butcher depending on the time of year. One of my first chores was to salt animal hides after slaughter. My father would cut off the meat, and I'd salt the hides to eventually sell to a tannery company. I can still smell the damn things, and I remember all the flies in the house. We'd collect, preserve, and save the hides until there were enough to sell.

My grandfather owned the town grocery store in Smithers. My grandfather, my dad, and my uncles are all pictured in this 1943 photo. My dad, Joe Sr., is on the right. My grandfather is between my uncle Wilf (who later taught me how to skate) and my father.

My father would buy the hides for about two dollars and then sell them to Helford's Hides in Edmonton. He'd receive about ten dollars.

One of my childhood chums, and still a friend to this day, Larry Miller, also has vivid memories of my dad when we were kids.

"All the Watsons—the whole family, including Joe, his dad, his brothers, and his uncles—were very strong physically. Joe's dad, Joe Sr., was just this backwoods kind of man. Always wore a Mackinaw. How northern BC can you get, eh? You had to be tough to survive back then. I remember the hides and the beaver and fox pelts. Joe Sr. had this little farm. Chickens running around, that sort of thing. But that wasn't too unusual back then," Larry recalls.

My mom, Mary, had a small restaurant of her own and then went to work for other people. For several decades, she was a waitress at the Northern Star Café on Main Street, located around the corner from our house. The restaurant is still there, in fact, but nowadays it serves Chinese food as well as Canadian food on the menu.

"Mary was a nice lady. Very spirited. Her restaurant was downstairs from where my grandparents lived. The other thing I remember is that she went to every hockey game not only when her boys were growing up but also long afterward. She had her own special reserved seat. In fact, it had her name on it," Larry recalls.

My father was born in Owen Sound, Ontario. He was two and a half years old when his parents trekked west across Canada. They went to Prince Rupert by train. From there, they took a ferry to Hazleton. Somehow, they eventually settled in Smithers; the rail station wasn't even there yet at the time. My mom's family came to Canada from Yugoslavia.

I love Smithers and am proud to be a native "Smithereen." It was a good community in which to grow up, and I still enjoy my visits. Some of my family remains. My formative years there instilled in me the three guiding principles that have governed my entire life: desire, discipline, and dedication.

My work ethic and my unapologetically old-school world views were instilled in me in Smithers. Whatever you do in life, put your heart and soul into it, don't expect anything to be handed to you for free, be punctual, and be invested in the group and not the personal accomplishments. That's probably where my love of hockey comes from; hockey certainly reinforced those beliefs for me.

My first real job outside the house was working in a lumber mill. I was never one of the taller boys among my peers, but I was physically sturdy. My job was to stand alongside the green chain and, as the logs moved along, to pull and pile them for grading, sorting, and drying. It was called the "green" chain because the lumber itself was green in color before it was seasoned.

It was hard, physically exhausting work. On the flip side, it helped build my body in an era long before sports science existed. Early on, I used to get up at 5:30 a.m. and ride my bicycle to the work site—a 10-mile trip from my family's house, with a lot of hills to climb. That was too much, though.

Thankfully, one of the workers onsite took pity on me and started picking me up in his Volkswagen and driving me to the site.

Why am I telling this story before I talk about anything else from my upbringing, including my early years in hockey? It's because, as much as I love Smithers and am grateful that I grew up there, I also knew early on that I didn't want to spend my entire life there.

I didn't want my future to be in a local lumber mill or, later, doing physical labor with the local public works department. I didn't want to take trips into town wearing boots caked in cow shit like my father did. I didn't want to survive on rotating seasonal work. I had many friends who never left Smithers. Some had no ambitions or desire to ever do so. Others had the dreams but not the drive.

Let me make this clear: It wasn't that I felt that Smithers life was beneath me. I know where I come from and am grateful for it. At the same time, I always felt there had to be a different path. That path inevitably meant leaving Smithers and making a life somewhere else.

You can't eat scenery, eh?

I was born on July 6, 1943. I am my parents' firstborn. Eventually, there were six Watson children, all boys. My brothers Fred, Steve, Jimmy, Glen, and Jerry came after me, in that order. Jimmy, who is nine years younger than me, would later become my longtime NHL teammate on the Philadelphia Flyers.

I was about two years old when this photo was taken of me outside my family's home. There were always animals running around, and I could often be found chasing after them. I was as wide as I was tall in this photo!

There wasn't a hell of a lot to do in Smithers, at least compared to living in a city. But I never lacked for company. I had a great circle of friends who were my age or close to my age: Larry Miller, Teddy Veenstra, and "Stubby" McClain among them.

"Joe and I have known each other since we were about five years old," Larry Miller recalls. "We both had big families. We were both altar boys at our church; actually, all of us were until we were about 14 or 15 years old."

Yup, that's right. Let it never be said there were no altar boys among the Broad Street Bullies!

Faith was an important part of life in Smithers. Actually, my father had hopes when I was a kid that I'd someday pursue the priesthood. He wasn't too wild about it at first when I chased after my hockey-playing dreams instead. I knew, though, that the priesthood wasn't going to be for me. From the very beginning, my mom was supportive of my goal to pursue a hockey career.

What else was there to do in Smithers apart from school, church, and hanging out with friends? Sports was the biggie.

A lot of the fellas loved swimming, too. That wasn't my thing.

As a matter of fact, I never learned how to swim. On August 1, 1968—during a summertime trip home after my first season with the Flyers—I damn near drowned.

Recalls Stubby McLean, "One hot summer day, we went up to my in-laws' house for a swim in their pool. That particular day, my mother-in-law was hosting a bunch of her older lady friends. We made ourselves comfortable at poolside.

"Keep in mind that Joe can't swim. When the ladies had all moved out of the pool, he decided to get into the shallow end and walk around. That was OK for about five minutes, until he ventured out to the slope of the deep end. Suddenly, he was gasping and splashing around. The gals all thought this was quite funny. But then I realized he was in trouble. He was drowning!

"My brother-in-law and I both jumped into the pool and pulled him to the side of the pool where a group of ladies could help pull him out to safety. He was so strong that it was difficult to get near him without being dragged down. It was a scary couple of minutes for all of us. He was a bit traumatized but tried to laugh it off.

"All ended well. This is where it got humorous. The three ladies who helped pull him up onto the pool deck were Mrs. Garlic, Mrs. Pepper, and Mrs. Green. Joe said, 'Well, shit. It sounds like I was just saved from drowning by a goddamn salad!' That's Joe's sense of humor."

My favorite summertime sports passion was baseball. I could hit for power and average. My team, representing Terrace, played for the British Columbia senior championship in Victoria when I was 16. There, I was approached by a Seattle-based scout for the New York Yankees by the name of Eddie Taylor.

That shocked me. I had no idea I was being scouted! Taylor asked if I'd be interested in going to Fort Lauderdale, Florida, on a tryout basis to earn a professional baseball contract in the Yankees organization.

I was flattered, but it felt like too much of a pipe dream. I didn't like my chances of traveling quite that far away to compete against who knows how many American kids. This was back before Canadian players had a foothold in the U.S. minor leagues, much less Major League Baseball. I thought my chances were better in hockey.

I've never lost my love for baseball, though. I became a big fan of the Detroit Tigers when I was young. The way that came about was that I took a seven-day train trip to visit my cousin Jimmy in Bessemer, Michigan. It was the middle of summer and unbearably hot. But I had a chance to see the Tigers play the St. Louis Browns. Years later, during the NHL offseasons, I'd play men's league baseball in British Columbia. There were some good players in that league—quality semipros.

While the summers in Smithers were short, the winters were, well, exactly how you'd expect them to be living that far north. Winters were long, dark, and frigid. Temperatures routinely fell to 20 degrees below zero.

Skiing, tobogganing, and curling were all popular sports during the winter. Of course, there was plenty of hockey, too. We had only one rink back then, which was outdoors. Later, the town of Smithers purchased an old airplane hangar and converted it into an indoor rink. My mom, Mary, was very active and supportive of that campaign.

My uncle Wilf was a fine athlete in his own right in his youth. He was recruited by the Vancouver Lions hockey team and also excelled in tennis, baseball, and curling. He once dreamed of attending McGill University to study electrical engineering, but the death of my grandfather Fred changed the plans. He went to work instead at the grocery store my grandparents owned before he went into the hotel business.

Uncle Wilf was the first one to get me out on the ice. I was three and a half years old. He put me on double-runner blades at first. Then I held onto a chair and pushed it around. Before long, I was skating. I was never an exceptionally fast skater—in my head I can hear the late Fred Shero in heaven saying, "That's an understatement, Joe!"—but I had a low center of gravity and good balance.

We couldn't stay outside for long periods of time. We'd put on our tuques, gloves, and jackets, skate for two minutes, and retreat to an indoor building to warm up before our next shift.

Recalls Larry Miller, "I played some hockey with Joe when we were kids. I liked it but not as much as Joe. He was obsessed with it. I remember one Christmastime when we were about seven or eight years old. We'd gotten hockey gear for Christmas. Santa was very good to us. Well, the very first chance he had, Joe drug me to the outdoor rink. It was nearly 20 degrees below zero. I gotta admit, I didn't love that, eh? But Joe ate it up. Also, he was ambidextrous, and that certainly helped him in sports. He was just a great all-around athlete."

When we weren't on the outdoor rink, we would play shinny on Lake Kathlyn when it froze up solid in the winter. If we didn't have a puck, we'd use frozen horse turds. Many years later, Jimmy told the late Jack Chevalier (the *Philadelphia Bulletin* beat writer who first dubbed our team "the Broad Street Bullies"), "True frustration was when the ice was beautiful on Lake Kathlyn and it was your turn to go break off a piece of turd."

That wasn't just a humorous line for the newspapers. That was truly what we did. My uncle Wilf operated a hotel along Lake Kathlyn called the Lakeside Motel.

Another one of my dad's brothers, my uncle Walter, was a fireman in Smithers.

Larry Miller recalls, "I started in the fire department myself when I was

16. Walter was a veteran in the department, and he showed me a lot. He was another guy who was damn tough, eh? Strong as an ox. I seen him pick a grown man up on his shoulders and carry him down the ladder."

Larry's father died when he was still a kid, so he had to go to work at a very young age to help support the family. As I noted earlier, I worked, too, because it was expected of all of us, but I had my hockey to look forward to.

Early on when I played, I was a winger. One time, I skated through all five players on the other team and scored a goal. I remember that our coach, Claude Munson, who was a local druggist as his "real-life" job, said to me, "Joey, if you can keep doing that, you'll play in the National Hockey League someday."

Well, I couldn't keep doing that. A subsequent coach, Joe Tennant (railroad engineer was his main line of work), asked me to switch positions and play defense. We were going to a place called Quesnel—best thing that ever happened to me.

Let's be honest: I was not going to be a big goal-scoring forward as I moved up the ladder, but I could play pretty solid defense. Besides, it meant a lot of ice time. I never switched back and never regretted it.

In 1959, a local community group in Smithers pooled the money to purchase a World War II aircraft hangar at Terrace Airport (a.k.a. Northwest Regional Airport Terrace-Kitimat) for the cost of one dollar. It was hauled to Smithers and converted into a rink. My mom was one of the volunteers who showed up every day to help build the rink, wielding a hammer and nails. The rink did not get artificial ice until 1963, but that was well after I was gone. There was no glass above the boards.

My mom was a regular attendee at hockey games. She went to every game she possibly could, not just to watch me and then my brothers play but to watch all the local boys. To put it mildly, she got very emotionally involved in the games. I got that from her, I guess.

This is a legendary story in Smithers, but I promise you that it's not exaggerated: When I was 14 years old, an opposing player named Marty Terhersky from Prince George checked me hard into the boards—a little too roughly for my mom's liking. In a flash, she reached over the boards and grabbed the other kid by the hair.

"No one touches my boy!" she hollered, yanking his head back with both hands.

I am one of six boys born to my parents, Joe Sr. and Mary. There were three of us at the time of this photo with my mother: me, Fred, and Steven. Jimmy, Glen, and Jerry came along later.

Long after my brothers and I were grown, my mom still attended every game. She always sat in the same seat, which said "Reserved for Mary Watson"—not that anyone would have dared try to take it from her.

Another time, years later, my brother Jimmy was playing a baseball game our mother attended. He was running the bases, rounding second and heading for third, when he lost his balance and fell. Our mom was sure the other team's second baseman tripped him when he went past. Mom marched directly onto the field, wielding her ever-present, oversized orange handbag and preparing to thrash the other team's player with it. Jimmy was mortified but calmed her down.

People I meet, especially Flyers fans, always ask me about my relationship with Jimmy when we were growing up. Keep in mind that Jimmy is nine years younger than me, and I left to play junior hockey when I was 16. It's probably fair to say that I grew much closer with him as we got a little older.

I have three main memories of Jimmy when we were kids.

First, he loved to tag along with my friends and me, especially when we went off playing sports or biking. If we were playing baseball, we made him the catcher. I would pitch and throw the ball as hard as I could at him. If we had a makeshift shinny on Lake Kathlyn in the winter, yes, he was the first one elected to go get a frozen horse turd if we needed a puck.

Second, Jimmy was, and still is, an even bigger sports junkie than I am. I'd go off with my friends at night or have a game. When I'd come home, there was always a sheet of paper on my bed. My brother, Steven, did it, too. They'd listen to the radio and write down the baseball scores and let me know which players had a good game. He, too, was a Detroit Tigers fan.

Finally, Jimmy was always my biggest fan. He'd get the newspaper, cut out any articles about me, and give them to me. He's often told people that I was his hero. Over time, I would say the roles reversed.

Jimmy was one hell of a natural athlete: a smooth and polished shortstop in baseball and a very smart and talented two-way hockey player—an excellent skater, a strong defender, and very smooth at moving the puck up to the forwards.

I'll talk more about Jimmy as a hockey player later, but I will say for now that it was a privilege to see my kid brother evolve into an NHL prospect and then to be his teammate as he became a five-time NHL All-Star.

As a matter of fact, I think Jimmy could excel even in the current-day NHL game. He had the feet to play at today's faster pace and the abilities on both sides of the puck to earn his coach's trust in a lot of different situations.

If Jim had ever cared about individual offensive stats rather than team wins and losses, he'd have put up more points than he did. He was never a selfish player at all, just a consummate team player who played the game the right way at all times. Physically, he was a couple inches taller than me.

Four of my five brothers played hockey when we were growing up: Glen, Steven, Jim, and Jerry.

Glen later went on to coach minor and junior hockey for many years. Jerry was a really good player in his youth, too, but he was the youngest and the last one to leave the nest.

My parents got divorced. I don't know if they ever formally obtained a divorce, but they permanently separated. Jerry didn't want to leave Mom alone to go off playing hockey. He stayed in Smithers for her sake. I give him a hell of a lot of credit for that.

Our brother Fred did not play much hockey. Steve, a high-scoring center and excellent puckhandler as a youngster, later went to work in the same restaurant where my mother worked. To this day, Steve has a heart as big as the Canadian tundra—just a caring and gentle soul and a religious man.

This was taken around 1947 or early 1948.
I'm about four years old in this picture.

The Watson home was chaotic and noisy. My five brothers and I were widely spaced in age, so there wasn't sibling rivalry in that sense. Of course, we had the usual spats that brothers do, then we'd forget about them and move on.

In 1957, a buddy of mine and I went out for a drive in his convertible on a Sunday after church. We had a serious accident, and I was thrown from the vehicle. My brother Fred discovered me face down and bleeding. He rescued me. I was rushed to the hospital and had 54 stitches in my head. This was long before the days of pagers or cell phones, and my mom did not find out for hours what had happened.

I was lucky that I wasn't severely injured or even killed in the accident.

As some of you may know, Smithers has gained a reputation over the years as a breeding ground for NHL players. In addition to me and Jim, there were the Flockhart brothers, Ron (who later played with Jim and me on the Flyers) and Rob (who, sadly, passed away in early 2021 at age 64).

We knew the Flockhart family very well. In fact, I worked for Ron and Rob's dad, Verne, for a time.

Former NHL players Alan Kerr and Ron Homenuke hailed from Hazleton, BC, which is 38 miles from Smithers as the crow flies and 46 miles by car. However, both played in Smithers when they were young.

I was a proud member of the Smithers Elks. This is one of my earliest hockey photos.

More recently, native Smithereen Dan Hamhuis had a 1,148-game NHL career as a defenseman. Dan is nearly 40 years younger than I am, but I always liked the way he played the game.

I've met Hamhuis several times at the annual Smithers Celebrity Golf tournament. He's a nice guy. The tournament is organized by a longtime friend of mine named Kent Delwisch (you'll meet him later), who has raised a lot of money for local charities over the years, especially the Smithers Child Development Centre, with which my old friend Larry Miller was deeply involved.

Smithers was a finalist—finishing in the top five—of the 2007 Kraft Hockeyville competition, which was televised each week on the CBC during Hockey Night in Canada broadcasts. The grand prize was cash to upgrade the local arena and the chance to host an NHL preseason game

(New York Islanders vs. Atlanta Thrashers). Unfortunately, Smithers didn't win. North Bay, Ontario, took the prize.

Prince George had a game in Vanderhoof in 1958. Due to an injury on the team, I was offered a chance to play for Vanderhoof. I accepted. I thought these were the best players I'd ever seen.

In 1960, I was offered fifty dollars to play for Vanderhoof. My cousin Jim Eby drove to Vanderhoof in his Volkswagen. We got stuck in the snow and had to dig his car out. I also got to play in the BC Juvenile championship. We made it to the finals before losing 6-3 in the championship game.

I was disappointed but not for long. In addition to getting paid to play hockey—the first time in my life that happened, and quite a thrill, I must admit—I soon found out that there was a scout from the NHL's Boston Bruins in attendance. I had no idea at the time, but he approached me and gave me his card. He also gave his card to two of my teammates: Butch Morris, a center, and Brian Collison.

On July 16, 1960, shortly after my 17th birthday, I was invited by the Bruins organization to try out for the Estevan Bruins, a junior team the NHL club owned in Estevan, Saskatchewan.

There were two hitches: First of all, I wasn't guaranteed a spot. I'd soon find out that there were 104 tryout invitees competing for four roster spots. Second of all, I had to get myself to Estevan. That's a nearly 2,800-mile drive from Smithers. I didn't own a car, so my coach Joe Tennant drove me to Estevan.

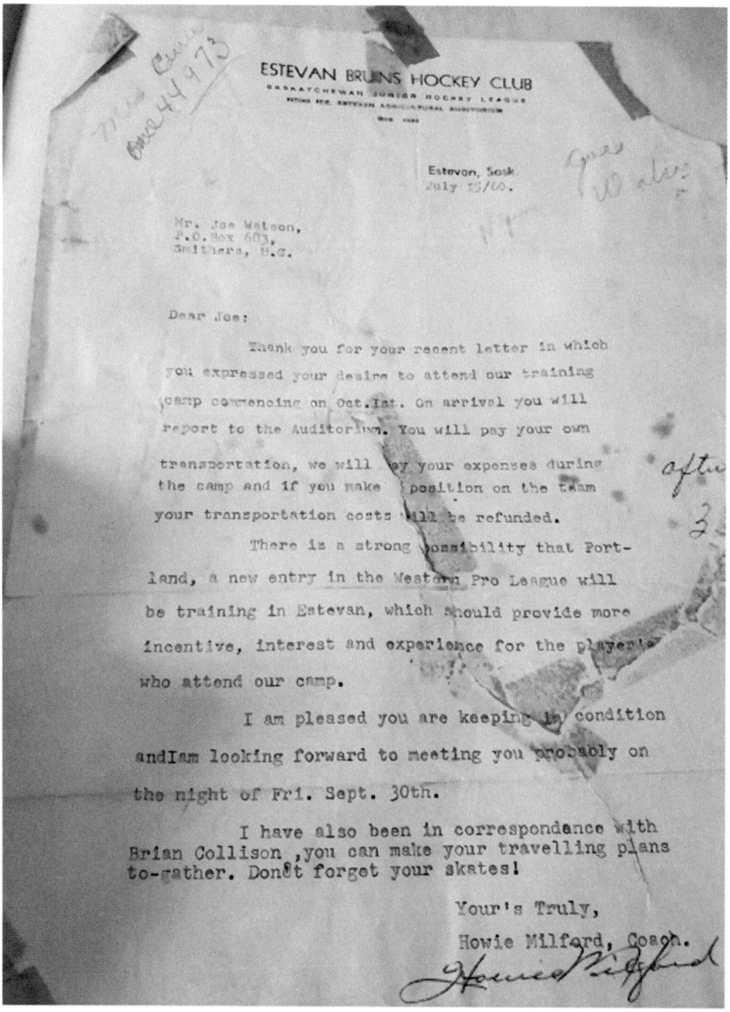

ESTEVAN BRUINS HOCKEY CLUB
SASKATCHEWAN JUNIOR HOCKEY LEAGUE

Estevan, Sask.
July 15/60.

Mr. Joe Watson,
P.O. Box 603,
Smithers, B.C.

Dear Joe:

Thank you for your recent letter in which you expressed your desire to attend our training camp commencing on Oct. 1st. On arrival you will report to the Auditorium. You will pay your own transportation, we will pay your expenses during the camp and if you make a position on the team your transportation costs will be refunded.

There is a strong possibility that Portland, a new entry in the Western Pro League will be training in Estevan, which should provide more incentive, interest and experience for the player's who attend our camp.

I am pleased you are keeping in condition andIam looking forward to meeting you probably on the night of Fri. Sept. 30th.

I have also been in correspondance with Brian Collison ,you can make your travelling plans to-gather. Don't forget your skates!

Your's Truly,
Howie Milford, Coach.

This letter, inviting me to try out for the Estevan Bruins, changed my life. There were 104 players invited. Only four were offered spots. I didn't think I had much chance at first, but I was one of the four who made it.

CHAPTER 2

Have Skates, Will Travel

When I first received the invitation to go to Saskatchewan to try out for the Estevan Bruins, I was extremely excited. I knew of the Saskatchewan Junior Hockey League team and that it was a feeder club for the NHL's Boston Bruins. I knew vaguely there had been a major riot in Estevan—a violent clash between striking coal miners and the Royal Canadian Mounted Police in which three people were killed—some 12 years before I was born. I didn't know all the particulars, but newspapers throughout Canada would still harken back to it whenever there was labor unrest that threatened to escalate.

I knew that I was a good defenseman for someone my age and that I was physically a little stronger than most of my peers. Back in Smithers, apart from the physical labor I did to earn a little money for my family, I used to do pushups every day to build my upper body, and I used to go running. My friends thought I was nuts—even most of my fellow hockey players. In the 1950s, very few trained that way.

Actually, I remember a few times in my midteens when I'd go out running. Buddies of mine would ride slowly past in a car, waving beer bottles at me. At heart, I was still one of the guys—I liked grabbing a babalooey [beer] or two as much as the next red-blooded Canadian male, and I certainly had just as much interest in the girls as they did—but I guess I was just a little more driven to play sports than they were. Hockey and baseball weren't just fun distractions or hobbies to me.

Larry Miller recalls, "Joe never took himself seriously. He loves to laugh and can laugh at his own expense. But when it came to sports, he was extremely serious. He hated to lose at anything. Hated excuses for losing. Hated anyone giving less than 100 percent because he always gave his all. Something else that was always real important to Joe for as long as I've known him: being on time for everything. Lateness drove him nuts."

One thing I didn't fully grasp when I first got the invite to try out for Estevan was just how far away it's located from Smithers. Estevan is in southernmost Saskatchewan, about 10 miles north of the United States border. It's a short drive from Estevan to Noonan, North Dakota.

I spent five days riding in the car with Joe Tennant to get to Estevan. We traveled nearly 2,800 miles, mostly down unpaved roads.

I think that experience helped me start gaining a deeper appreciation of just how expansive Canada's geography really is. It's one thing to see on a classroom map, but physically traveling some of those distances by car, bus, or train gives you a more vivid sense of how big the country is. Over the years, I've had countless similar revelations in minor-league, NHL, and NHL Alumni hockey. Even all these years later, though, I marvel at how our world is so big in terms of size and yet so small in terms of human nature. People are basically the same wherever you go.

Something else that I was uncertain about when I first went to Estevan for the tryouts was this: I didn't know how I compared as a hockey player to the pool of teenage players in Canada beyond my home region in British Columbia. As a matter of fact, I was upset at first when I was informed that I was one of 104 players trying out for the Estevan Bruins. There were also players a year or even two years more experienced against a wider array of competition mixed in among the pool of hopefuls. I'd soon find out that there were only four open roster spots.

"Why would you bring me to something like this?" I demanded.

I was told this: If the Bruins' scout didn't think that I was capable of winning one of the spots, he wouldn't have wasted his time or mine with the invitation. I had to just be myself on the ice: Don't try to be flashy to impress the Bruins. Play sound defense. Compete hard. If I gave it my best and I fell short, so be it.

My first year in Saskatchewan, I was assigned to Estevan's feeder team, the North Battleford Beaver Bruins. I was still too young to play for Estevan. We won the championship, and I got an eye-opening experience about how ruthless and tough hockey could be even at that level.

While in North Battleford, I'll never forget the experience of seeing former NHL player Fred Sasakamoose—playing in a Saskatchewan Ice Hockey Association game—run roughshod on the ice. He even slugged a referee. I had barely turned 17 years old. Yes, it was scary as hell.

The next season, I had the chance to earn a spot with the main club in Estevan. I'm sure you've heard the term "roster battles" used in a variety of different team sports, both in yesteryear and in current times. Nowadays, it's just a figure of speech. Back then, especially in hockey—from junior to the National Hockey League and everywhere in between—it was an apt description in the literal sense. Throughout my active hockey career, training camps were not for the faint of heart. Things got very rough. Fights were a daily occurrence and not always limited to the ice.

At the camp, I got into fisticuffs several times with a player named Harvey Roy. We had three or four full-blown fights. Here's the thing: all eyes were on you.

The coach wasn't necessarily concerned with whether you won or got beat, but he was taking stock of whether you got intimidated or stood up for yourself. If you were in that first group—and got labeled a "chickenshit" player—it didn't matter how naturally skilled you were as a stickhandler or passer unless those skills were off the charts. I wasn't one to start fights, but I didn't back down if someone challenged me.

Same thing with the way I approached checking. I was never a "put 'em through the boards" kind of hitter, but I knew how to angle my opponent to the boards and take him out of the play. I always took pride in this as a player: I was a physical defender as well as being strong enough to

Before I progressed to the Estevan Bruins, I was assigned to the feeder team, the Beaver Bruins, in North Battleford, Saskatchewan. We won the league championship, and I had a blast.

win most positional and stick-to-stick battles, but, unlike many "defensive defensemen" of my playing era, I never took a lot of penalties at any level of the game.

I never had even 60 penalty minutes in any season of junior, minor league, or NHL hockey. I felt I was more valuable on the ice than in the penalty box. When you aren't a big scorer, you need to contribute in other ways to play regularly. The best way I knew how was to be reliable positionally and physically competitive on the boards and in front of the net but to play within the rules as much as I could.

Each day, the ranks of tryout hopefuls thinned. By the end of day five, there were 100 guys gone. There were four left, and I was one of them. I was now officially Boston Bruins property. That's how it worked before the creation of the NHL Entry Draft.

Until 1968, NHL teams sponsored junior teams across Canada and laid claim to their players' NHL rights. Technically, the practice ended in 1963 with the creation of the NHL Entry Draft. However, the NHL grandfathered in their recognition of the six preexpansion teams' rights to certain players. In the province of Quebec, for example, the Montreal Canadiens had a virtual NHL-rights monopoly on all the best young French-speaking junior players in the province.

In the case of the Bruins, the team laid claim to players in Ontario from the Niagara Falls Flyers and Oshawa Generals (including future Hockey Hall of Famer Bobby Orr). The Estevan Bruins were a prospect feeder team in the west. Honestly, the western kids were not as highly regarded by the Bruins as our eastern counterparts. The Niagara Falls Flyers landed more prized recruits and won Memorial Cups, and its alumni tended to get stronger NHL consideration than most of the farm kids from western Canada who toiled for Estevan.

That was certainly the case, at least, when Leighton "Hap" Emms moved on from the owner/GM/coach of the Niagara Falls Flyers to being the Boston general manager. He made no pretense about the fact that he didn't think much of the western kids, on or off the ice, and preferred the crew from Niagara Falls. In those early days, however, I was blissfully ignorant to how organizational politics worked within NHL clubs in the six-team league.

Our coach and GM in Estevan was the late Roderick "Scotty" Munro, a prolific junior hockey coach who was instrumental in the establishment of what's now the Western Hockey League (WHL). He was a short and stocky kind of guy. First time I met him, he took a drag on a cigarette and introduced himself to us before a team meeting.

"Listen, boys," he said. "We had a very good team last year, and we're gonna be good this year. We're looking for four players. That's all we'll need."

When I made the team, Scotty called me into his office.

"I'm proud of ya, Joey," he said. "We've never had a kid come from where you're from who made it on our team. You're the first. We wanna sign you to a contract."

"A contract?" I asked.

My friend Brian Collison made it, too.

I was thrilled to be wearing the Estevan Bruins' uniform, competing against more challenging competition, and making big money for it. Well, big money to me at least.

I got $150 a month ($75 every two weeks) to play for Estevan. My billet family was our trainer John MacDonald's household. I paid $120 a month for room and board and had $30 left over for spending money.

Thirty dollars to spend? Holy smokes, I was in hillbilly heaven! I've never been a big spender, anyway.

Remember that famous episode of *The Cosby Show* where the Heathcliffe Huxtable character uses Monopoly money to teach his son, Theo, the value of a dollar? The teenager gets cocky when he has some money left over after his dad subtracts from his "take-home pay," and Theo takes a little back, saying he'll skimp on rent, transportation, and food.

"You plan on having a girlfriend?" the father asks.

"You better believe it!" the teenager replies.

The dad nods and takes away every dollar of the remaining money.

At each level of hockey I played, from junior to pro and then after our on-ice careers, I had my share of teammates who spent money faster than they made it. I liked to have a good time, too, but even as a teenager in Estevan, I was always aware of how much I had available to spend and when the next time would be that I'd get paid. In those years, I wasn't thinking about hockey from a financial standpoint. I was just thrilled to get paid at all. I also knew that I had to stretch out my spending money for as long as possible.

It's just how I grew up. I saw my parents scramble for every dollar they made. To this day, if I see a quarter lying on the ground, I'll pick it up and pocket it.

Anyway, I settled in fast in my temporary home. I was fine with living so far from home during hockey season, although it severely limited my opportunities to go home to visit. But the hockey life suited me well, and I liked playing for Estevan.

Scotty Munro was a real colorful character: gruff at the rink but usually jolly away from the ice. In his youth, he'd been a two-sport standout in hockey and baseball for the Moose Jaw Canucks. As he told anyone who'd listen, the Boston Bruins once clamored for his services as a goaltender until a serious injury suffered at his off-ice workplace—an oil refinery explosion from which he survived but suffered second- and third-degree burns over his legs—prematurely ended his playing days.

Munro moved the former Humboldt Indians club to Estevan, which built a new rink to house the club. The building cost $250,000 to construct. Tickets in those days cost $1 per adult, 50 cents for kids ages 12 to 18, and 25 cents for children under 12.

As a coach, Scotty was a fiery sort of guy. He had a tree-stump build and weighed in at 210 pounds. He expected his players to be tough, both physically and mentally. A Lethbridge Herald reporter hit the nail on the head in a 1966 article in which the journalist described what Munro was like in the locker room, speaking to us players in a "sand-blast bark" tone of voice.

"Pointing a stubby finger," the journalist recounted, "Munro bulls into the dressing room and growls: 'You [bleep], you! You didn't play worth a damn out there!'"

I remember one time that Scotty was so angry at the way we played in a road loss that he made us skate at 1:00 a.m. after we arrived back in Estevan. Even by old-school standards, he was a hard-driving coach.

Munro admitted to the reporter that his players' description of him was true, but he only did it to motivate. "I never yet let one of my kids go to bed feeling bad about it," Munro said.

That was true, too. He cared about his players. As a strategist and practice coach, Munro was never in the same realm as a coach as the legendary Freddy Shero. But in his own way, Munro was a creative, outside-the-box thinker.

Back in 1958–59, he was suspended for the season due to an incident during an Estevan game against Moose Jaw in which Munro physically assaulted referee Don Inglis when a heated argument over a call escalated into a physical confrontation. Undaunted, Scotty announced the appointment of his wife, Rose, as the Bruins' new coach. He gleefully told the newspapers that he'd scoured the league's bylaws, and there was nothing that said a woman was ineligible to coach.

In 1961, Munro hired Howie Milford as the new Estevan coach but reassumed the job behind the bench when Milford resigned to take a higher-paid job with the Omaha Knights. Around that time, Munro tried to gain a competitive edge by placing a walkie-talkie-like speaker and receiver in players' equipment, in the style of an NFL football team. That idea lasted one game before it was ditched.

As I said, Scotty was quite the unusual character. But I was a better player for my time playing for him. We had a strong roster, but we came together as a team under our coach. Scotty died from cancer at age 58, a few months after the Flyers won the 1975 Stanley Cup.

We had one hell of a goalie on Estevan: a guy by the name of John Wayne Norris, whom we all called Jack. He was my roommate and a good friend.

Jack later broke into the National Hockey League in Boston and spent parts of four seasons in the NHL, but his career was not what it could—and should—have been. In an exhibition game against the Chicago Black Hawks, the goalie got struck in the head by a Bobby Hull shot. Do the math: maskless goaltender plus banana curve stick plus one of the hardest shooters of all time firing a rising puck at him. The equation added up to a horrifying scenario.

Jack could have been killed. He survived the injury, thank goodness, and had a 13-year pro career but was never the same caliber of goaltender again after the on-ice accident. It was a damn shame.

Norris was once a prospect with potential that was comparable to some of the other guys who followed in the Bruins system—future Hockey Hall of Famers Bernie Parent and Gerry Cheevers (who originally got his start with the Toronto Maple Leafs). At least Norris had a lengthy pro career.

In 1961–62, we had a very good team in Estevan, posting a 34-10-12 record. Center Phil "Skip" Krake was a prolific goal scorer who later broke into the NHL in Boston and played about 450 combined games between the NHL and World Hockey Association. Ron Willy was a very good minor-league forward for many years after turning pro. Right winger Art Chiupka became a fan favorite later as a member of the minor-league Philadelphia Ramblers and Jersey Devils. Left winger Ron Boehm had a lengthy minor-league career, too, and we later played together for a time with the Minneapolis Bruins.

Another teammate of mine in Estevan was a fellow by the name of Terry Simpson. He didn't have a long playing career, but he eventually became an NHL head coach, including a season with the Philadelphia Flyers in 1993–94. He also had stints behind the bench with the New York Islanders and the original Winnipeg Jets.

We had a good staff as well as good players. John MacDonald was one of the better trainers in the Western League and served a long tenure that spanned until his retirement in the early 1970s (the Estevan team's second incarnation). I think that people who have not played—or at least worked closely with—a hockey team don't quite realize how instrumental the trainers/equipment guys are to the staff. They really are a vital part of the team and of players' day-to-day lives. I was well treated when I boarded in the MacDonald family's house.

Our team doctor was Dr. Robert Inglis. He was something of a legend in Estevan during a medical career that spanned 41 years. Dr. Inglis was an old-school sort of doctor that simply doesn't exist anymore: the kind who made house calls, knew most everyone in the community by name, and could do anything from treating hockey injuries to delivering babies.

During the early 1940s, Dr. Inglis shared a medical practice in Estevan with Dr. Jim Creighton, who'd served in the Royal Canadian Horse Artillery and was later a surgeon and physician during World War I. The doctors' office had one of the first telephones in Estevan. Their phone number was "3." I thought nothing of it. Growing up in Smithers, our house phone number was "19."

Hard to forget those kinds of phone numbers, eh? I remember that the local operator worked a switchboard, and she—it was always a woman—or pretty much anyone could hear your entire conversation.

For many years—from Estevan through the minor leagues and up to when I played in the NHL—I'd call home to my family in Smithers most every Sunday. There were two reasons why Sunday was "Call Day."

Firstly, we didn't play games on Sunday back then. I'd go to mass on Sunday morning and then phone home at night. Secondly, calling on Sunday was cheaper than on any other day of the week. Couldn't call as often as I'd have liked. Long-distance calling charges were damn expensive! So I did the once-a-week calls to update my family on how I was doing and tell my mom about how our team was playing since we last spoke.

Our team made long road trips. None were longer than the 600-mile jaunt to play the Flin Flon Bombers. At the time, Flin Flon was the most northerly junior team in Canada, and Estevan was the furthest south. Ordinarily, we traveled to road games in a small school bus—hardly spacious even before the hockey gear was loaded and packed to the gills once we

This was our Estevan championship-winning team from the 1962–63 season. I am seated on the bottom row, second from the right.

were all aboard. For trips to Flin Flon, at least, we had a proper full-sized bus. I remember thinking how nice it was.

Something else I remember in hindsight about going to the Whitney Forum in Flin Flon. I found out years later that the Bombers' stick boy in the early 1960s when I was playing for the Estevan Bruins was a kid by the name of Robert Earle "Bobby" Clarke. Clarkie is six years younger than me, so he was about nine or 10 years old at the time.

Hockey is a small world, but it's a vagabond's lifestyle. Have skates, will travel.

We played some exhibition games against the MJHL's Winnipeg Rangers, which featured a high-scoring center named Jimmy Johnson. I subsequently played against him in each step up the hockey ladder. Later, from 1967–68 through about half of the 1971–72 season, we became teammates and friends on the Flyers. Jimmy was then traded to the Los Angeles Kings in an eight-player deal that, among others, brought Ross Lonsberry to the Flyers.

Ross, who was nicknamed "Roscoe" or "Rabbit," was a guy I played with primarily as a teammate. We very briefly played together (one game) in Estevan, then later in the minor leagues for Minneapolis. In the NHL, we were teammates on the Bruins, opponents when he played for LA, then teammates again in Philadelphia.

I'll discuss both of those guys in more detail later. But I just wanted to show how in hockey, and in any workplace, you tend to encounter the same people over and over. I'll also say here that both Roscoe, who passed away in 2014, and Jimmy, who died in 2021, were good men and rock-solid hockey players. I miss both guys and other members of our hockey fraternity who are no longer with us.

The rivalries in our league were fearsome. The crowds in a lot of the mining communities and cattle towns got riled up at the games, and things got rough on the ice, too.

Gordie Howe, who was already an NHL star when I was a kid, was the prototypical western Canadian player that most every kid, for decades to come, emulated. Of course, no one could score like Gordie, and few were nearly as physically strong and tough as him, but they sure could let the elbows fly pretty good. You always had to be alert.

As I said, the crowds could get pretty ornery. Let's put it this way: Years later, I was not surprised by what happened in Regina, Saskatchewan, during the 1980 Memorial Cup tournament. My own NHL career was over and done by that point, but not much had changed in the rough-and-tumble western junior towns since I'd played there 17 or 18 years earlier.

In case you're unfamiliar with the 1980 Memorial Cup, the tournament pitted the Western League's Regina Pats against the Ontario League champion Peterborough Petes (coached by Mike Keenan) and the Quebec League champion Cornwall Royals (coached by Doug Carpenter). Regina was the host city. With a trip to the championship game at stake, Peterborough played Cornwall and was a big favorite to win. That would set up a final between the Petes and the Pats. One day earlier, Regina crushed Cornwall, 11–2.

On this day, the Petes got out to a big lead and then rested most of their best players. A funny thing happened, though: the Royals came back to win the game and set up a rematch with Peterborough in the championship game. The Pats were out.

The Regina locals were furious. They tried to storm and overturn the Peterborough team bus. Locals who'd bought tickets for the championship game—expecting to see their beloved Pats play the Petes but ending up instead with the team from Quebec—came armed with dozens of eggs and rotten potatoes, tossing them at the Peterborough bench the whole game.

Hearing and reading about what had unfolded made me flash back to my own days playing against Regina. We reached the Western Canada championship game in both 1961–62 and 1962–63. During the playoffs in the latter year, we played Regina on the road. A fan threw a construction bolt at our bench, and it struck Scott Munro. When the Memorial Cup incident happened 17 years later, I mused that at least the Petes' bench only had to dodge eggs and potatoes rather than bolts.

We defeated Regina and went on to beat the Melville Millionaires to win the 1963 SJHL championship. Melville was coached by Don Abel and featured a strong-as-an-ox right winger by the name of Bill Flett. "Cowboy" Bill, who was a legitimate rodeo cowboy, later became my Flyers teammate in the same trade that brought Roscoe to Philly and sent Jimmy Johnson to Los Angeles.

In 1963, we played the Edmonton Oil Kings. The Oilers were coached by Buster Bradshaw.

The Oil Kings had a big, tough, nasty defenseman by the name of Pat Quinn. Quinner and I would later work together in Philadelphia when he was head coach and I was doing advanced scouting and serving as a training camp instructor. I came to like him, but I definitely did not like playing against that big son of a bitch.

During the 1963 championships, Quinn broke Phil "Skip" Krake's leg. Skip was one of our two best offensive players, along with Lyle Bradley. Krake was also a tough and feisty guy, but he was five-foot-ten and 165 pounds, to Quinn's six-foot-three, 215 pounds. Even by today's hockey standards, Quinn was a big guy. By the standards of the 1960s, he was freakin' Goliath.

Apart from Quinn, the Oil Kings' squad had some other players whose names are probably familiar to most fans. Their roster had future NHL coach, player, and executive Glen Sather (later a teammate of mine with the Oklahoma City Blazers and Boston Bruins in 1965–66 and 1966–67), future longtime NHL defenseman Bert Marshall, and future Detroit Red Wings defenseman Bob Falkenberg. They also had right winger Greg Pilling, whom some folks in Philly may remember as the head coach of the NAHL champion Philadelphia Firebirds in the mid-1970s.

Like I said, small world, eh?

Both the Edmonton Flyers and the Oil Kings played their home games in the old Edmonton Gardens. That place, nicknamed "the Cow Barn," was quite an experience. First of all, the ice dimensions were huge, including a 212-foot length from end to end. Second of all, it dated back to 1913, and a $60,000 renovation project in the early '60s hardly modernized it. The girders leaked water onto the goddamn ice surface, creating hazardous mounds. The lighting fixtures were outdated, so the building was dark. If pucks weren't usually shot and passed along the ice in those days, someone would have gotten severely injured or killed.

The old Cow Barn lasted until 1974. It was torn down in 1982.

Losing in the championships to Edmonton in '62 and '63 was heartbreaking to me. In '63 the final game was played in Estevan, and we lost 2–1. I can't describe the pain of getting that close to your ultimate goal and falling just short.

Sather, who was on the victorious Edmonton side and went on to win the Memorial Cup in 1963, recalls how tough that series was.

"We were glad we had Quinn on our side. He was knocking their guys over like bowling pins. Look, '63 was a long time ago. But I remember it got rough at times. In one of the games, Pilling swung his stick like a bat at one of their guys. But Greg himself got sliced up pretty good. Estevan had a very loyal and tough group of fans. We had to haul ass out of town on our bus. This part I remember clearly. We didn't have a doctor on our bus, and Pilling was still bleeding. I was the one who stitched Greg up. Needle and thread. No Novocain," Sather remembers.

"I played against Joe, and I played with Joe later on. It was definitely better to be his teammate. He played clean, but he played tough. He was a smart defenseman who kept a mental book on everyone he played against. I remember that I respected him even as an opponent, and we became friends later on when we became teammates."

I was always worried first and foremost about playing my defensive position, protecting my goalie, and getting the puck to safety. Any points I earned offensively were strictly a bonus. Even so, I had a strong offensive playoff run in '63. I posted 12 points (two goals, 10 assists) in 11 games. It was just a situation where we had some banged-up players, and the rest of us had to step up any way we could.

Would I have traded every one of those 12 postseason points for a championship for my team? Of course I would. If we'd beat Edmonton in '63, we'd have played the Niagara Falls Flyers for the Memorial Cup: Bruins affiliate vs. Bruins affiliate. It wasn't meant to be, I suppose.

After the 1962–63 season, the Bruins offered me a professional contract to play for one of their minor-league affiliates, the Minneapolis Bruins of the Central Hockey League. I signed after a long and difficult negotiation that lasted, I'd estimate, a whole two seconds.

They offered me $3,000 for the 1963–64 season, plus $1,000 to sign the contract. I grabbed the pen and signed. That was it. I felt like I was on top of the world.

This was one of my earliest hockey publicity photos as a prospect of the Boston Bruins.

CHAPTER 3

Hockey from Coast to Coast

In my first two pro seasons, 1963–64 and 1964–65, I played for the Minneapolis Bruins of the Central Hockey League. Originally, though, I wasn't supposed to play for Minneapolis, which was where the Boston Bruins typically sent most of their top prospects.

Initially, I was told to go to training camp in Calgary to try out for the San Francisco Seals, a Bruins farm team in the Western Hockey League (WHL). Not to be confused with the modern-day Western Hockey League, which is a major junior league, the WHL of the early 1960s was a pro hockey minor league. The Seals were coached by Bud Poile, who left the Edmonton Flyers after a championship 1961–62 season to coach San Francisco.

During camp in Calgary, I met many of the Bruins' top prospects. This was where I first made the acquaintances of Terry Crisp and Gary Dornhoefer. When we got to San Francisco, we were put up at the Fairmont Hotel on Nob Hill, owned by Mel Swig. While at the hotel, I met basketball legend Wilt Chamberlain. I had no idea who he was—someone told me shortly thereafter—but he was the tallest person I'd ever met.

I made the team. Bruins scout Harold "Baldy" Cotton then recommended me for Minneapolis. Cotton held a good deal of sway with the Boston organization at the time. Cotton was an interesting character and a hockey guy with strong opinions.

Born in 1902 in Nanticoke, Ontario, he got a bit of a late start in pro hockey because he moved to Pittsburgh to attend Duquesne University and play for the semipro Pittsburgh Yellow Jackets. "Baldy" was a tenacious and feisty checking winger who later played 12 seasons in the NHL from the mid-1920s to mid-1930s, winning the Stanley Cup with the Toronto Maple Leafs in 1931–32.

One time, Cotton got into an argument with Maple Leafs roommate Charlie Conacher over being a puck hog and rarely passing. Cotton threatened to retaliate.

As Cotton later told it, the bickering escalated to the point that the much bigger and stronger Conacher dragged his teammate, who had a fear of heights, over to an open window on the 20th floor of the Hotel Lincoln in New York. When Cotton still refused to shut up, Conacher picked him up by the feet and dangled him out the window. Cotton screamed a frantic apology. Conacher calmly pulled him back to safety and went to bed.

Fear for his life made Baldy relent to Conacher, but there weren't many points he conceded. As with Happ Emms, Cotton had a general disdain for "hayseed" western Canadian farm kids, or at least a strong preference for the players from the eastern-based leagues.

I believe it was Cotton who ultimately recommended my assignment to San Francisco rather than Minneapolis. I'm not sure what changed Baldy's mind about me, but after being informed that I'd made the cut for the Seals' roster, I was told to pack up and go to Minnesota instead. That was good news. The Bruins sent their better prospects to Minneapolis to play for Harry Sinden.

Off I went to Minneapolis. Sinden was our coach as well as a defenseman on the team. I learned a lot from Harry, on and off the ice, about playing my position, especially about reading the play before it developed into a dangerous scoring chance. Things move faster and faster each rung you move up in hockey, and Sinden helped me with details of the game such as playing through the puck carrier rather than getting mesmerized by the puck.

Recalls Sinden, "Joe fit in right away. I liked him as a player, and I liked him as a person, both as his coach and his teammate. He was a smart player. Very exuberant. Very competitive. Always well prepared to come play. He was also a fun-loving guy off the ice. Big heart. Great sense of humor. Just an easy guy to like, and someone you wanted on your team."

Here I am serving a penalty while I was a member of the Oklahoma City Blazers. Whatever the penalty was for, I'm pretty sure I didn't do it.

Apart from being instrumental in helping me get ready to play in the NHL, Harry and I became lifelong friends off the ice. He's a fine gentleman with a great family. I always felt like he was in my corner as a player, and he was a man of his word. I saw how he approached playing and how he approached coaching, and he was a true leader.

To me, a true leader is someone who knows the way, goes the way, and shows the way. That was Harry Sinden, as well as Fred Shero, Bobby Clarke, and some of the other great leaders with whom I was fortunate enough to be associated.

We had a good team in Minneapolis, not quite as good as the roster of the Omaha Knights (coached by Scotty Bowman and then by Bill

McCreary) but roughly on par with the St. Paul Rangers (with Fred Shero behind the bench and Marcel Pelletier in goal). The Rangers finished one point ahead of us in the regular season.

Our club had one of the league's top scorers in little French-Canadian center Jeannot Gilbert and a winger from the Maritimes named Gerry Ouellette. Along with myself, the contingent of young players joining our team included names such as J. P. Parise, former Niagara Fall Flyers forwards Gary Dornhoefer and Terry Crisp, Winnipeg native Ted Irvine, and center Ron Schock (who joined us after his junior season with Niagara Falls and five NHL games with Boston). Future NHL/WHA goalie George Gardner was our main starter in net, but my former Estevan teammate Jack Norris also spent some time with Minneapolis my first year.

Teddy Irvine and I hit it off as friends quickly, and we became roommates for a couple years in Minneapolis and Oklahoma City. Unfortunately, we never played together in the NHL because the LA Kings grabbed him in the 1967 Expansion Draft.

"Me and Joe had a great time. We were always laughing about something on the bus. Joe was a guy who hated to lose, but he also loved to win. Those are the best kind of teammates. He was serious about hockey, but he had fun. Maybe we pushed the curfew a time or two, had a few beers, shot some pool, and whatnot. I remember that he had this camera he took everywhere on the road. He liked to see different places. A good friend, a great teammate—but, damn, he had the loudest voice I've ever heard in my life," Irvine recalled in 1977.

This was still minor-league hockey, so we weren't making much money. The NHL was, of course, my ultimate goal, but I felt like I had a good life in Minneapolis and made some good friends off the ice as well as on. I had a very pretty girlfriend, too, and she came up to visit me back home after the season.

The Minneapolis franchise was run by Walter Bush Jr., Robert McNulty, and Gordon Ritz. Bush, an attorney by profession, was a legendary name in local and national hockey, including a stint as the general manager of the 1964 Olympic hockey team for Team USA.

We played our home games uptown at the Minneapolis Arena (2800 Dupont Ave. South, adjacent to Lake Street). Formerly the home of the old Minneapolis Millers as well as the University of Minnesota Golden Gophers, the facility was a decent one by minor-league standards of the era, although it was getting a little long in the tooth (it opened back in the mid-1920s). The stands held 5,500 fans. The highest-priced tickets cost $2.50, while the cheap seats were just a buck-fifty.

Relatively speaking, we got pretty good fan support, although the team was only around for two seasons before we relocated to Oklahoma City as the Blazers. The support was at least decent enough that the NHL awarded an expansion franchise (the Minnesota North Stars) to the community in 1967. Bush, McNulty, and Ritz headed the ownership group that landed the franchise that became the North Stars and, later, the Dallas Stars.

In the 1964 playoffs, we ran into Omaha, which was a Montreal Canadiens farm team at the time. They had plenty of talent, including my future Philadelphia teammate Garry Peters, forwards Claude Larose and Norm Dennis, and Ernie Wakely and Cesare Maniago in goal. Their defense was stacked with a combination of talents like Jim Roberts and Bob Wall, as well as sheer nastiness brought by Barclay Plager and Noel Picard.

Yes, that's the same Barclay Plager (later reunited with brother Bob Plager) and Noel Picard who later tormented and beat up my early Philadelphia Flyers teams as members of the St. Louis Blues in the 1968 and 1969 playoffs—the gang that made Flyers owner Ed Snider insist that the Flyers find tougher players who could stand up to the rougher teams in the league.

Picard, who was a physical monster for that era at six-foot-one and 230 pounds, was a despicable player in my point of view. Being tough and physically intimidating are part of the game, but Picard was also a cheap-shot artist. The two worst sneak attacks I ever witnessed in my playing career were both perpetrated by Picard.

Many older Flyers fans know that Picard sneak-attacked my teammate Claude LaForge in the 1968 playoffs, ending LaForge's NHL career. Years earlier, when I played for Minneapolis and Picard played for Omaha, he pulled a similar stunt against Sinden.

"Picard sucker punched me when we played against Omaha," Sinden recalled. "He got me pretty good. I was woozy, but I managed to swing and hit him."

Unfortunately, the Knights more or less dismantled us in that playoff series. They took us out in five games, shutting us out, 5–0, on our home ice on March 31, 1964, to close out the series. Omaha went on to beat Shero's Rangers in the finals to win the league championship.

I went home to Smithers for the summer, took a summer job, did a little fishing, and caught up with my friends. I felt it had been a good season for our team and for my own development—Harry showed trust in me, and I saw continuous improvement—but I was kind of pissed about the playoff series against Omaha. They were the best team in the league, but I felt like we could have made a better showing than we did. We gave up four or more goals in four of the five games (including our 6–4 win that avoided a sweep). They were a high-scoring team, but we'd been one of the better defensive teams during the season.

The next season, we were again one of the top three clubs in the league, along with St. Paul and Omaha. Much of the same squad remained on our roster from the previous year with a few additions, including my old Estevan teammate Skip Krake and defenseman Brent Hughes (yet another future Philadelphia teammate). Eighteen-year-old Ross Lonsberry was called up briefly from Estevan late in the campaign.

I spent most of the 1964–65 season with Minneapolis. But on December 17, 1964, my lifelong dream came true: I was called up for one game to the NHL, joining Milt Schmidt's last-place Boston Bruins for a road game against the first-place Detroit Red Wings.

At the time, strange as it may seem nowadays, I was only the 14th player from British Columbia to play even one game in the NHL. The notables that came before me included Hall of Fame goalie Tiny Thompson and Lester Patrick's sons Lynn (himself a Hall of Famer) and Muzz. Within my playing era, there was Len Lunde (a veteran by the time I broke in), hard-nosed John Ferguson, goalie Cesare Maniago, and my subsequent Flyers teammate Larry Hale. Bert Marshall broke into the NHL with Detroit in 1965–66.

I remember putting on my Boston Bruins uniform for the first time and stepping out on the ice at the Detroit Olympia. Looking out at the ice, I saw the likes of Gordie Howe, Ted Lindsay, Alex Delvecchio, and Norm

Ullman. It almost felt surreal. The Red Wings also had a 20-year-old Pit Martin and young center Eddie Joyal.

The Bruins, as usual for that era, entered the game in last place, dragging a 5-17-4 record into the "Old Red Barn." The Red Wings, coached by Sid Abel, occupied the top spot in the NHL and were undefeated by the Bruins so far that season (four wins and one tie). One night earlier, the Red Wings flew past the Rangers at Madison Square Garden, 7–3.

On this night, however, the Bruins outworked and outplayed the Red Wings. We skated off with a 5–3 win. I'm sure I was nervous early in the game, but I settled in. I wasn't on the ice for any Red Wings goals. After the game, Red Wings defenseman Gary Bergman approached me and introduced himself.

"Just wanted to tell you that you played a good game," Bergman said.

That meant a lot to me. I was sent back to rejoin Minneapolis shortly thereafter, but I would get another call-up late in the season for the final three games. I played in a 5–2 home loss to the eventual Stanley Cup champion Montreal Canadiens. I was on the ice for two Montreal goals, one of which was scored by the legendary Jean Beliveau. The next game, the Bruins earned a 6–2 win at the Montreal Forum. In the season's final game, I picked up my first NHL assist and was plus-two in a 3–1 home win over the Chicago Black Hawks (the team spelled its name as two words, not one, in those days).

Here I am returning home from Minneapolis for an offseason visit with my family in Smithers. My mom, three of my brothers, and a female friend of mine at the time are pictured with me.

My first taste of NHL hockey was an incredible thrill. It left me wanting more. Back with Minneapolis for the Central League playoffs, we once again lost in the playoffs in five games to the eventual league champions, this time St. Paul. In the final round, Fred Shero's team got revenge on Omaha from the previous year, prevailing in six games.

I experienced another thrill in 1965 that marked a personal milestone of sorts: I purchased my first car, a Pontiac Grand Parisienne. I bought it in Toronto from a guy named Brian Cullen. He formerly played in the NHL for the Maple Leafs. I paid $1,900 at the car dealership Cullen owned with his brother, Barry.

I went to training camp with the Boston Bruins in September of '65. The first order of business was obtaining a contract for the season. It didn't go well.

Harry Sinden recalls, "Back then, the young players would get their contracts in camp; they'd step into the general manager's hotel room and work out a deal with Lynn Patrick or Happ Emms. I told Joe that I thought he could get a $500 or $600 raise for the season. A little later, I saw him, and he was crestfallen.

"I asked him what was wrong, and he said, 'I asked for a $600 raise. They told me to go home.' I told him not to worry and that I'd help him out. Joe got, I think, a $300 or $400 raise. Sounds pretty silly nowadays to put a kid through that over a couple hundred dollars for the season, but that was how it was back then."

I did not make the Bruins' NHL roster out of camp. I was disappointed but not shocked. The only question was where I'd be playing: in the NHL for the Hershey Bears or back in the Central League, where the Minneapolis club had relocated to become the Oklahoma City Blazers.

I was not the only young player who received this treatment. None of us were sure where we'd be playing until the Boston organization told them where to report.

My buddy Terry Crisp was told, "Get in your car and start driving west. When you stop, give us a call, and we'll tell you where to go."

I never owned a car of my own before 1965. Purchasing my first car from my minor-league earnings cost $1,900. I bought it from former NHL player Brian Cullen.

Pretty lousy way to treat someone—making him wait to find out where he'd be living and playing—but that was how the business of hockey worked in those days.

As for me, cue the Rodgers and Hammerstein music: Oklahoma it was.

I enjoyed my season with the Blazers. Off the ice, I've always liked to visit new places. By now, at age 23, I'd literally played hockey from coast to coast: British Columbia and San Francisco on the Pacific coast; Boston on the Atlantic coast; Estevan, Minneapolis, and now Oklahoma City in between. That doesn't even count the road trips to far-flung places on our team buses. As I said previously, the hockey life is basically a vagabond's life.

As a member of the Blazers, I took my first-ever trip to Dallas. It was a memorable experience for me, especially seeing Dealey Plaza, where John F. Kennedy had been assassinated just a few years earlier. To this day, I keep photos from that trip in an album at home.

We had a very close-knit team in Oklahoma City. A lot of us had been together for three seasons at that point. We all respected Harry as a player and coach, and the rest of us got to know each other very quickly. The NHL's Bruins may have been a perennial last-place team, but help was on the way from what was becoming one of the deepest farm systems in the six-team league.

Recalls Sinden, "I can't say that I knew we'd eventually build a Stanley Cup champion. That seemed a long way off, and you never know how things will come together as you move players up the system to the NHL, but I could see we had good young talent. It really wouldn't be until Bobby Orr reached the NHL and the Bruins made the big trade for Phil Esposito [in 1967] that everything really started to come together. But I knew in Oklahoma City that we had quite a few players who were probably going to make it to the NHL and stick there."

Our roster in OK City had a lot of familiar names: Skip Krake, J. P. Parise, my roomie Ted Irvine, and Ron Buchanon (who joined Minneapolis late in the previous season). Defenseman Dallas Smith was another mainstay. Other Blazers teammates included a couple guys I'd play with again later in Philadelphia: checking center Terry Crisp and winger Keith Wright.

Teenage forwards Don Marcotte and Derek "Turk" Sanderson of the Niagara Falls Flyers passed through Oklahoma City briefly. Meanwhile, our team was stacked in goal with Gerry Cheevers and Doug Favell. Favie's old Niagara Falls teammate and close friend Bernie Parent primarily played in the NHL with Boston that season, but he also appeared in three games for the Blazers.

One of my new teammates was an old rival from junior hockey: Glen Sather. Playing against Slats when he was with Edmonton, I hated the sight of him. He was a miserable SOB to play against—a total rat. Now that he was on our side, I got a new slant on him both on and off the ice. You had to appreciate his tenacity and competitive drive, especially in tough buildings on the road. Off the ice, we became friends, and the friendship has endured for more than half a century.

Recalls Sather, "As a teammate, you knew Joe was totally committed. Never took a thing for granted. He hated to lose. Competed his ass off. Never took a game off, and he didn't put up with anyone else doing it. All he wanted to do was win. Away from the ice, we had a lot of fun together. You could hear him from the next room; he talked and laughed so damn loud. He's never changed. Joe was a smart hockey player and, to this day, a good friend."

I hated playing against Glen Sather when we were in junior hockey but befriended him as a teammate in Oklahoma City. Slats and I remain friends to this day. It's absolutely true that sometimes the most despised rivals make for the best guys to have on your side. The late Pat Quinn was another such player.

Teammates nicknamed me "Whispers" because I lacked an "inside voice." Later on in Philly, I became "Thundermouth."

I was a league All-Star that season. We finished in second place during the regular season, five points behind the Minnesota Rangers. In the playoffs we took out the St. Louis Braves in five games to set up an all-Oklahoma final series with the Tulsa Oilers.

In the first game of the championship series, we captured a 5–1 win on home ice, following it up with 4–2 and 5–2 wins on the road. In the final game, we ended the suspense early, building a big lead and going on to an 8–4 blowout to capture the championship.

No matter what the league or level of play, championships are special. The experience forms a lifelong bond with every one of your teammates. The postgame beer tastes just that much better after clinching the win. The post-championship party, or at least what you remember of it, is a joyous experience.

After having lost the Western League championship in junior hockey and falling short in the first round twice with Minneapolis, I can tell you winning the championship with Oklahoma City was a feeling that I craved again and again for the duration of my playing career. It was wonderful.

Unfortunately, I had a little too much fun at our championship celebration in Oklahoma City. Got behind the wheel of the car after having too much to drink, and I caused a car accident. Not my smartest or proudest moment.

The mayor of Oklahoma City, Jim Roterer, was on the board of directors of our hockey team. He advised me to get out of town, and he'd make sure things would be all right. So I did.

My only hockey-related disappointment from the 1965–66 season was this: I did not play in a single NHL game for the Bruins. I had a scheduled recall, but it was canceled. A certain roommate of mine turned off the alarm clock when we got in, and I ended up missing my flight to rejoin the Bruins. Boston kept me in the minors the rest of the season.

That's OK, Teddy. It all worked out OK in the end.

CHAPTER 4

On the Shore with Orr

The first time I met Bobby Orr, he was still a junior hockey player with the Oshawa Generals. We'd all heard about him. The Bruins owned his rights, and even pro players were aware of the stories about how dominant he was at both ends of the ice against older teenage players.

I hadn't seen him play yet, but Harry Sinden believed with absolute certainty that Orr would be a force in the NHL before too long. That was good enough for me. Harry was sharp as a tack and not someone to overhype a player.

That said, my first impression of Bobby was, "Geez, this kid is skinny."

The next time I saw Orr was the Bruins' 1966 training camp in London, Ontario. His body had transformed. At age 18, he was now rippling with muscles, especially in his lower body. He'd put on the good kind of weight. He had tree-trunk quadriceps, Popeye-like calves, and well-defined arms.

No one looks like that without putting in a whole lot of hard work. I had to ask him how he did it.

"I bought a rowing machine," he said simply.

I remember thinking, "Well, hell, everyone should do that."

During the summer of 1966, Sinden sent a letter to all the Bruins players and prospects about the importance of offseason training. To this day, I still have the letter (dated June 30, 1966) at home.

Dear Joe:

I trust this letter finds you enjoying the summer.

You will find enclosed a set of exercises which we feel will be beneficial to you for pre training camp and the coming hockey season.

First, they will be of great benefit in the prevention of training camp injuries. I am referring to such things as groin pulls, sore backs, hamstring muscles, rib cartilages, etc. Injuries like these, sustained at training camp, often hamper a player's performance for many weeks into the playing season and, in some cases, he has failed to make the team because of them.

Secondly, if we spent a month or two on these exercises, it will enable us to conduct a camp in which you would be able to display your talents to [your] advantage. Exercises and calisthenics cannot be eliminated from camp, but how much of it is needed depends to some degree on the condition in which we arrive at camp.

These exercises are the result of extensive research by noted physical therapists. They are not original. How much they have to do with the success of other organizations, we will never know. It is as simple as "players on championship clubs are requested to do them—why not us?"

It is not my intention to ask you to embark on a rigorous offseason training program but to emphasize to you that a sound training camp is so very important to veteran and rookie alike. We feel these exercises are the first step toward this.

Looking forward to seeing you in London this fall.

Very sincerely yours,

Harry

The enclosed exercises were copied from the 5BX manual developed for the Royal Canadian Air Force; 5BX stands for "Five Basic Exercises." The five exercises were 1) stretching, 2) sit-ups, 3) back extensions, 4) push-ups, and 5) running in place.

Throughout the suggested exercise charts, the five types of exercise are the same. However, they become more difficult as variations are introduced for higher levels of physical fitness.

I took the letter seriously. I felt that, coming off strong seasons in Minneapolis and Oklahoma City (including the Adams Cup championship) in 1964–65 and 1965–66, I was on the brink of earning a full-time spot at the NHL roster. Harry Sinden knew my game, and I knew he had trust in me. That's huge for any young player.

Back then, most contracts for the upcoming season were done in assembly line fashion. The general manager summoned you to his office—often just a makeshift desk in his room at the team's training camp hotel.

Harry Sinden was in his first year as Bruins' coach, replacing Milt Schmidt. Boston had missed the playoffs for six straight years, usually finishing in last place in the six-team league. In other words, we had a long climb ahead of us, but we had a lot of young talent coming in, too.

"It was another year until we got [Phil] Esposito from Chicago. Orr and Esposito transformed our team. But that first year with Bobby Orr, our record maybe didn't show it yet, but we were improving. What I remember about Joe was that he was very competitive and he was a good defense partner for Orr," Sinden recalled.

During training camp, I was not paired with Orr. Gilles Marotte started out alongside Bobby. During the early part of camp, according to news clippings, I played with Teddy Green. Later, Harry put me with Orr. Our schedule was as follows:

September 23, 1966: Bruins 1 – Toronto Maple Leafs 1 (London, Ontario)
September 24, 1966: Bruins 6 – Oklahoma City Blazers 4 (Oshawa, Ontario)
September 29, 1966: Boston 4 – Detroit Red Wings 2 (Hamilton, Ontario)
September 30, 1966: New York Rangers 3 – Bruins 0 (London, Ontario)
October 1, 1966: New York Rangers 3 – Bruins 0 (Kingston, Ontario)
October 2, 1966: Bruins 3 – Toronto Maple Leafs 1 (Peterborough, Ontario)
October 7, 1966: Detroit Red Wings 3 – Bruins 1 (London, Ontario)

October 8, 1966: Bruins 5 – Rochester Americans 2 (Rochester, New York)
October 11, 1966: New York Rangers 3 – Boston 1 (Boston Garden)
October 12, 1966: Bruins 3 – Montreal Canadiens 0 (Boston Garden)

At the start of camp, we had 38 players. Emms and Sinden agreed that the Bruins should give extended looks to young players, with the auditions ongoing into the early season.

I don't remember exactly how many of the 10 preseason games I played in, but it was most of them. That was a good sign, from my perspective. It was when a roster hopeful only dressed in a couple preseason games that he had reason to worry about not being in the team's plans.

My old Minneapolis and OKC buddy and roommate, Ted Irvine, only got into a few preseason games in September of '66 and was cut. He'd spend the 1966–67 season in Oklahoma City and then join the fledgling Los Angeles Kings the next year after LA selected him in the Expansion Draft. He went on to have a 724-game NHL career. I'd have loved to play with Teddy in Boston, but it wasn't to be.

In the October 1 game against the Rangers in Kingston, Orr suffered a shoulder injury. In response, Forbes Kennedy went after one of their guys, and there were several fights that resulted. Actually, Forbie was cut from the roster after either the next game or the last one before our team crossed the border to go to the United States. Next time I saw Kennedy, we were teammates on the brand-new Philadelphia Flyers. Orr missed a few games but was soon back in the lineup.

Along with several other young players, I made the NHL team out of training camp. That accomplishment felt good, but Harry made it clear that we'd have to keep proving ourselves. Except for Orr, the young guys on the opening-night roster were in the NHL basically on a tryout basis.

That was our reality. I understood that I'd have to earn my keep, and I had no intention of going back to Oklahoma City or being sent to the AHL team in Hershey. It's tough to get to the NHL and just as hard to stay there.

When we got to Boston, the young guys on the team rented a house overlooking a beach on North Shore. In addition to me, my housemates were Orr, Ross Lonsberry, and Ted Hodgson. Wayne Connelly and Dick Cherry were also around the club as NHL roster hopefuls looking to earn full-time spots on the club. The five of us posed for a center-ice photo at the Garden.

We had a lot of fun together. Orr and I hosted some great parties at the house. We'd invite friends and teammates over, along with some lady friends. The local newspapers also sent along a photographer, and they took pictures of Orr and me setting up our black-and-white television, a group of four of us (Orr, Lonsberry, Hodgson, and me) having breakfast, and one of Roscoe and Orr posing by the telephone in our kitchen.

Originally, I shared a rented house with fellow Bruins rookies Bobby Orr, Ross Lonsberry, and Ted Hodgson. After Roscoe and Teddy were assigned to Oklahoma City, it was just Bobby and me for the rest of the season. Our house was a team hangout headquarters, however.

In hindsight, I'm glad these photos were taken and preserved. I also snapped some color photos with my own camera (side note: even all these years later, it looks strange to me to see words like "colour" spelled the American way, without the "u").

One vivid memory I have from living at that house is this: the "Boston Strangler" panic. Albert DeSalvo had been in police custody since the fall of the previous year. He was awaiting trial for being the perpetrator of killing spree of 13 women in Boston between June 14, 1962, and January 4, 1964.

But there was still considerable fear in the community, especially among women. There were widespread rumors of copycat criminals and local urban legends (which many folks believed) that DeSalvo himself had escaped and was plotting another wave of home invasions, sexual assaults, and murders.

None of it was true, but the fear itself was real. The Bruins had a security detail provided, and several female friends and neighbors stayed at our house for a time to be safe from the Boston Strangler.

Meanwhile, as Harry had made clear would happen, some of the young players who started out the season on the NHL roster wouldn't be in Boston for long. Hodgson was sent to Oklahoma City after four games. "Roscoe" Lonsberry, who was still only 19, lasted only about 10 games (dressed for eight and scratched in the others) before he went to Oklahoma City.

Now it was only Orr and me in the house. Bobby did the cooking. I lied to the press and told 'em my buddy was a good cook. He was actually a lousy cook! But that's OK. I certainly was no chef either. My chores consisted of watering the plants and straightening up after myself.

There were other young players who ended up sticking around with the Bruins for most or all of the season—just not the guys who'd been our housemates. French-Canadian forward Hubert "Pit" Martin, 22, had a 20-goal season before being part of the big trade with Chicago for Esposito the next summer. Ron Schock, 22, had played for a while as my teammate in Minneapolis and played his first full NHL season with the Bruins in 1966–67. Morotte, 21, was in the NHL all season. So was Connelly.

Other friends and minor-league teammates of mine passed through Boston that year or joined later in the season. Bernie Parent split the season between Oklahoma City and Boston. Skip Krake spent 15 games with the Bruins and the rest in OKC with the Blazers.

Starting with a 6–2 home win over Detroit on opening night, the Bruins exceeded preseason predictions by getting off to a 6-6-3 start through the first 15 games. We lost our second game, 3–1, to the Canadiens at the Montreal Forum on October 22. Even so, the night provided a personal thrill for me.

The game was scoreless through the end of the first period. In the second period, Montreal's Ted Harris (later my Flyers teammate on our second Cup-winning team) and Bobby Rousseau scored power-play goals to give the Habs a 2–0 lead. At 14:30, after Connelly won a draw back to me at

Goalie Bernie Parent bailed me out with a big save on Henri Richard on this play. It was a pleasure—both in Boston and Philly—to play in front of the Hall of Fame netminder.

the point, I put a shot through traffic that beat Hockey Hall of Fame goalie Lorne "Gump" Worsley to cut the gap to 2–1. It was my first NHL goal.

Every player recalls for life the details of his first NHL goal. In my case, it's no secret that I wasn't an offensive-minded defenseman. I scored 38 regular season goals in my 835-game NHL career, plus three goals in 84 games in the Stanley Cup playoffs. The upside was that when I scored one, I remembered it.

On this play, I simply wristed a shot along the ice, and it went in the net. Sinden always preached shooting low. He said it gave you the best chance at something sneaking through or creating a rebound. Harry was right.

Although the goalie position has evolved (more than any other position on the ice) over the decades, some things still ring true to this day. Even with the massively improved equipment and old standup-style long since having been replaced by butterfly and hybrid styles, low shots can be effective.

They're more deflection friendly, for one thing. For another, they're more controllable and less likely to wildly miss and then rim around the boards out of the zone. Last but not least, shooting right at the goalie's feet can create rebound chances for teammates if the puck catches the right spot. Sometimes, they'll even leak through the pads or skates. If the goalie stops it and freezes the puck, you still get an offensive zone faceoff out of it.

Old-school hockey isn't always outdated or wrong. Anyway, I digress.

Back in those days, of course, there was no cable television or sports highlight shows. By way of NHL game broadcasts, there was only Hockey Night in Canada, rebroadcasts of older games, and whatever games were shown locally.

One of the neatest things about my first goal was the timing of it. The Canadiens vs. Bruins game from the Montreal Forum was slated to be broadcast on TV the following weekend in Smithers. I told my mom, and my family was able to catch the broadcast on Can Television and see my goal. She'd have watched, regardless.

Going into the third period of that game, Sinden felt like we were in decent shape. We had a late-period surge in the second after my goal, and we took a carryover power play into the third period. Unfortunately, we weren't able to build from it. Montreal killed off the penalty, and several shifts later, Leon Rochefort (another future Flyers teammate) scored an insurance goal.

Incidentally, in the afternoon, there was a Boston Celtics vs. Philadelphia 76ers basketball game. Philadelphia Eagles junior executive Ed Snider attended the sparsely attended game. Seeing the advance-sales ticket line for the last-place Bruins, he made up his mind to go full steam ahead on an NHL expansion team venture in Philadelphia. That's how Mr. Snider told it to me years later, at least.

The next night we rematched with the Canadiens in Boston. It was another hard-fought game. Martin scored a nice goal in Worsley in the first period. In the third period, Orr notched his first NHL goal to tie the game at 2–2. That's right—I beat Bobby to our respective first tallies in the NHL. He'd have to settle for scoring "only" 238 more goals than I did in 178 fewer career games than I played.

At 17:27 of the third period, we went on the power play. We had a golden chance to win the game or, at worst, leave with a tie. Instead, we turned a puck over, and Jean-Guy Talbot beat Eddie Johnston on a breakaway for a shorthanded goal. We lost, 3–2.

Despite the back-to-back heartbreaking losses to the Canadiens, our team seemed to be improved early in the season. Our longtime star John Bucyk was still a great player at age 31 and had become team captain following the departure of Leo Boivin via trade. We had a lot of youthful energy on the roster, and Harry was a damn good coach.

Overall, for the first month of the season, things went about as well as could be realistically expected. At one point in early November, we shut out Toronto at Boston Garden, 4–0, and then beat Montreal, 2–1, a couple nights later. We followed those games up with a 3–3 tie against the Rangers and a 5–3 win over Detroit.

We felt good about ourselves—that is, until November 23, 1966. On that night, we were in Manhattan to take on the Rangers. Before the game, general manager Emms stopped by our locker room.

You've no doubt heard of motivational speeches. I guess that was Emms's intent. But what he delivered was a "demotivational" speech. He told us how lousy we all were, that it was a disgrace that we had our third-line guys (Connelly, Ron Schock, and veteran Ron Murphy) leading our team in scoring at that juncture. He said we'd been lucky to pull together a few wins, but we had to be a lot better than that to have any prayer of competing.

In my entire career, I don't think I ever saw the mood in the dressing room sink as suddenly and dramatically as it did after Emms finished telling us how terrible we were. Coincidentally or not, we lost to the Rangers that night and went on from there to go 2-14-4 in a freefall that lasted through New Year's Day of 1967.

I learned a lesson from that experience. It's one thing for a team manager to point out specific ways a club needs to improve and get to work trying to upgrade the roster when possible. It's quite another to plant negative thoughts in the team's head.

Even though Emms's probable intent was to piss us off and get us to find ways to keep winning ("We'll show that SOB!"), it backfired spectacularly. We were a largely young team with still-fragile confidence. He stomped on it for no good reason.

Amid all the losing, we had a game in December against Toronto. Orr, as he was so good at doing, rushed the puck down the ice. He was met by veteran defenseman Marcel Pronovost, who hit him low and wedged Bobby's left knee into the boards. Orr suffered torn ligaments, the first of, sadly, several serious knee injuries he'd suffer. Over time, his knees degenerated, and it shortened his Hall of Fame career.

As Orr's defense partner, I saw the play unfold before me. Bobby missed 19 games that season. Even so, he was still obviously a budding superstar with many Norris Trophies in his future as the NHL's top defenseman. In 1966–67, it would have been a crime if anyone else had won the Calder Trophy as the NHL's rookie of the year.

To this day, Orr is still the best all-around defenseman I've ever seen in my life—slightly better than even Larry Robinson or Raymond Bourque or Nicklas Lidstrom or Chris Pronger. Orr could do it all, offensively, defensively, the physical game, strength or finesse, hockey smarts. Being his partner on defense was pretty easy. Play my position, be sure not to get in his way, and then just marvel while watching him at work.

After our six-week spell of almost constant losing, we were buried in last place. We'd stay there the rest of the season (17-43-10 record), but we eventually started to play some decent hockey again.

In mid-to-late January of '67, we put together a 5-4-0 stretch that included two wins over the Habs at the Forum, a victory over Toronto at Maple Leaf Gardens, and a 6–2 blowout win over the Rangers in Boston. I had the first multipoint (two assists) game of my career in the win against the Rangers. I was credited with an assist on an Eddie Westfall goal, and later, Ron Stewart deflected my point shot past Eddie Giacomin.

The biggest individual game of my time in Boston happened on March 12 in a 7–3 home win against Detroit. In the first period, after Gordie Howe outmuscled Orr (not many people could truthfully claim that) and scored the game's first goal, we exploded for four unanswered goals. Orr tied the game, and then we got a tally from Murray Oliver and back-to-back goals by Bob Dillabough. I didn't do anything special, but I was credited with secondary assists on the Oliver goal and the second Dillabough marker.

In the second period, Krake answered a Floyd Smith goal to restore a three-goal lead for the Bruins. With 1:03 left in the middle stanza, I scored on a power play for my second (and final) goal of the season to give the Bruins a 6–2 lead and myself a three-point game. Westfall had the lone assist for the second of his three points on the night. The two teams traded off a goal apiece in the third period.

I've said it before, and I'll say it again: hockey has a way of keeping you humble. Our next game after the victory over Detroit was another trip to the Forum to play the Canadiens. They kicked our butts, 11–2. I was on the ice for power-play goals by Ralph Backstrom and Yvan Cournoyer as well as even-strength goals by Rochefort and Bobby Rousseau.

We closed out the season on another losing streak: 0-6-0 over our final six games. We finished the 70-game season with 44 points: 14 points less than fifth-place Detroit, 28 points less than the fourth-place Rangers (the lowest-ranked playoff team), and 50 points behind first-place Chicago. The Maple Leafs won the Stanley Cup.

I dressed in 69 of the 70 games that season. The only one I missed was the next game after Toronto's Eddie Shack relieved me of four front teeth with a single reckless swing of the stick. Tim Horton put the puck around the boards and hollered "look out!" Too late.

My mouth was full of blood. I was taken back to the dressing room, and our trainer said the remnants would have to come out. He asked if I wanted my mouth numbed.

"I am numb!" I mumbled as best I could. "Hurry up!"

The first two came out easily enough. The others, which still had live roots, created a level of agony I can't describe and wouldn't wish on anyone. I screamed and nearly passed out.

Then I returned to the game. We only used five defensemen, and it was expected back then that, short of being hospitalized or something being broken, a player returned to the ice. Except for the career-ending leg injury I suffered in my final NHL game more than a decade later, that was just about my most painful experience on the ice.

At the end of the season, minus four teeth, I felt like my first NHL campaign had been a success. I finished fourth in the Calder Trophy voting; honestly, that was also a testament to Orr as well as a bit of personal recognition. If I couldn't play well with Orr as my regular partner, I would've been something less than an NHL-worthy defenseman.

As things turned out, I only played one year with Orr as my teammate. But he was a great teammate, a tremendous roommate, and a wonderful friend. Subsequently, he was my best man at my wedding in Smithers.

Life takes people in different directions. I don't see or talk to Bobby much nowadays, but the friendship bond is still there. It was my privilege to be his teammate and my honour...sorry, "honor"...to call him my friend.

Cartoon drawing in my honor during my rookie season. It seems like I'd already been "relieved" of my four front teeth by Eddie Shack by the time this was created.

CHAPTER 5

Where They Get Rid of the Bodies

I took a summer job with the Smithers Public Works Department when I returned home from my rookie season with the Bruins. My boss was Vern Flockhart, a family friend and the father of future NHL players Ron (later a Flyers teammate) and Rob.

I was in good spirits and looking forward to the 1967–68 season. In my personal life, I had a steady girlfriend. Professionally, the last season had gone well from my standpoint. I spent the whole year in the NHL. That was huge.

Boston had once again finished in last place in the NHL standings (28 points out of the playoffs), and it felt only like a matter of time until the group that we were building—Orr, Martin, Westfall, etc.—would start to gel. We were well coached by Sinden. John Bucyk was aging but still a high-end player. We had a lot of young players who only figured to get better with experience. Orr was still a teenager. Players like Bill Goldsworthy, Ron Schock, Gilles Marotte, and Krake were in their early twenties. I was about to turn 24. One of our better prospects, Lonsberry, was only 20 and had made his NHL debut. Wayne Cashman showed a lot of promise in the minor leagues, as did Sather. We had good young goalies in the NHL and on the farm, too.

On May 15, 1967, the Bruins made a major trade with the Black Hawks. Chicago sent Phil Esposito, Ken Hodge and Fred Stanfield to Boston in exchange for Marotte, Martin, and Jack Norris. The trade would, of course, help Boston immensely in the years to come.

Meanwhile, I was aware that the National Hockey League would be expanding from 6 to 12 teams the next season, with new franchises joining in Philadelphia, Pittsburgh, St. Louis, Minnesota, Los Angeles, and Oakland. However, I can't say that I'd given much thought to the upcoming Expansion Draft, which was to be held on June 6 at the Queen Elizabeth Hotel in Montreal.

This was a different era of hockey and a different era of media coverage. There were no newspaper articles, even in Canada, speculating on which players would be protected or exposed to the Expansion Draft. The Draft was not a television or radio event. I don't recall even knowing how the rules worked, except that the existing NHL teams could only protect so many players, and the rest were eligible to be taken by one of the expansion teams.

As I later found out, each Original Six team could protect one goalie and 11 skaters before the 20-round Draft. Any player born before or on June 1, 1946, was exempt from selection (most importantly, this meant in Boston's case that Orr did not have to be protected). After the first, fourth, and seventh rounds, teams could add one additional protected player to their lists. Thereafter, over the remaining 13 rounds, any time a team lost a player to an Expansion Club, they could add an additional protected player, if they so desired.

I had no idea, until after the fact, which players the Bruins protected. In goal, they protected Cheevers and left veteran Eddie Johnston and young goalies Bernie Parent and Doug Favell exposed. The 11 protected skaters were Bucyk, Ted Green, Westfall, Tom Williams, John McKenzie, Don Awrey, Hodge, Esposito, Stanfield, Eddie Shack (recently acquired from Toronto in a trade for Murray Oliver), and Gary Doak.

The first round of the Draft, which entirely consisted of goalie selections by the six expansion teams, saw the Philadelphia Flyers take Parent. The Bruins protected Johnston. Round 2 also consisted exclusively of goalie picks. Philly once again selected from the Boston system, taking Favell.

In Round 3, with the 16th overall pick, the Flyers plucked Van Impe off Chicago's unprotected list. In Round 4, the Flyers chose me with the 25th overall pick. Overall, the Flyers would go on to make a total of eight picks from the Bruins' organization—more than they chose from any other organization. Philly also took the likes of Gary Dornhoefer (14th round, 81st overall) and Dick Cherry (11th round, 61st overall) from the Bruins. The rest of the NHL was slower to recognize what the Flyers hockey operations brain trust—general manager Bud Poile, player personnel director Marcel Pelletier, and coach Keith Allen—already recognized about the stockpile of young talent in the Boston system hidden below the surface of annual last-place finishes at the NHL level.

In the meantime, I was blissfully unaware of what had gone down in Montreal. I went to work, flagging traffic, the morning after the NHL Expansion Draft. A few hours later, a driver recognized me and called over to me as he rolled slowly past.

"Hey, Joe! I just heard your name mentioned on the radio a little while ago," he said.

I was curious.

"Really? What'd you hear?" I asked.

"You were taken in the Expansion Draft by Philadelphia," he said.

I was in a state of shock momentarily. I went through all the stages of grief, minus acceptance. Nah, this can't be true. Maybe the Bruins will get me right back. But why the hell didn't they protect me in the Draft?

I felt sick to my stomach. Total depression set in. Now I was going to have to start all over again with this Philadelphia Flyers team. Where is Philadelphia, anyway? (The only thing I knew about the city at the time was that it was the home of the Phillies, and their slugging outfielder, Johnny Callison, had hit a home run to win the All-Star Game for the National League a couple of years earlier). Who else is going to be on this team? No way they're going to be any good.

My head was a mess. I found Mr. Flockhart, told him what had happened, and asked him if I could be excused from work for the rest of the day. He said OK.

Gathering some friends, I went to the bar at the Smithers Hotel. I hosted an impromptu self-pity party, drinking all day and deep into the night. I have no idea how much alcohol I consumed, but it was a whole lot. The next morning, I felt as lousy as you'd think. I was in no condition to work. I had to call Mr. Flockhart and ask for another day off. He was very unhappy with me.

"Well, maybe if you didn't drink all the beer in Smithers yesterday, you coulda got yourself to work today," he said.

I apologized. I knew he was right.

"OK, take today off," he said. "But that's it."

With my head pounding, I mumbled a thank-you and hung up the phone. Then I slept most of the day.

Later, I heard from Harry Sinden. He wrote me a gracious handwritten letter, which I've kept ever since and is still in almost pristine condition.

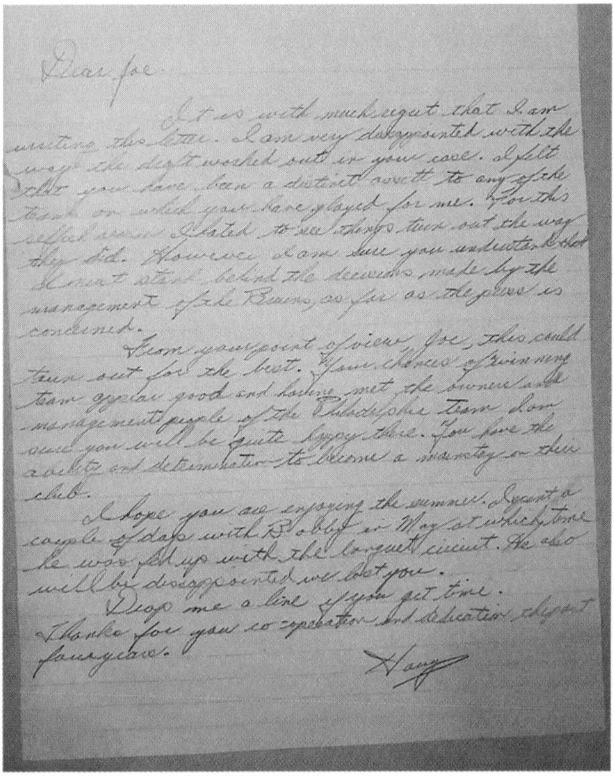

Dear Joe

It is with much regret that I am writing this letter. I am very disappointed with the way the draft worked out in your case. I felt that you have been a distinct asset to any of the teams on which you have played for me. For this selfish reason I hated to see things turn out the way they did. However I am sure you understand that I must stand behind the decisions made by the management of the Bruins, as far as the draft is concerned.

From your point of view, Joe, this could turn out for the best. Your chances of winning team appear good and having met the owners and management people of the Philadelphia team I am sure you will be quite happy there. You have the ability and determination to become a mainstay on their club.

I hope you are enjoying the summer. I spent a couple of days with Bobby in May at which time he was fed up with the banquet circuit. He also will be disappointed we lost you.

Drop me a line if you get time.

Thanks for your co-operation and dedication the past four years.

Harry

Dear Joe,

It is with the utmost regret that I am writing you this letter. I am very disappointed with the way the draft worked out in your case. I felt that you have been a distinct asset to any of the teams for which you played for me. For this selfish reason, I hated to see things turn out the way they did. However, I am sure you understand that I must stand behind the decisions made by the management of the Bruins, as far as the press is concerned.

From your point of view, Joe, this could turn out for the best. Your chances of a winning team appear good and, having met the owners and management people of the Philadelphia team, I am sure you will be quite happy there. You have the ability and determination to become a mainstay on their club.

I hope you are enjoying the summer. I spent a couple of days with Bobby [Orr] in May, at which time he was fed up with the banquet circuit. He also will be disappointed we lost you.

Drop me a line when you get time. Thanks for your co-operation and dedication the past few years.

Harry

I have always appreciated Harry's kindness, hockey wisdom, and teaching ability. The letter meant a lot to me, and it still does. However, I still had one nagging question: Why? Why did the Bruins' management leave me exposed to the Expansion Draft but protect some players I'd beaten out for playing time the previous season.

The next time I spoke to Harry, he explained that upper management had left me unprotected in the Draft because they figured they wouldn't lose me. To be honest, that didn't make me feel any better.

Harry then said that the Bruins attempted to reacquire me from Philadelphia after the Flyers took me in the fourth round. However, the Flyers "wanted too much" in return.

That didn't make me feel better, either.

Nowadays, more than 55 years later, Harry can't recall the discussions that let up to the Bruins deciding to leave me exposed to the Expansion Draft.

"I remember we had a lot of discussion about the list, and Joe's name came up a few times as someone we were thinking about protecting. Why we didn't protect him at the end, I don't recall. I remember that I said he was one of the players that we should protect, in my opinion. It was tough losing him to Philadelphia. I was fond of Joe. He was a good player and a good man. The Flyers did their homework on all of our players, so that's to their credit. They built a very strong team, and a lot of it was with players they selected from the Bruins, such as Parent, Dornhoefer, Favell, and Joe," Siden recalled in April 2021.

Over the rest of the summer of '67, I had to come to grips with the fact that I'd be with an expansion team the next season. What other choice did I have? At least I'd still be in the NHL.

I tried to keep an open mind. Turn the page, Joe, you're a Flyer now. All six expansion teams would be grouped together in the newly created Western Division. Whichever expansion team won two rounds of playoffs against the other Western clubs would advance to the Stanley Cup Final to play whichever Original Six team won the East. Maybe Philly could be that team.

The Flyers' first training camp was held in Quebec City. There were some familiar faces in the other players who'd been selected from the Bruins in the Expansion Draft. Among my new teammates who'd come from other

I wore No. 3 my first two years with the Flyers before switching back to No. 14, which I wore during my years in the Boston organization. This photo was taken during pregame warmups.

NHL organizations, I hit it off quickly with Van Impe. I also saw that my new coach, Allen, had a sharp hockey mind and was a straight shooter. He commanded respect.

During camp, I saw a young, well-dressed man with salt-and-pepper hair and glasses. I asked someone who he was. That was when I was introduced for the first time to Ed Snider, the youngest, most energetic, and most ambitious member of our team's original ownership group. I didn't believe it at first, because he didn't look the part. I'd learn soon, though, that he got very wrapped up emotionally about the hockey side of our organization and not just the business end. From day one, the Flyers were his greatest passion, and he was our team's number-one fan. He took wins and losses as personally as I did. I think that's a big reason why we always got along and understood one another.

Apart from Ed Snider, the ownership group also consisted of Bill Putnam, Jerry Schiff (married to the identical twin sister of Ed's wife, Myrna), and legal counsel Earl Foreman (married to Ed's sister, Phyllis), who temporarily owned a small share of the team. There'd be an acrimonious split with original cofounder Jerry Wolman, with hard feelings lasting between Wolman and Snider the rest of their lives.

I wasn't privy to any of the behind-the-scenes drama, of course, but the Flyers nearly folded before playing a single game. Wolman was in deep debt and asked his business partners to sign off on leveraging the new NHL hockey team as collateral on a loan. Ultimately, there was a takeover by a reconstituted group of owners. Longtime Ballantine beer distribution executive Joe Scott, a wonderful man, stepped up to help the fledgling team get off the ground. He later became team president and one of Ed's most trusted confidants. Foreman also bought a small share, which he soon sold to his brother-in-law.

By the way, it feels strange to this day to refer to Ed Snider by his first name, rather than as Mr. Snider. He always strongly preferred to be called by his first name, but we all held him in such high esteem—for reasons I'll explain later—that we felt it was more respectful to refer to him as Mr. Snider. It's just easier here when referring to various members of his family to use the first names. But I never really got used to calling him by his first name, even long after my playing days as our friendship grew deeper.

During camp, general manager Bud Poile sent me a contract to sign. He lowballed me, offering $18,500 per season to sign a two-year contract. Eddie Van Impe was also unhappy with the contract he received. Figuring there was strength in numbers as well as the fact that we'd both had measures of success in the NHL the previous year, we jointly decided to hold out for more money.

A lawyer by the name of Alan Eagleson, who built a reputation as the NHL's first superagent before his reputation and career came crashing down amid scandal, offered to represent me in the negotiation with the Flyers. I accepted.

Poile, who was hot tempered and used to getting his way, told Eddie and me to leave camp. "Go take a drive, and when you get to your destination, call me," he said. No doubt he figured that we'd both come to our senses and return to the team ASAP. Van Impe and I went together to Erie, Pennsylvania, then split up. I got a plane ticket and flew to British Columbia to see my girlfriend, Marianne, in Kamloops.

When I got to my destination, I called Poile and identified myself.

"OK, so what do you want?" he said impatiently.

"You told me to call you when I got where I was going," I reminded him. "I'm in BC."

I could have sworn that I heard a thunderbolt on the other end of the receiver.

"You're where?!"

"I'm back in British Columbia," I said. "In Kamloops."

"Why the f-k would you go there? Are you out of your goddamn mind?!"

"You told me to go away from the team, so I did," I said.

"Yeah, but I didn't tell you to go that far away," Poile shot back.

Bud proceeded to do almost all the talking. Actually, there was very little conversation. Mostly, Bud burned up the phone line hollering and cursing at me.

Ultimately, I agreed to a two-year contract totaling $20,000 per season. However, Eagleson took a $1,500 commission off the top, so I ended up receiving the same $18,500 for 1967-68 that the Flyers offered me in the first place. Shrewd, eh?

It's strange the way that life works out. I never would have predicted at the time that I'd end up living most of my life in Philadelphia and spending 54 years working almost exclusively for the Flyers. I'll never forget the first impression I had of Philadelphia immediately after my arrival.

I got a ride from the airport. From the passenger side, near the Penrose Avenue Bridge (later renamed the George Platt Bridge), I saw a chop shop. Machines grinded automobiles down to scrap. Car parts lined the ground.

"What's this place? What're they doing?" I asked.

"The mob owns it," I was told. "They use it to get rid of the bodies after they kill people."

I gulped audibly. Welcome to Philadelphia, buddy.

We're getting ready to depart for the first regular-season road trip in Flyers team history. This photo was taken on October 9, 1967.

Anyway, we started our inaugural season on the road, with games against the Seals in Oakland on October 11, 1967, and in Los Angeles against the Kings three nights later. Bing Crosby was on the ice in Oakland before the game.

In the opener, it was miserably hot outside. Inside, the ice was in rough shape. Apart from a goal by Bill Sutherland that briefly tied the score at 1–1 midway through the second period, not much went right for the Flyers or for me individually. Eddie and I were still working our way into game shape after missing time in training camp, and we both struggled, especially in the latter stages of the game. Our defense pairing was out for several goals against as we trailed 3–1 by the end of the second period and went on to suffer a 5–1 defeat.

In Los Angeles, Sutherland scored again, this time on the first shift of the game. Eddie Hoekstra then knocked a Jean Gauthier rebound past Wayne Rutledge to make it a 2–0 lead with 10:52 left in the first period. We had two goals on five shots. After that, well, it was ugly.

Over the final 50 minutes of the game, we got outshot, 34–11, and outscored 4–0. It was another tough game for Van Impe and me, too. I felt bad for Favell, who was under siege after we took the short-lived early lead. He was bombarded with 19 shots in the second period alone and stopped 18 of them. Somehow, we went into the third period leading 2–1 thanks to Dougie, but LA soon tied the score and then went ahead to stay. The final LA goal was an empty netter.

Throughout my career, I wasn't one to fraternize very much with opposing players. But it was nice seeing and saying hello in LA to my old friend and former roommate Ted Irvine, who'd been taken by the Kings from the Bruins in the Expansion Draft. He made his Kings debut on this night (only the second NHL game of his career) and got an assist along with a few shots on goal. Needless to say, Ted was in better spirits than I was when the game was over. I finished the night at minus-one and had taken a holding penalty late in the first period that I would have avoided if I'd had my game legs under me.

We had four days off until our next game: a road match against the St. Louis Blues. That game would be our third as another expansion team's home-opener opponent. After the way our team played in getting outscored by a combined 9–3 in our first two games, I have to admit that I was worried about whether the Flyers could even compete with the other expansion teams, let alone the Original Six.

Where was the goal-scoring going to come from? Sutherland was a capable offensive player but no superstar, despite scoring in each of the first two games. He was a well-traveled minor leaguer. Brit Selby had won the Calder Trophy with Toronto two years earlier and was still just 22 years old, but he wasn't going to be a top-of-the-lineup forward. Our captain, Lou Angotti (taken from Chicago in the Expansion Draft), was our one and only forward who'd spent the entire 1966–67 season in the NHL.

During the time off between the LA game and the trip to St. Louis, we returned to Philadelphia. The city proclaimed October 16, 1967, to be "Philadelphia Flyers Day." We were told that we'd be greeted by Mayor James Tate and then have a welcoming parade down Broad Street to check out our brand-new digs at the newly constructed Spectrum. An open-to-the-public practice was scheduled, followed by a meet-and-greet event with the fans.

This is the first-ever "team photo" of the Philadelphia Flyers. It was taken at a city hall ceremony to welcome our team to the city. We were welcomed by Mayor Tate no-showing the event and by a very sparse (and, in some cases, hostile) group of onlookers during a subsequent "parade" down Broad Street to our new arena in South Philadelphia, the Spectrum. Nowhere to go but up, eh?

When our contingent got to city hall, we were taken to the mayor's reception room. Mayor Tate, however, did not show up. After a delay, we were greeted by City Representative Fredric Mann. We had no idea who he was, which was fair because he had no idea who we were. I doubt he'd ever seen a hockey game in his life. The arts were his main passion, as I learned years later. He's the guy for whom the Mann Music Center is named. We took a few photos, and Mann excused himself.

The subsequent parade was, well, humiliating. We rolled south down Broad Street. Without exaggeration, there were maybe two dozen people watching, and most were construction workers on their break. Very few smiled or waved.

One guy standing by the curb, in fact, derisively flipped us the bird. Then his young boy, standing next to him, followed suit. Like father, like son, eh?

Another guy cupped his hands by his mouth and bellowed, "You bums will be in Baltimore by December!"

No doubt, the heckler was referring to rumors the previous year that Baltimore would get an NHL franchise. The Philadelphia group, called Philadelphia Hockey Club, Inc., was initially considered a longshot bidder, but the NHL ultimately awarded them a franchise. Philadelphians, especially sports fans, can be cynical and pessimistic. That's still true to this day. That October day was the first taste I ever got of the phenomenon that nowadays is called "Negadelphia."

The built-in local cynicism honestly never bothered me much. It's not actual hostility. It's a self-defensive reaction of fans whose hearts had been broken many times before. Besides, people predicting our new team's failure gave us all extra motivation to succeed. Sure enough, I learned that under their tough exterior, the Philadelphia sports fans and community as a whole treat you and your family incredibly well once you win their hearts. I love the Philadelphia fans. One way or another, they let you know they care.

The handful of guys from the original team who were around for our first Stanley Cup parade in 1974—Bernie, Eddie, Dorny, and me—could appreciate just how much things had changed in the seven years since that welcoming parade. When we won the Cup, over two million people came out for the parade, and every one of us was treated like a hero. Actually, we still are, all these years later.

Anyway, getting back to our original parade, we rode south down Broad

Street and arrived at the Spectrum for our first practice. I wish I could say the place looked like a hockey palace, but the truth of the matter is that the place wasn't fully finished yet on the inside. This was due to a labor dispute about overtime pay from the city. The work got done but behind schedule and mighty close to our upcoming home opener.

When we suited up and stepped onto the Spectrum ice for the first time, there were some workmen still painting. We also didn't have the boards installed yet on the ice. Other workers installed the final few seats. Just to keep those guys loose, we shot a few pucks up at 'em. I've got to say—they moved quicker than some of our players!

As I said earlier, the practice was supposed to be open to the public, with fans getting a chance to meet the players afterward. Only problem was that there were two players to each fan that day, so it wasn't much of a meet-and-greet. The only attendees were the surviving members of the old Ramblers minor-league hockey team fan club who'd signed pledges to become the first members of the Philadelphia Flyers fan club. Super nice people. They were thrilled to have a new local team to adopt. We'd need a lot more of 'em to avoid going the way of the long-forgotten Philadelphia Quakers, Philadelphia Arrows, Philadelphia Rockets, and various incarnations of the Ramblers.

At least we were starting to feel more like a team. We might not have been the most talented bunch, but we bonded as a group. Angotti was a good choice for captain: hard working and a true pro. One of my favorite off-ice memories of Lou is that he didn't trust safe-deposit boxes at hotels, and he didn't carry a wallet, so he'd travel with his money rolled up in his sock.

Our hard-nosed, rawhide-tough veteran forward, Forbes Kennedy, took the lead in finding a good hangout spot for the team after practices and games. He knew all the local bars and restaurants. Although it is our "Broad Street Bullies" teams of the 1970s that are primarily associated with hanging out at Rexy's in Mount Ephraim, New Jersey, it was originally Forbie who befriended the establishment's owner, Pasquale "Pat" Fietto, and brought teammates along. Rexy's became our drinking establishment and eatery (the food was damn good, too) for years and years until the 1980s Flyers adopted Kaminski's Bar and Grill in Cherry Hill as their generation's hangout of choice.

Our two goalies, Parent and Favell, were like two peas in a pod. They're both out of their minds, like most goalies. I say that lovingly, of course. On the ice, they were our team's biggest strength. Off the ice, they were fun loving and (sometimes unintentionally) hilarious. The two of them got along great, which isn't always the case with a team's goalies, and they'd been teammates at every level from the Niagara Falls Flyers in junior hockey to Oklahoma City in the minors and then in Philadelphia.

We also had Larry "the Rock" Zeidel, a 39-year-old journeyman tough-guy defenseman who'd played for Poile years earlier on the old Edmonton Flyers. Rock was a great guy off the ice and became my frequent defense partner that season. He also had a few screws loose, and the bomb could explode at any time.

I still had no idea how many games we'd be good enough to win that season. We were, after all, off to a 0-2-0 start and looked bad in the process. But I started to realize that we had a good group of guys.

Keith Allen preached a defensively sound style of play due to our goaltending and an abundance of players who made smart decisions without the puck. We weren't a big team. We weren't an especially tough team, except for a few players. We didn't have blazing speed. We didn't have lots of scorers. But we were getting closer to gelling as a team that could keep the score down and scratch out just enough offense to win or tie.

On October 17, we flew out to St. Louis. The next night we won for the first time, 2–1. Favell outplayed Hall of Fame goaltender Glenn Hall, and Hoekstra broke a 1–1 tie in the third period. I was on the ice for both of our goals and was not on for the only Blues' goal.

There wasn't much time to celebrate, because we had our home opener on the eighteenth against the Pittsburgh Penguins. We all had a couple babalooeys on the plane, though. The conversation flowed much smoother, punctuated with laughter, and the beer tasted better on the plane ride after a win. I was never a cigar aficionado, but we had a few of them on our team, including Bernie and Forbie. They lit up stogies on the plane. It was, after all, a legitimate reason to kick back for a few hours: our first win in franchise history.

The next day, October 19, we had our first-ever home game at the Spectrum. We were nearly short one player. The security guard initially refused admission to Bill Sutherland because he didn't believe the poor guy was a professional athlete. Bill was about 33 years old, but he was one of those guys who looked considerably older than his age. Good thing they let Bill in, too.

In those days, there wasn't yet a third deck at the Spectrum. We drew an OK crowd (7,812) but there were still a lot of empty seats—again, a huge contrast to the full houses we played to every night a few years down the line. We were introduced to the fans by Gene Hart, who actually started out as our public address announcer at the Spectrum before quickly moving to the broadcast booth.

Gene pronounced everyone's name right on our team, even our guys with French-Canadian names like Jean-Guy Gendron, Rosaire Paiement, Leon Rochefort, and Jean Gauthier. About half the people cheered the introductions. Hey, at least no one booed.

Then we had a ceremonial first faceoff, with NHL president Clarence Campbell (who later heard plenty of boos whenever he showed up during our Broad Street Bullies days because we weren't exactly his favorite club) dropping the puck in between our captain, Lou Angotti, and the Penguins' captain, Ab McDonald.

The game got underway. It was very defensive in nature, and the crowd was quiet. The loudest sound was Gene talking during stoppages of play to explain things like power plays, icings, and off-side calls. There weren't a lot of shots on goal for either team (just 14 apiece through the opening 40 minutes), and we had to kill off four of the game's first five penalties. Favell had no problem with the few shots he saw.

Early in the third period (at the 2:59 mark), the Penguins tried to clear the puck, but we held it in the zone. A few seconds later, Sutherland scored a rebound goal past Les Binkley, to give us a 1–0 lead. We held on the rest of the way to christen the Spectrum with our first home win and our first shutout.

Not long after I met Ed Snider for the first time, in Quebec City during training camp, I met two of his kids: sons Craig and Jay. They were still very young, and they had the run of the facilities, including running around the top of the arena on game nights. To be completely honest, I didn't love that at first, or at least I wasn't used to it.

Traditionally, team facilities were strictly off limits to families except for rare occasions. But that was different on Ed Snider's Flyers. Myrna Snider made sure the wives and kids felt like they were part of the family, too. They forged strong bonds of their own, just as the players did. Ed himself made sure that we players had everything we needed, and he got to know us as people as well as players. That was something rare in hockey. It was something that I really came to appreciate.

With Ed Snider at the helm, the loyalty was genuine. It was a two-way street. As a Flyer, you came to know that he cared about your well-being both professionally and personally. The wives knew Myrna cared about them. As players, we knew that our owner rode the same gamut of emotions that we did on the ice, all game and every game. He wore his heart on his sleeve: agonized when we lost, exalted when we won.

Mr. Snider didn't make himself a stranger, and he really came to know the game of hockey itself. There are very few owners in any sport you can say that about. Of course, we all knew that hockey is a business, but most players were far happier to come to the Flyers than they were when it was time to leave. That all started with Ed Snider and his first wife.

We were still a brand-new hockey team, but I was starting to feel at home. Our crowds at the Spectrum weren't overwhelming, but I started to recognize the faces and enjoy their enthusiasm. The fans embraced us once we got going, and they were, well, Philly crowds: passionate, loud, and never left you wondering how they felt. We got along great.

At least as far as the other six expansion teams went, I felt like I'd landed in the best possible place once we started to gel as a team. On November 4, 1967, we played our first game at the Montreal Forum against the Canadiens. It was made clear before the game even started that the other side didn't think we even belonged on the same ice as the Habs. It wasn't quite Harlem Globetrotters vs. Washington Generals, but the clear-cut vibe was that everyone in the building expected us to get our doors blown off by the mighty Habs. Before the Canadiens knew what hit them, we had a quick 2–0 lead.

Rochefort and Parent, both local boys, stole the show that night. Leon scored a hat trick (the first in our team's young history), and Bernie outplayed Rogie Vachon by a wide margin, stopping 34 of 35 shots. At the end of the night, the Canadiens' fans heckled their own team for losing to our lowly expansion team, but they also gave a well-deserved round of applause at the end of the game to Parent and Rochefort, who'd certainly earned it.

The next night, the Canadiens came to Philly. They came in a little less cocky and arrogant than they did one night earlier, and we played a very disciplined game. Early in the second period, Eddie Hoekstra broke a scoreless tie. Parent took a shutout into the latter portion of the third period before Yvan Cournoyer got a lucky bounce to tie the score. The game ended up 1–1. Still, getting three of four points against the Canadiens opened a few eyes around the league.

As big as the November 4 game in Montreal was to Parent, that's how big our trip to Boston on November 12 was to me. There's always extra motivation when you play against your former team, and I had a lot of friends still on the Bruins, including Orr and Sinden. On my first shift of the game, just 1:12 after the opening faceoff, I put a shot at the net from the point that found its way past Cheevers: my first goal as a Flyer and the third of my NHL career.

I had a good night defensively, too, and Parent erased most of the few mistakes we made for two-plus periods. Second-period goals by Rochefort and Sutherland built a 3–0 lead. Boston made a late push in the final five minutes of the game, as Sather and Esposito cut the gap to 3–2. Finally, Don Blackburn scored an empty-net goal in the final minute to seal a 4–2 win for us.

Our win at the Boston Garden in our first game would be the only one we'd earn in that building until Game 2 of the 1974 Stanley Cup Final. I guess you could say we made 'em count, at least. I do remember that it was a real fun night afterward and a miserable follow-up game in Pittsburgh. The Penguins whipped us, 5–0, because we hadn't come ready to play.

Keith Allen warned us before the Pittsburgh game that we had to churn out the same kind of effort again that we did in Montreal and Boston. Plain and simple, we weren't a good enough hockey team to overlook the Penguins. We received the ass-kicking we deserved. We'd just beaten the Canadiens and beaten the Bruins, and we had a game upcoming against the New York Rangers after playing the Pens.

With a fresh team-wide lesson in humility, we got right back on the horse when the Rangers paid a visit to the Spectrum on November 16. Things got testy as we built leads of 2–0 and 3–1 on goals by Van Impe, Rochefort, and Hoekstra. The Rangers had one of the NHL's toughest players in Reggie "the Ruffian" Fleming (who later played for the Flyers), and Reg not only was one of the few guys in the NHL who was unafraid to get Eddie Van Impe pissed off at him, but he also traded off high sticks with our Pat Hannigan and scored a goal for New York. Even so, Favell made a dozen saves in the third period, and we nailed down a 3–2 win over Eddie Giacomin and company.

We'd now beaten three of the so-called Original Six teams, and it was only mid-November. After beating the Rangers and batting the Minnesota North Stars to a 2–2 road tie, we rattled off four more consecutive wins. Each of the games was memorable to me in its own right.

On November 19, Scotty Bowman's St. Louis Blues came to town. While we certainly had a few tough guys on our team—Forbie, Rock, Eddie, and Dorny—they had the bigger, more physical, nastier, and meaner team. From my minor-league days, I already knew full well that the late Noel Picard was a dangerous and ruthless player. It was also no damn fun playing against the likes of the Plager brothers, Bob and Barclay.

Quick side story here before I get to the game: Although I hated the Plagers as opponents, similar to how I used to dislike Glen Sather and Pat Quinn when they were on the other side, we got to be friends off the ice. I particularly liked Bob as a person once I got to know him. Bob once told me a great story that's a perfect example of how us rough-around-the-edges Canadian boys might have had plenty of hockey toughness, but we didn't always have a ton of street smarts.

When Bob was playing for the Baltimore Clippers in the American Hockey League, the guys went out for a few pops after the game, and he wore a new leather jacket. A guy brushed into him and, unprovoked, challenged him to fight. Not about to turn down a challenge, Bob took off the jacket and rolled up his sleeves. The other guy promptly grabbed the jacket and ran like hell. Plager never caught up to him. He always made me laugh whenever he retold that story.

Anyway, our first home game against the Blues was a precursor to what would become the Flyers' fiercest rivalry during our early seasons. Yes, it was St. Louis we hated the most, and not the Rangers or Penguins or Bruins or any other team that later got associated with a history of bad blood with Philly. We built up a 3–0 lead on goals by Blackburn, Angotti, and Van Impe, and then held on for a 3–2 win behind Parent. In the third period, we checked the hell out of them. The Blues got frustrated.

Not surprisingly, it was Noel Picard who started trouble, first with a questionable hit on Hoekstra and then tangling with Dornhoefer. At the end of the game, Picard instigated a melee that resulted in the first line brawl in our team's history—the first fighting majors, in fact, which went to Zeidel and Hannigan on our side and Picard and Gord Kannegiesser. Plager earned himself 29 minutes worth of penalties in the third period alone.

I was damn happy we'd won that game. I was chosen second star of the game. It is always a good feeling to be recognized for your contributions to a winning effort, especially when you are not a goal-scoring player.

Three nights later, we hosted the Detroit Red Wings. What I recall about this game was that the line of Angotti, Sutherland, and Dornhoefer outplayed the likes of Gordie Howe and Alex Delvecchio and were instrumental in us making Detroit the fourth preexpansion team that we beat

In this photo from a November 30, 1967, home game, teammate Bill Sutherland carried the puck over the attacking blue line as I tried to join the attack.

in a inaugural season. Sutherland scored two goals, and Dorny was like a man possessed on the forecheck.

In another game against the Red Wings during my rookie year, Gordie broke my nose. A few years later when I was with the Flyers, Howe and I both went down awkwardly on the ice. Unfortunately, Howe suffered cracked ribs.

"Don't move!" Gordie hollered.

"Don't worry," I replied. "I can't!"

Anyway, getting back to my first year in Philly, Angotti was a very good choice for our inaugural captain. He was a true pro, had a tremendous work ethic, and embodied the sort of unselfish and team-oriented approach that Keith Allen wanted to become central to our team identity. He wasn't big (five-foot-nine, 170 pounds), but he played with heart and competitiveness. Lou only spent one year in Philly, but he made it count.

Lou was also very good about making sure we bonded as teammates. We were all new to Philadelphia, but we had each other. He made sure everyone felt included. That's one of the responsibilities of a captain, and it came naturally to him. He wore the "C" with pride and understanding of what the role required.

After we beat the Red Wings, we traveled to St. Louis for our season series rubber match with the Blues. Early in the first period, Dornhoefer shrugged off a cross-check from Barclay Plager and scored on a Sutherland rebound. It didn't take long for things to heat up after that. Forbie Kennedy and Picard traded off stick work. Ron Attwell boarded Wayne Hicks. There were several retaliatory spearing penalties (both teams were guilty) in the second period, culminating with Dorny fighting Ron Stewart in response to getting a stick blade to the gut. Midway through the third period, Angotti got his stick up with Frank St. Marseille and skated off with a cut under his eye.

Oh, and we won the game 2–1. Only a goal by my old Oklahoma City buddy and future Flyers teammate Terry Crisp got past Parent among the 47 shots on goal he faced. Yup, this win felt good, too.

On November 26, we won yet again. This time it was a 7–2 rout of LA at the Spectrum. Seven different Flyers, including myself, scored once apiece.

Bernie had a pretty easy night in goal. As I've stated before, we were far from a high-scoring team, but we were firing on all cylinders at the time. Coming to the rink every day was fun. Our crowds at the Spectrum were starting to grow, too. We were now drawing about 11,700 per game, and we were getting onto the front page of the sports section in the newspaper with some regularity.

We had a decent month of December. The Original Six teams were a little better prepared for us now, but we usually beat the other expansion teams, including a couple more wins against the Blues. We finished out the calendar year with back-to-back wins over the LA Kings. On New Year's Eve, we crushed LA, 9–1, in the most lopsided win of our first season. Even the Rock scored a goal on this night—the only goal he scored as a Flyer and the third and final tally of his NHL career.

Too bad we couldn't spread out some of those extra goals from the LA game in January. We went 4-7-2 largely because goals were hard for our team to come by most of that month. But our January 24 game at Maple Leaf Gardens was a huge one for our team. Doug Favell and Bruce Gamble waged one hell of a goalie battle, and Favie came out ahead. We sandwiched an early first-period goal by Hoekstra and a mid-third-period score by Claude LaForge, created by the hustle of Forbes Kennedy in between 46 saves by Favell in a 2–1 win. We now had at least one win over five of the six Original Six teams. Only the Chicago Black Hawks remained.

On February 3 at the Spectrum, I had my only multipoint game of my first season in Philly. I was credited with a power-play goal off a faceoff and an even-strength assist as we defeated Chicago, 5–3. To this day, I take pride in the fact that the Flyers were not only the lone 1967 Expansion team to beat all six preexisting teams in the inaugural season but that it took most of the other new teams several seasons to do so. For good measure, right after we beat the Black Hawks, we knocked off Toronto again. This time, it was by a 4–1 score at the Spectrum.

I've always associated good times with playing winning hockey. In upcoming chapters, I won't have as much to say about the 1968–69 to 1971–72 seasons because I've largely blocked those out of my mind over the years. Those weren't fun times from a professional standpoint. But those first five months of our inaugural season were the most fun I had until our

Flyers team became a Stanley Cup contender and then a champion. We were a close-knit, overachieving team.

And then the roof blew off the Spectrum. I mean that literally. On March 1, 1968, during a performance of the Ice Capades, high winds caused a chunk of the roof to blow off the building. Our home rink was closed for the rest of the season and would not open again until the playoffs.

For the rest of the season, we lived like vagabonds. We played "home games" at Madison Square Garden in New York and Maple Leaf Gardens (where Leafs owner Harold Ballard charged the Flyers such an extortionate rental fee that Ed Snider nearly canceled the game). The rest of our home games were played at the Coliseum in Quebec City, the home rink of our AHL farm team, the Quebec Aces. Although the Aces were a good team, and, in fact, reached the Calder Cup Finals in both 1967–68 and 1968–69, they didn't get much fan support at their games.

With little money coming in via the gates, Ed Snider (who was traveling with our team) was worried about whether our organization could survive the arena closure. He always leveled with us players, and he told us the finances were becoming dire.

"I don't know if I can keep the team going," he said aloud one night.

Fortunately, the Flyers had a very understanding and committed lender in Girard Bank, especially executive Bill Baer, who was a Harvard graduate from Boston and a lifetime hockey lover. The bank loaned Mr. Snider an additional $2 million to get them over their financial crisis. Some old-time Flyers fans likely remember how Girard Bank was always one of our team's most visible and devoted sponsors in our early years, but they may not know that they probably saved our team from early extinction. Mr. Snider later became independently wealthy, but he never forgot what the support of people like Joe Scott and Girard Bank meant to his success. Ed spent a lifetime paying that forward.

While Ed Snider was worrying about keeping our team afloat financially, we started to feel like the Western Division race could slip away from us. We started out the month of March by going 0-3-1. On March 7, one night after the Maple Leafs put a 7–2 beating on us, we were the "home" team in Toronto against the Bruins.

Because we were a brand-new expansion team, everyone on the Flyers had to pitch in to try to generate fan interest in our club, off the ice as well as on. Here, I was enlisted to make a lottery drawing.

Apart from losing the game, 2–1, this match had one of the ugliest and craziest incidents I ever witnessed in my half century plus in the sport: the infamous stick fight between Larry Zeidel and Eddie Shack. I was paired on defense with the Rock.

As was very often the case back in those days, there was a lot of bench jockeying—trash-talking, chirping, whatever you want to call it. It still goes on to this day, but the boundary lines have shifted over the years. Larry, being the only Jewish player in the NHL for much of his career, heard a lot of ethnic slurs, as did the Italian-Canadian Phil Esposito, the league's French-Canadian players, First Nation players—whoever stood out as different. Not too much of anything said on the ice was considered off limits if it could get someone distracted or get them to blow their cool. Different times, I guess.

On this occasion, someone on the Boston bench apparently crossed the line with Zeidel, at least in Rock's retelling of it, by mocking the fact that Larry had lost relatives in Europe to the Holocaust twenty-some years earlier. I didn't hear what was said or who said it. Larry himself wasn't sure who said it, but he reacted so vehemently that I never doubted he was telling the truth about what he heard. I'd seen Rock lose his temper before but never quite like this. He had a nearly homicidal look on his face.

Eddie Shack was not the culprit in whatever vile comment directly set off Zeidel. Larry always said he was sure of that much. But Shack was the perfect proxy from Zeidel's point of view. Those two had quite a history of doing battle with one another and needed little provocation to go at each other's throats. Years earlier, those two had a stick fight in Niagara Falls that started near the benches, spilled over into the stands, and resulted in both players being arrested by the local police. Now they were ready for round two.

I held onto the nearest opposing player, my former Bruins teammate Ted Green, as was standard during on-ice fights. But Rock and Shack weren't satisfied with fisticuffs. They started jousting with their sticks and swinging them like baseball bats at each other's heads.

Ted and I got the hell out of Dodge, as did everyone else but Larry and Eddie. Both men were badly bloodied but continued to swing what had been virtually reduced to jagged twigs at each other. They were ejected and escorted to the respective locker rooms for repairs at 9:33 of the first period.

During intermission, as I returned to the locker room, Zeidel came barreling out into the hallway. He still had stitching needles sticking out of his head. Someone had told him that Shack was in a nearby room, and Larry was intent on finding him to continue the dispute. I don't know if Shack was there or not, but Larry was removed from the scene before he could find out. Both players were fined and suspended by the NHL.

I always liked Larry. For all his eccentricities, he was a good man with his heart in the right place. It also goes without saying that he was one hell of a tough guy to make it in hockey for as long as he did and to work his way back into the NHL in his late thirties after many years in the minor leagues. I enjoyed his company and always knew he had my back: two important qualities in a good teammate.

Despite all the trials and tribulations, we managed to hang on and clinch first place in the Western Division. We did it on March 30, 1968.

With the Spectrum yet to be reopened, we visited the Penguins at the "Igloo" in Pittsburgh. We sustained a 2–0 loss in front of 5,569 fans. A first-period goal by Leo Boivin held up until Earl Ingarfield added an empty-net goal in the final minute of the game. Pittsburgh goalie Les Binkley recorded a 23-save shutout. Doug Favell stopped 21 of 22 shots in a losing cause.

Later that night, however, the second-place Kings played to a 2–2 road tie against the Oakland Seals. Playing the final game of the regular season, Los Angeles gained one point (their 72nd of the season) but remained one point behind the Flyers. That clinched the West for us and rendered meaningless a rematch against the Penguins in the final game of the season.

When we learned of the outcome of the Kings game, Ed Snider convened a team celebration at the Radio Artist Club. Most of us partied through the night, including Mr. Snider and me. Our free-spirited goalie, Doug Favell, was a little disappointed in the timing, however.

"Did we have to clinch now?" Favell griped. "I just took three sleeping pills, and *The Slime People* is on the Late, Late Movie."

We played the Blues in the Stanley Cup Quarterfinals, just as the Spectrum reopened.

It was a very hard-fought series, which we lost in seven games. The Blues brought Hockey Hall of Famer Doug Harvey out of retirement at age 43, and damned if he didn't assist on what proved to be the series-winning goal in St. Louis' clinching victory. Red Berenson added a late empty netter to seal a 3–1 final.

More than any other play in that series, though, the most historically important moment came during the third period of Game 5. A brawl erupted at 9:03 of the third period. Noel Picard blindsided and viciously assaulted Claude LaForge, who happened to be the closest bystander. Claude, a five-foot-eight finesse player, was totally unsuspecting. He crashed face first to the ice and was left unconscious in a pool of blood. He lost 13 teeth.

Ed Snider privately vowed that he'd never again see a Philadelphia team manhandled in that manner. In the years to come, the Flyers assembled the team that became known as the "Broad Street Bullies." LaForge did not play again in the series and was out of the NHL shortly thereafter.

No one felt sympathy for Claude LaForge or the Flyers when the Blues victimized him. So we got bigger and tougher as a team and took care of our own business. That's why I never had much time or patience for our team's critics during our glory years.

CHAPTER 6

Bernie and the Bear

I had a visitor in Smithers during the summer after my first season with the Flyers. My teammate, Bernie Parent, traveled out west to enjoy the outdoors and have a little bit of offseason fun. As it turned out, Bernie spent as much or more time hanging out with my dad as he did with me and my hometown friends.

My father and Bernie hit it off instantly. They smoked cigars, drank a few babalooeys, and probably sat in front of the black-and-white TV in the house to laugh at the antics of Moe, Larry, Curly, and Shemp on the old Three Stooges films that had started airing in syndication on Canadian TV a few years earlier. Parent always loved the Stooges.

Bernie was—and still is—an avid outdoorsman. Apart from hockey, our mutual love of fishing was one of the things that we bonded over as friends. Bernie has long enjoyed hunting, too. As a child, Bernie used to go on fishing and hunting trips with his late father, Claude, to Mont-Laurier in northwestern Quebec. He loved that area and quickly felt at home, too, in and around Smithers.

Those who know Bernie best will attest to the fact that he's a very spontaneous type of guy. He goes with the flow, and he often does whatever comes to mind in the moment. While he was in Smithers, he decided he wanted to go bear hunting. Joe Tennant, my old hockey coach and railroad engineer by trade, offered to take Bernie.

Bernie was thrilled. He got to combine a train ride through beautiful northwestern British Columbia with a chance to go hunting. Somehow, Bernie decided, and got Joe Tennant to agree, to bag a bear while on the train—an illegal activity, mind you—after seeing a young bear near the tracks.

Bernie's first shot missed and frightened the hell out of the bear, which weighed less than 100 pounds. It started running down the tracks. Eventually, Bernie pumped the poor thing so full of lead that it died from lead poisoning and sheer fright by the time it fell.

Now that he'd bagged the bear, Bernie had to figure out what the hell to do with it. With some assistance, he strapped the carcass to the roof of his car. He ended up driving around with it for several days. It was a bloody mess, literally, and soon attracted flies. Not a pretty sight, believe me.

I'm pictured here in early 1968 with my Flyers teammates Forbes Kennedy and Bernie Parent. Bernie came to Smithers that summer to visit me. He had quite the adventure while he was there.

While my Flyers contract was far from lucrative, I was now at least making enough money that I didn't need a second job to tide myself over until the next season. Apart from Bernie's visit, I was able to spend time with my girlfriend, Marianne, during the summer of '68 before reporting to the Flyers' training camp in Quebec. During camp, we lived at the Laurentides Motel in the Quebec City suburb of Beauport.

Several weeks before we reported to camp, as was typical in the NHL at the time, the Flyers players received a precamp letter from general manager Bud Poile. The letter outlined the expectations for us once we arrived. It was standard stuff for the time but nowadays makes me chuckle to reread. Here is the text from the two-page letter:

1. After checking into your rooms, please report to Dr. Stanley Spoont and Dr. Gendron Marcoux for your medicals.

2. Players with automobiles can arrange with the front desk for parking facilities that are available. Automobiles may be used to go to practice. However, bus transportation to and from the Colisee has been arranged for your use. Check the lobby for schedule.

3. Please submit your travel expenses to Bud Poile. (*Note: We had to front those costs ourselves for the team to approve and reimburse.*)

4. You are responsible for all long-distance telephone calls, laundry, and dry cleaning charged against your room. Any charges must be paid within 24 hours. *(Note: Thank goodness for those Sunday long-distance rates back then. Calling Marianne or my family in Smithers was an expensive proposition, especially on our salaries of the time.)*

5. Check each evening in the lobby. Your shift times will be posted by 10 p.m. Be on time for all practices and travel. *(Note:*

I am habitually punctual or a bit early. Growing up in the hockey realm conditioned me to this. Especially in the old school days, but nowadays as well, lateness for any team activity or travel was frowned upon by a hockey team. Many years later, when I was managing the Flyers Alumni Team, I maintained these same punctuality expectations for my teammates and myself.)

6. Curfew at training camp will be 11:00 p.m. That means being in your own room. If a player is absent, he will be subject to a fine. *(Note: This is an age-old cat-and-mouse game. Yes, we had our share of guys who regularly bent or broke curfew. I wasn't a saint, either. In reality, so long as you were on time for everything else, showed up ready and in condition to play or practice, and weren't too blatant about what you did at night, there was leniency. We had no star players, but star players, of course, got even a little more leeway.)*

7. You are responsible for placing your own wakeup calls. *(Note: After my experience of missing out on a Bruins callup due to a snafu with the alarm when I roomed with Teddy Irvine, I always made damn sure I was awake in plenty of time.)*

8. Be sure your equipment is ready for workouts, and all protective equipment must be worn. If repairs are needed, be sure to tell the trainers. Players must be properly attired for all practices. Help out your trainers by hanging up all equipment. It only takes a minute. *(Note: Protective equipment back then, for most players, did not include a helmet. We had our shoulder and elbow pads, jocks, shin guards, etc., but the melon was unprotected. I never wore a helmet in my pro career, but my brother Jimmy did wear one for portions of his. It really should have been common sense to wear one, I admit. As for the second part of the instruction, you can tell a lot about a player's character by how he treats the trainers/equipment managers. These guys are*

part of the team and help the players tremendously in a largely thankless role that no one ever got rich doing. Guys who treated the trainers like servants were almost inevitably bad teammates, too. Thankfully, not many players were like that.)

9. Following practice, skates to be sharpened must be left in the middle of the room. *(Note: All I can really add to this is something that relates to my last comment. Trainers get to know exactly how players like their skates to be sharpened: some want them razor sharp at all times, others not quite as sharp. Things such as stick-taping preferences may seem trivial to outsiders but are very particular and personalized. If a player breaks a stick midshift, it's the equipment staff that has to quickly retrieve another one of yours from the rack and hand it to you with an absolute minimum delay. The really good trainers are worth their weight in gold to a team and are usually great guys off the ice, too. I had great trainers in Philly over the years such as Frank Lewis and Jim McKenzie, and the Flyers Alumni Team has an outstanding one in Dave Culp.)*

10. Injuries, however slight the player may think they are, must be reported immediately to the coach, the team doctor, or trainer and regarded with the same importance as a team function. *(Note: This was always a dicey proposition. If you can play, you play. There's also the old saying "You can't help the club in the tub" that we and other teams had posted in our trainer room. No one wanted the rep of being a guy who was taking treatment constantly or complaining about every little ache and pain. Serious injuries were another matter, but this instruction from the precamp letter really didn't jibe with the real-life way of doing things in hockey.)*

11. Smoking is not permitted in the dressing room, and cigars are not permitted on the bus. *(Note: Most teams in that era,*

including ours, had their fair share of cigarette and cigar smokers, as well as tobacco chewers.)

12. Your weight will be checked periodically. *(Note: Conditioning standards nowadays are much more stringent.)*

13. Sticks must not be given away, taken from the dressing room, or broken in fits of anger. *(Note: This rule makes me chuckle, but not as much as the next one.)*

14. Many youngsters as well as adults attend practices, games, etc. Let us curb bad language. *(Note: Yup, this one was broken on a daily basis! Wherever hockey players hail from originally, we all speak fluent profanity.)*

15. Please dress in sport shirts or dress shirts when around the motel, restaurant, or Le Colisee. A shirt and tie are mandatory for all travel or home games. *(Note: There's still a dress code nowadays around NHL teams. The main difference is the players own more suits to travel in because they're making a hell of a lot more money.)*

16. Drinking of intoxicants is forbidden. Players are not to enter taverns or other drinking places. There will be a minimum fine of $100. *(Note: I don't think I need to say much about how strictly this rule was followed or enforced. In the real-life hockey world, the main rule of thumb as players was to make sure you didn't go to the same bars as the coaches and GMs.)*

17. No gambling. *(Note: But if a few friendly wagers during card games slipped in among teammates, well, no one was going to snitch.)*

18. A player must make himself available for all press radio-TV

> interviews, personal appearances, and still photographs and motion pictures when requested by the club.

An additional page expanded a little further on the dress code, travel, and media availability policies. In regard to dress code, there was a note that coach Keith Allen and general manager Poile were fine with players being comfortably dressed while lounging around during camp but requested "you refrain from wearing t-shirts, dungarees, et cetera" in public at any time and added, "Remember, you are not only a representative of the Flyers and Aces but all of hockey."

As related to travel, we were told that for all road trips, we'd travel as a team. Further, "in order to preboard planes, the team must be at the assigned gate 20 minutes before takeoff."

Regarding being accessible to the media, we were instructed to "please cooperate with these men." Additionally, "if it is impossible to be available at the time requested, try to accommodate that person as soon as possible thereafter."

Not only because there were no women covering hockey in the newspaper, TV, and radio media back then, this instruction seems quaint nowadays. But we came to know pretty well most of the reporters who covered our team back then; in fact, many of us became friends over time. There wasn't nearly the same degree of tension or mistrust back then or fear over what would get printed or repeated. This was mutually beneficial in some ways and, I suppose, bad in other ways. I do miss the rapport—being on a first-name basis and chatting with the main reporters we saw throughout the season about nonhockey stuff as well as the game.

The precamp letter ended with this: "Let's work together for another successful season. Good luck."

Well, we'd need all the luck we could get in our second season. A lot of us came in optimistic that we could build on what we did in 1967–68, perhaps even be the team that came out of the West Division in the playoffs to play the winner of the East Division for the Stanley Cup.

Instead, we went backward. Keith Allen preached the same formula as the previous year: play sound defense, keep the score low, and score just enough to win games. Offensively, despite some minor roster changes, we were pretty much the exact same team that scuffled to put the puck in the net. We scored 173 goals in 1967–68 and 174 in 1968–69.

Perhaps the most notable change on our roster, at least from a perspective of hockey history, was that Poile brought in defenseman Allan Stanley to replace Larry Zeidel. Allan was a Hockey Hall of Fame player. Thing is, he was already 42 years old at that point—two years older than the Rock—and was nearing 1,200 regular season games and more than 105 games in the Stanley Cup playoffs.

Stanley ("Sudden Sam," as I called him) played decently, but he was no longer the same player who formed half of one of the NHL's most illustrious defense pairings with the late Tim Horton. I'm from the generation that remembers Horton as a brilliant hockey player and not just the guy the donut shop franchise is named after. Allan, who passed away in 2013 at the age 87, played only the final season of his career in Philly. He retired after the 1968–69 season.

The other main difference between our inaugural and second roster was that Lou Angotti was gone via trade, and Ed Van Impe stepped in as the captain. During the 1968 offseason, Poile traded Angotti in a three-way deal with Pittsburgh and St. Louis. Gerry Melnyk and Darryl Edestrand came over from the Blues organization to Philadelphia.

Melnyk never got to play in a game for the Flyers. He suffered a heart attack in training camp that forced him to retire at age 34. In a stroke of fate that would pay Philadelphia huge dividends in the future, Gerry became a scout. He'd been a decent hockey player, but he turned out to be one of the best scouts in NHL (not just Flyers) history. Among a slew of others, it was Melnyk who lobbied in 1969 for the draft selection of Bobby Clarke and, years later, recommended Pelle Lindbergh and then Ron Hextall.

Edestrand, meanwhile, went on to have a respectable 455-game NHL career but mostly played for the Quebec Aces during his two seasons in the Flyers' organization. He got into two games as a Flyer.

As hockey trades go, this deal didn't help the Flyers much. But I guess you could say it worked out in the end because of the impact Gerry ended up having for the Flyers organization on the scouting side.

One of the biggest differences in our team in year two was the comparative play of our goalies. During our first year, Bernie (16-17-5 record, 2.48 GAA, four shutouts) and Dougie (15-15-6 record, 2.27 GAA, four shutouts) played strong seasons behind us and were pretty much interchangeable. In year two, though, Favell struggled (3-12-5, 3.56 GAA), while Parent kept us in most games (17-23-16, 2.69 GAA). We won 11 fewer games than our first year and had 10 more ties instead. For whatever reason, we especially struggled to score when Bernie was in net. We played lots and lots of 1–1, 2–2, and 3–3 games when Parent started.

We got off to a slow start in October, going just 1-5-2 in our first eight games. However, very briefly, we started to feel like we just might recapture the form we had the previous year. On November 2, we went into Toronto, and two goals by Jean-Guy Gendron plus 32 saves by Parent lifted us to a 3–2 win over the Maple Leafs.

The next night, we were in Montreal. We shook off goals by Hall of Famers Jean Beliveau and Henri Richard before coming back to win, 3–2. Our French-Canadian line of Simon Nolet, rookie center Andre Lacroix, and veteran Gendron led the comeback before Jimmy Johnson scored the game winner and Forbes Kennedy punctuated the win with a doozy of a fight against Terry Harper. Parent made 33 saves and won first-star honors.

Hockey, though, has a way of keeping you humble. After we beat the Habs, we got crushed by the Bruins at the Boston Garden, 7–1. The next night, November 7, 1968, we played St. Louis at the Spectrum. I remember that date by heart because I was an unwitting part of hockey history that night. We might have been playing the Blues, but I was seeing red—Red Berenson, that is.

On this night, Berenson tied an NHL record by scoring six goals, including five in a row over the first and second periods. Unfortunately, the defense pairing of Eddie Van Impe and me were on the ice for all six Berenson goals. Ed gave him a two-hander on the leg after the last one. We lost 8–0.

To this day, I cringe whenever one of those "Today in Hockey History" segments pops up on NHL Network or TSN on a November 7. It's not a fun memory. The Flyers fans booed us and applauded Red at the end, which was a justified response.

To make matters worse, I injured my shoulder and was out for 13 games after undergoing surgery. At least our team won some games. Right after the roller coaster ride plummeted during the ass-kickings we took from the Bruins and Blues, it climbed again as we won three of the next four games. Favell shut out the Penguins in a fight-filled game. Even more satisfying for the boys, we beat the visiting Bruins in the next game, 4–2. Parent had 31 saves, and fellow ex-Bruin Gary Dornhoefer notched a pair of goals and an assist.

The worst stretch of our season followed shortly thereafter as we went 11 straight games without a win (0-9-2). I was still rehabbing my shoulder injury and sidelined for most of it. I discovered that when your team is losing but you're at least healthy and playing in the lineup, you feel like you can at least control your own performance. When you are sidelined and the club is losing, you feel helpless and useless. There was a newspaper photo of me sitting in the stands during a game played amid our winless streak, and the look on my face told the story of all my emotions: it was a miserable time.

Bud's infamous temper boiled over around this time, too. He read the team the riot act in the dressing room after we got shut out by the Seals, 4–0, in front of just 3,166 fans in Oakland. Truthfully, I couldn't blame him for it. Still in an ill humor, Poile got into a verbal altercation with Blues broadcaster Gus Kyle when St. Louis visited the Spectrum on December 8. We learned about it after the fact.

At this point in our history, we were still the ones getting bullied. Noel Picard boarded Don Blackburn of our players on the game's first shift. In response, on his second shift of the game, Forbie Kennedy mixed it up with Barclay Plager. Shortly thereafter, Picard high-sticked and cut one of our guys. Pat Hannigan stepped up and fought Picard. Late in the period, Picard was at it again and butt-ended Kennedy.

Already frustrated with our winless streak and worked up over the antics of Picard in particular, Poile paced the press box. When he overheard Kyle's broadcast commentary, which was slanted toward the Blues, Bud exploded. Without waiting for the end of the period or a stoppage of play, Bud stormed into the broadcast booth.

"Why don't you tell the truth?!" Poile demanded. "Go get your eyes fixed!"

We trailed much of the game, battling back from deficits of 2–1, 3–2, and 4–3. Stanley scored his first goal as a Flyer to even up the game at 2–2 and then set up Nolet late in the second period to create a 3–3 tie. After Picard scored to put the Blues ahead again, Forbie got a measure of revenge as he beat Picard to a Hannigan rebound and forced the puck over the goal line past Glenn Hall. The game ended in a 4–4 tie.

The next day, the Blues filed a complaint with the NHL about Poile's outburst. Bud refused to pay the ensuing fine.

I returned to the lineup the next game. We lost that one to Toronto, 1–0, running our winless stretch to 10 straight games. Two nights later, Bernie waged one hell of a goalie's duel in Montreal with Tony Esposito. Parent stopped 46 shots. Only a puck off the stick of Canadiens' tough guy John Ferguson got past Bernie. Unfortunately, we didn't beat "Tony O" even once on 25 shots. The result was yet another 1–0 loss. Our season record fell to 6-17-4.

I'll say it again: Nowhere to go but up, eh?

Over our next 11 games, we only lost twice. Mind you, we only won three. Yup, that's right, we played to six ties in that stretch, including four in a row in one point. At least it was better than losing. Additionally, one of our youngest players, Lacroix, was starting to put up points with some regularity. For the first time in our team's short history, we had a player who could make plays with the puck. Andy went on to lead our goal-starved team with 24 goals (13 on the power play) and 56 points.

The inordinate number of tie games became a recurring theme throughout the rest of the regular season, but the wins remained scarce. It got mind numbing, to be totally honest. Without much scoring pop at his disposal beyond our French-Canadian line, all that Keith Allen could do as coach was stick with the program and encourage us to try to win games by 2–1 or 1–0 scores.

For different reasons, Bud was starting to grate on the players' nerves, as well as Keith's and Ed Snider's nerves.

Mr. Snider was already getting to be a student of the game of hockey, much more than your average team owner. Poile found Ed's inquisitive nature threatening and thought nothing of telling his boss to mind his own business, stop asking so many questions, and let the GM run the team. That was *not* the way to deal with Ed (or any boss, really).

In Keith's case, our team morale was pretty low by this point, and he was doing all he could to get us up for games. Bud wasn't helping by haranguing our players constantly and telling the reporters that our team had collectively misplaced our work ethic (which was also an indirect criticism of our coach).

For that matter, even many of the players' wives were mad at Bud. As recounted in Jay Greenberg's book *Full Spectrum,* he publicly included the wives in the blame game for why the team was struggling.

"Players shouldn't be babysitting or taking their wives and girlfriends on shopping trips during the season. These girls like the nice clothes that hockey buys, and they like to go to Florida after the season. They have to sacrifice if they want that. They should let the players concentrate on hockey during the winter," Poile said.

Yeah, that stuff went over with the wives about as well as you'd expect.

On January 30, the Black Hawks tore us apart, 12–0. Shortly after that, Favell was briefly replaced on the roster by Quebec Aces goalie Dunc Wilson before rejoining the Flyers two weeks later. That disaster started another winless streak. This one was a nine-gamer (0-6-3). I scored my first goal of the season on February 8—once again in Boston—but we fell to a 6–5 loss.

The next night we were supposed to play the Rangers in Madison Square Garden. Meanwhile, heavy snow and high winds rocked the entire northeastern seaboard of the United States. Somehow, we were able to catch a train, but an electrical malfunction forced the engineer to make a stop in Pelham, New York. It was uncertain when—or if—we'd get moving again.

Keith borrowed a pair of snow boots from Dorny. He got off the train and disappeared out in the storm to go find a pay phone to call Rangers general manager and coach Emile Francis to inform him that our team was currently stranded in Pelham and we might not make it to Manhattan for the game.

However, the issue was quickly fixed. Keith noticed that the train was about to take off and ran back to get aboard just as it slowly started to pull away. He was covered in snow, red faced, and out of breath but safe.

We finally arrived at Penn Station, just across from MSG, some eight hours after we left South Station in Boston and barely an hour before our game against the Rangers. The game itself ended—you guessed it—in a tie. But this was an especially galling tie. We had a 3–0 lead midway through the third period on goals by Gendron, Donny Blackburn, and Lacroix. The Rangers, who outshot us 18–5 in the third period, scored twice to cut the gap to one goal. With their goalie pulled for an extra attacker, Bob Nevin scored through a heavy screen in the final 42 seconds to create a 3–3 tie.

A 4–3 win at the Spectrum over the Seals finally ended our winless streak. It didn't come easily. We spent the last several minutes on the penalty kill. Forbie snapped late in the game, high-sticking and then spearing a Seals player. Escorted to the penalty box, he charged out to go challenge the Seals bench and threw a glove at their coach, Fred Glover. Kennedy was tossed from the game. Three big saves by Parent with the Seals on a six-on-four attack enabled us to hold on for the win.

After the win against the Seals, we went winless in our next six games, losing three and tying three. Meanwhile, Keith Allen had a very public falling out with Kennedy, who griped about his declining ice time and the fact that our team kept spinning our wheels. That's what happens on hockey teams when the wins are too scarce, nerves get frayed, and the team's mentality becomes one of waiting for something bad to happen.

Things between Keith and Forbie finally came to a head when a verbal confrontation almost became physical. Poile suspended Kennedy for insubordination, and he went home to Prince Edward Island in the Maritimes to await a trade. On March 2, he was traded to Toronto along with Brit Selby. In exchange, the Flyers reacquired Bill Sutherland (whom the Flyers had lost in the intraleague draft after the 1967–68 season) and also picked up Gerry Meehan and Mike Byers. The same day, Poile sold the contract of another player who'd grown unhappy, Pat Hannigan, to the Vancouver Canucks (then a Western Hockey League club, not the subsequent NHL team of the same name).

For those of us who remained, there was a clearing-the-air meeting. There were only 12 games left in the season, but the playoffs were still in reach because of how weak the Western Division was overall. We finally got a hot streak during the heart of the stretch drive. We won seven games, including four in a row and one point, and tied three others. One of three ties was a 3–3 deadlock on the road against the North Stars on March 15. My second and final goal of the season evened the score midway through the third period.

Our late surge of 17 points was sufficient for the Flyers to leapfrog Minnesota and Los Angeles to finish third in the Western Division. Once again, we drew St. Louis in the Stanley Cup Quarterfinals. Unfortunately, unlike the nip-and-tuck series of the previous year that went the full seven games and could have swung either way, this series was no contest. The Blues swept us in four games: 5–2 and 5–0 in St. Louis and by scores of 3–0 and 4–1 in Philadelphia. St. Louis once again went on to reach the Stanley Cup Final, where they lost in four straight games to Montreal.

After we came to camp with high hopes, the 1968–69 season was a disappointment both for me and for the team. Following the season, Marianne and I got married in Smithers. Bobby Orr was my best man. Orr's arrival was treated locally like a visit from royalty. Unlike Bernie Parent's visit, the bears were also safe with Orr in town.

This family photo was taken at my wedding in Smithers. With me are my mom and my brothers Fred, Steven, Jimmy, Glen, and Jerry.

CHAPTER 7

Check but Don't Check

My brother Jimmy left Smithers for Alberta at age 17, where he joined the Calgary Centennials for the 1968–69 season. He was coached by my old coach from Estevan, Scotty Munro. Scotty hadn't changed a bit: he was just as gruff and hard nosed but as caring to his players underneath the tough shell as he'd been when he was my coach.

Although Jimmy was a more naturally gifted hockey player than me, it took him time to thrive in Calgary. I'll let him tell the story.

"I probably didn't have my priorities straight for a while. It was kind of a rude awakening because things weren't going like I hoped. We had another kid on the team my age, Ron Homenuke, who was from Hazelton, BC, which is adjacent to Smithers. I knew him, of course. He ended up playing one game in the NHL for the Canucks before he had a severe accident while hiking that ended his career. He later became a missionary. We had a few older players from BC as well. So I wouldn't say homesickness was the issue," Jimmy recalled.

"For a while there, though, I wasn't motivated enough. It took time to find myself. I was thinking about quitting hockey and going home to do something else. Then Joe invited me to spend time with him and the Flyers. I went along with him on a road trip to Montreal. Saw the Flyers play at the Forum. Saw that Joe was happy and living a pretty good lifestyle in the NHL. He told me that if he could do it, I certainly could, too. That was a big turning point for me when I got back to Calgary. I got more serious about doing the right things every day, continuing to work on my game and getting stronger."

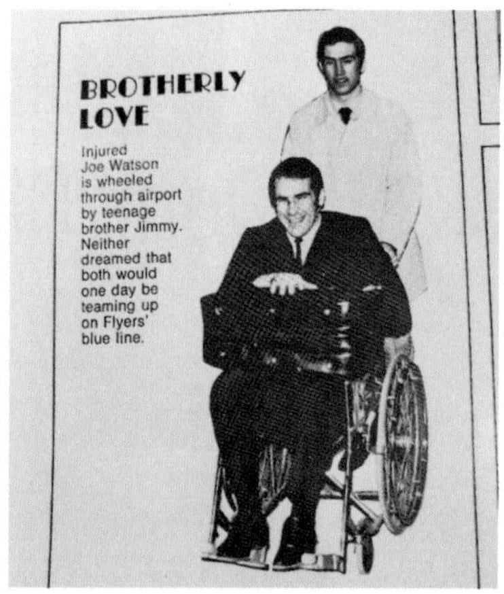

My brother Jimmy was playing junior hockey in Calgary at the time this photo was taken. Years later, the Flyers published the picture in the team yearbook.

For me, Jimmy's visit was one of the few hockey-related highlights of the end of the '60s and the start of the '70s. Things took a turn for the worse in my career and with the Flyers as a team. In 1968–69, we got hot late in the season to get into the Stanley Cup playoffs before we got swept by St. Louis. I hadn't been happy with my own season.

Looking to make a fresh start, I requested a sweater number change. I switched from No. 3 to No. 14, which I'd worn throughout my years in the Boston organization.

After the 1968–69 season, the Flyers replaced Poile as general manager. Allen moved from the coach's office to the GM chair. The Flyers then promoted Quebec Aces coach Vic Stasiuk to the team's new NHL coach. Stasiuk had some success before becoming Flyers coach. The Aces reached the Calder Cup Finals both in 1968 and 1969, losing out to the Rochester Americans (four games to two) the first year and the Hershey Bears (four games to one) the second.

It's kind of strange in hindsight that the Aces were more successful on the ice during that time period than the parent club in Philly. Financially, it was a different story. The Flyers lost money operating the Aces, who perpetually struggled to sell tickets.

With Stasiuk coming to Philadelphia, the Flyers hired Hockey Hall of Famer Walter "Turk" Broda to take over the coaching duties in Quebec. I didn't really know all that much about Stasiuk when we went to camp in 1969. Several of our guys who'd come up to the Flyers through the Aces were not fans of Stasiuk, but every coach has certain players he doesn't like and vice versa. Knowing that, I kept an open mind about how my player-coach relationship would be with him.

As old-school as I am in my beliefs, Vic's views of the game were straight out of the 1940s. He was an interesting guy. Not a bad guy at all away from the ice, but he was not a very good coach at the NHL level from a preparation or X-and-O standpoint.

For example, that first season under Vic—the date was February 26, 1970, and I was scratched that game—we trailed Chicago 3–2 in the waning seconds. Bobby Hull scored a pair of goals, and my former Bruins teammate, Pit Martin, scored the other. Nothing unusual about that. But with four seconds left in the third period, we had an offensive zone faceoff. For whatever reason, we hadn't pulled our goalie for an extra attacker as the players lined up five on five for the draw. Screaming from the bench, Vic hurriedly tried to make the extra-attacker-on-and-goalie-off substitution for a six on five, but it was disallowed.

Our strategy on the play was even worse. Stasiuk, who normally wanted one man working the walls, the second in the slot, and the third up high in case of a turnover, instructed two of our forwards to barrel into the corner to retrieve the puck. That's fine, but we still kept a third man up high. No one went to the net.

We won the draw, but time expired with the puck tied up on the boards. To this day, I don't know what Stasiuk was trying to accomplish. He must have lost track of the clock.

"Hell of an idea, Vic," I muttered to myself as I watched the play unfold in disbelief. "Great way to run out the goddamn clock!"

During his NHL playing days, Vic played for Detroit and Boston. For a time with the Red Wings in their 1954–55 Stanley Cup season, Stasiuk was teammates with Keith Allen and another future Flyers head coach, Bill Dineen. In Boston, he was part of the "Uke Line" with fellow Canadians from Ukrainian backgrounds—Johnny Bucyk and Bronco Horvath. Stasiuk took pride in that, understandably so.

Most of all, though, Vic was in awe of old teammate Gordie Howe. Can't blame Vic for that! Everyone was awed by Mr. Hockey.

Thing is, Vic applied the "What Would Gordie Do?" standard to all things and all situations. Nothing and no one could play up to that expectation of playing with Howe's toughness, physical strength, and skill. Vic was also obsessed with players' hands—not in the sense of their passing or finishing touch but based on a belief that it was a significant detriment if you had small hands.

"Kid, lemme see your hands," was a common greeting from Stasiuk when he'd be introduced to a new draftee.

Thankfully, my hands and my handshake grip, especially the latter, passed muster with Vic. We'd clash soon enough about other stuff.

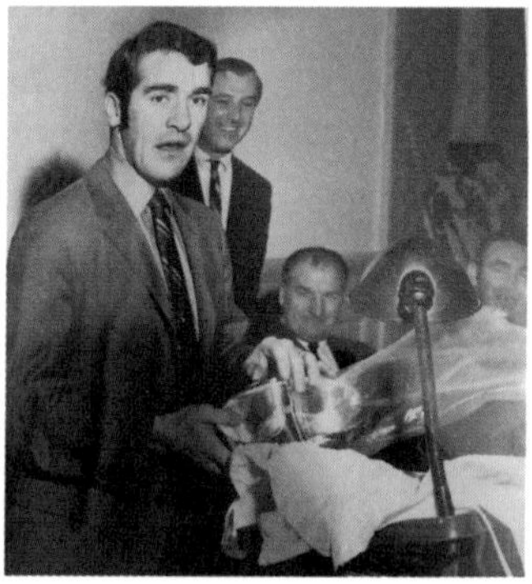

The leanest years of my Flyers career came during Vic Stasiuk's tenure as coach. We had our differences—hockey-related, not personal—over our two seasons together (1969–70 and 1970–71). Vic is in the background of this photo of me, as is Ed Van Impe.

With respect to coaching personality and temperament, Vic was excitable. A lot of words tumbled out of his mouth, but he wasn't very good at explaining exactly what he wanted you to do.

"Check but don't check!" was one of his pet refrains.

To this day, more than 50 years later, I still haven't figured out what that means.

If you've ever watched on YouTube the documentary footage of his stint coaching the California Golden Seals in 1971–72, it captures the way he coached us, too: a mixture of generic encouragement ("There's a goal in that stick!"), running commentary directed at no one in particular ("That's what you wanna…No! Watch it! Watch it!"), and fleeting disgust and screamed cliches ("Be tough! Be tough!"). If Vic got paid one dollar for every time he said "Get it out now!" when the puck went in the defensive zone and "Get it in deep! In deep! In deep!" every time you had the puck in the neutral zone, he'd have been the highest paid coach in the NHL.

When I was watching Vic's Seals footage many years later, there was a segment that made me chuckle. One of his players on the bench informed him that Montreal appeared to have too many men on the ice. Vic himself hadn't noticed it, but he immediately became livid and started hollering at the officials.

"How about too many men on the ice?! Can't ya count, you guys?!"

Watching that old highlight video brought back a rush of memories about what it was like day in and day out playing for Vic. He hollered nonstop, all game and every game. Drove all of us nuts. Again, he was a decent and likeable fellow as a person but more of a distraction than a help as a coach.

One big positive from our 1969 season was the arrival of Bobby Clarke. Gerry Melnyk pushed Keith Allen hard to select the Flin Flon Bombers' center with the sixth overall selection in the Entry Draft, but, as with every team in the NHL, the Flyers were scared away by the fact the player was a diabetic. Instead, the Flyers took right winger Bob Currier, who was never destined to play in the NHL.

Thank goodness. Clarke was still available in the second round when the 17th overall pick came up. This time, Allen went along with Melnyk's recommendation and chose the future Hockey Hall of Famer and franchise icon. It's hard and a bit scary to even imagine what Flyers history would be like had the Flyers not taken Clarke. In the meantime, the Flyers took Willie Brossart in the third round, goalie Michel Belhumeur in the fourth, Sorel Black Hawks left winger Dave Schultz in the fifth, and Regina Pats right wing Don Saleski in the sixth.

Talk about hitting a home run: this was a grand slam of a draft. All of these players eventually made it to the NHL with the Flyers, and, of course, the future "Hammer"(Schultz) and "Big Bird" (Saleski) were valuable role players on our two Stanley Cup winning teams. The Broad Street Bullies era was still a few years away, but adding players like Schultz and Saleski in the 1969 Draft and Bob "the Hound" Kelly in the third round in 1970 (after the Flyers took speedy center Bill Clement one round earlier) marked the first steps toward forging the identity of work ethic, toughness, and unselfish play that we'd come to embody a few years down the line.

Clarke immediately earned a spot on the NHL roster after two training camp scares where he went into diabetic shock after skipping breakfast before practice and our trainer Frank Lewis had to intercede. Thereafter, Frank and Clarkie worked out a complete dietary plan that Bob followed his entire career.

It was obvious pretty fast that Clarke was going to be a star NHL player as he gained experience. For now, though, we still had a weak team, and our rookie center had the normal ups and downs.

Vic put a big premium on players being physically and mentally tough. Very few who've ever played this game have been mentally tougher than Clarkie, so it wasn't a surprise that Stasiuk came to trust him even in his first NHL season.

In other cases, Vic was a little too quick to judge players as soft, and it was extremely hard to change his mind. Among others, Stasiuk never had much faith in young forward Serge Bernier. He had a very high skill level and decent size, but in coaching him with the Aces and Flyers, Stasiuk was convinced that the player wasn't competitive enough. Bernier was left in the AHL for nearly the entire 1969–70 season (except for one game with the Flyers), although we clearly needed more skill, and he was our most naturally skilled prospect in the farm system.

It wouldn't be until the next season, 1970–71, that Bernier cracked the NHL roster in his fourth pro season (23 goals and 51 points in 77 games). Vic rode Bernier particularly hard. That gave rise to one of the funniest and strangest situations I ever saw in hockey: a head coach arguing with a referee about a call that went in his team's favor.

Bill Friday was the referee in this game. His arm went up to signal a delayed holding penalty drawn by Bernier. Stasiuk, however, was more upset that Bernier hadn't made enough effort in his estimation to battle through the check. He summoned Friday to skate to our bench.

"What the hell was that, Billy?"

Friday was puzzled.

"Vic, you're getting a power play here," Friday said.

"I know that. That's not the point."

"Well, what are you complaining about?" the ref asked.

"I've been telling that [bleeping pansy] to fight through the checking all year! All year! At practice, in the games. fight through it! He was finally getting the message, and now you just set me back a month. Goddammit!"

With Vic, you learned quickly to expect the unexpected. He said and did off-the-wall things and had a penchant for verbally riding the officials all game. But that argument was surreal even by his standards.

Frankly, it's a testament to how skilled little Andre Lacroix was as a finesse forward that he mostly stayed in Vic's good graces. Not that there was much other choice. We were still seriously lacking in scoring punch, and Lacroix led our team in scoring in back-to-back seasons. I guess he'd built up some tolerance from Stasiuk because Andre wasn't the type of player that Vic normally liked. There were a few times when Vic would holler to "cut out that Fancy Dan stickhandling!" after a turnover, but he usually let Andre do his thing and make plays. Before Clarkie truly hit his stride in the early-to-mid-'70s, Andre was the best playmaker in our team's short history.

Gary Dornhoefer was more a prototypical Stasiuk type of player. Then again, he was the type of player any coach would like. Worked his tail off and battled for every inch of ice and for every puck. A no-frills north-south skater. Played physical. Played hurt without a word of complaint. Had your back. A quality person off the ice. Gary was normally pretty quiet and minded his own business. But he also had a good sense of humor and a sharp mind for the game. Dorny was an underrated needler, often keeping it humorous but getting his point across when someone needed a spark.

Gary led our team in scoring during Stasiuk's first year as head coach, and nearly all of his 26 goals were scored right around the net on rebounds or jam-ins. After Dorny scored just eight goals in 1968–69 and passed through waivers unclaimed at one point, it made me happy to see Dornhoefer start to have success. He followed his 26-goal year with a 20-goal season. He did this despite battling a back injury for much of the 1969–70 season and needing knee surgery after the season.

Lastly, I'd be remiss if I didn't mention how well Simon Nolet played in 1969–70. Simon has always been kind of an under-the-radar player in our team's history.

Nolet did a lot of things well on the ice but wasn't off the charts in one particular skill. He was another player with a good hockey mind. That's probably why he later became a very successful amateur scout for the Quebec Nordiques and Flyers. The Flyers acquired his NHL rights when they purchased the Aces franchise, and Simon bounced back and forth a few times between the AHL and NHL before he finally made it as a full-time Flyer in 1969–70. He posted a solid 44 points in 56 games (22 goals, one shy of his eventual career high set two seasons later) and had a good work ethic. He was also a likeable guy off the ice.

As for me, I found myself in a situation that no player wants to be in. During Stasiuk's first season, I played every game for half the season, and then he yanked me from the lineup for lengthy stretches of time. Larry Hale saw extended playing time, as did Terry Ball. Our team had acquired both of the Hillman brothers—Larry and Wayne—and they both played extensively.

I thought that I had a pretty decent individual season in 1969–70—significantly better than the previous year. But I only dressed in 54 of 76 games. I dressed in only one of the final 18 games of the season. Let's be totally honest here: that was the biggest thing that I was unhappy about with my player-coach relationship with Stasiuk.

If you're sitting out a lot, but the team is winning, you suck it up and deal with it. The team always comes first, and it's the coach's job to put out the lineup that he feels gives the club the best chance to win. That's how it's always been and always will be. For the sake of the club, a good team player must put aside his pride and ego, which we all have to some degree because we're only human.

However, if your team is losing—and we lost a lot of games—on top of you not playing, that's when you start to feel disgruntled. Favell bounced back compared to his 1968–69 season, and Parent had another pretty solid season, but the wins were even fewer and further between for our team.

We dropped from 73 points in our inaugural season to 61 our second year to 58 the first year under Vic. We won a measly 17 games all season, but we once again stayed afloat in the playoff race because we had 24 ties (a franchise record). As a team, we scored at a modestly higher clip but not enough to make a huge difference. That meant a lot of 1–1, 2–2, and 3–3 ties once again. It also meant a lot of tough losses where a point slipped away late in the game.

Due to our extremely high volume of ties, we entered the stretch drive holding a lead over the Seals for the fourth and final playoff spot in the Western Division. Then our team went into a nosedive. We were still in OK shape after splitting two games with the Seals on March 22 and March 25, 1970. But our 3–2 road loss to the Seals was the start of a four-game losing streak. I finally played again on April 2 at home against St. Louis. The losing streak moved to five straight games as we lost 1–0. The difference was a first-period shorthanded goal by Jim Roberts that stood up the rest of the way.

As a result, our playoff hopes rested on the outcome of the final game of the season on April 4 at the Spectrum against Minnesota. With 58 points, we were tied with the North Stars and Seals. Depending on how the weekend played out, we could finish third, fourth, or fifth in the division. Only the last possibility would keep us out of the playoffs.

For this Saturday-afternoon tilt, I was scratched from the lineup for the seventeenth time in the last 18 games. The Seals didn't play their final game until that night, while the North Stars had an additional game the next day in Pittsburgh against the second-place Penguins. If we beat the North Stars in this game or even played to our twenty-fifth tie of the season, we had a very strong chance of holding on to a playoff spot.

For two periods, Parent and Gump Worsley provided shutout goaltending for the respective teams. Then, at 7:38 of the third period, disaster struck. The sequence started with a face-off near the Minnesota blue line. Neither team was able to win the draw cleanly. North Stars defenseman Barry Gibbs then claimed the loose puck and lobbed it down the ice. Bernie Parent never moved, never flinched. The puck sailed over his right (stick side) shoulder and into the net.

Parent had been good for us all season and had been flawless in this game up to this point, but this was a catastrophe. Bernie later said that he lost the puck in the sun due to the afternoon glare pouring in from the concourse windows at the other end of the building. That explanation made folks laugh, especially in future retellings of the story, although Bernie wasn't trying to be funny in that instance. I struggled to see the humor, anyway.

I'll never know exactly what happened—there's no video footage—except that Bernie never reacted to the long-distance lob, and it all seemed to unfold in horrifying slow motion from my vantage point. Gibbs was no more of a sharpshooter than I was—it was only his 3rd goal of the season. If he tried that shot from that distance another 100 times, he probably wouldn't have put it in the net again even with Parent stationary. But this one went in, and we trailed.

Unfortunately, our offense couldn't bail out Bernie from his one mistake on the 35 shots he faced. Worsley completed a 30-save shutout, and we were done for the season. The North Stars moved two points in front of us. The Seals, who lost later that night, stayed tied with us with 58 points but finished in fourth place on a tiebreaker (they had 22 wins to our 17).

My contract expired at the end of the 1969–70 season. I was still unhappy with Eagleson because he took a $1,500 commission for himself (equal to my entire first-season raise) on my previous contract, so I went back to representing myself. We reached an agreement shortly before training camp, and I got a modest raise. It was about as good as I could hope for after playing in just 54 games. Although Allen could be a tough negotiator,

I thought he dealt fairly with me. It was a one-year contract, and it opened the door for something better a year later.

The 1970–71 season went better for the team. We won 11 more games, improved to 73 points, and finished third in the division. We still struggled on the road, but we were becoming a good team at the Spectrum. We had a 20-10-9 home record.

After wearing uniform No. 3 during my first two seasons with the Flyers, I switched to No. 14 for the remainder of my career. This photo was taken in 1971.

Midway through the campaign, Allen made a major trade. In a three-way trade with Boston and Toronto, we traded Parent to the Maple Leafs. The Flyers received top Bruins prospect Rick MacLeish as well as veteran backup goalie Bruce Gamble, minor-league forward Danny Schock, and a 1971 first-round pick (Pierre Plante) out of the trade. Mike "Shakey" Walton ended up in Boston via the Flyers.

Bernie had been immensely popular with the Flyers fans, and the trade angered much of the fan base at first. But it's no secret that Bernie ultimately benefited from his time in Toronto, where he was mentored by his childhood hero Jacques Plante. Meanwhile, for us, Dougie had his best year since our inaugural season, and Gamble was a decent backup.

Individually, I started out the season the same way I had finished the last one, with Stasiuk playing me sparingly. I was scratched in 5 of the first 10 games but then started playing regularly again until I had a minor knee injury in January that recurred in March. I missed 9 games that month, although I felt healthy enough to return sooner than that.

As a result, I only got to play in 57 games that season. But I had a plus-nine rating on a team that gave up a lot more goals than we scored. As a guy who didn't put up a lot of points, I think that was pretty good. I played a little bit with Ed Van Impe as my partner, some with new arrival Barry Ashbee and some with Larry Hillman. They were all good pros. I was just happy when I was in the lineup.

The Blues were still our biggest rival at the time and would stay that way for a few more years to come. It was easy to get up to play them, and I had come to detest playing against Picard and the Plagers. My old friend and Flyers teammate Bill Sutherland ended up on the Blues that year after starting out the season with us, having his contract sold to the first-year expansion Buffalo Sabres and then being flipped by Buffalo to the Blues. I didn't hate everyone on the Blues. Sudsy was one exception, and my old teammate Terry Crisp was another, but I couldn't stand the sight of that musical-note uniform on the other side of the ice.

After we played the Blues for the first time after Sutherland's arrival, he told the Philadelphia Bulletin, "Those guys beat us up pretty good when I was with the Flyers. Those were tough games. Now I'm on the other side. It still feels a little strange, to be honest, but I'm glad to be here."

For whatever reason, maybe the sheer adrenaline of playing against a team I hated but probably just a fluke, I scored three goals that season against the Blues. They were the only three I scored all season. On December 9, 1970, I snuck a low shot from the point through traffic and past Ernie Wakely to give us a 4–2 lead. We won, 5–2. Four nights later, we played St. Louis again in Philly. Damned if I didn't break a scoreless tie in the second period, beating Hall of Famer Glenn Hall through his pads. On December 30 in St. Louis, which we lost 5–2, I scored on a long rebound that came out to me and went off a Blues player's skate and past Wakely.

I mentioned Barry Ashbee a little while ago. He'd come over from the Bruins organization in the offseason. Although we were both in the Boston organization at the same time in the mid 1960s, I didn't know "Ashcan" all that well until we were in Philly together. We encountered each other in training camps for the Bruins, but he played in the AHL with Hershey, and I was in a different league when I was with Minneapolis and Oklahoma City.

This seems crazy in hindsight: Barry spent part of one season in the NHL with the Bruins in 1965–66 (I was in Oklahoma City) and then missed the entire next season due to injury. The Bruins held it against him and accused him of malingering. That's something that was 100 percent foreign to the character of Barry Ashbee.

The Bruins buried him back in Hershey for the next three years. He was an All-Star defenseman in the American Hockey League but couldn't get a sniff—not so much as a single game—at another NHL opportunity. Finally, during the 1970 offseason, the Bruins flipped Ashbee's NHL rights to the Flyers in a trade for Darryl Edestrand and Larry McKillop. Edestrand could play but deals like these were why Allen became known as Keith the Thief.

Ashbee instantly became a fixture on our blueline and a quiet leader in our dressing room. His style was different than mine. I was animated and talkative, whereas Ashcan spoke only when he had a message to deliver, but we had a solid bond of mutual respect. Barry was fearless, tough as nails without having to act out to prove it. Had one of the highest pain thresholds of any human being I've ever met. Cared only about winning. Plus he was a damn solid defenseman—what would be called nowadays a shutdown defenseman.

In short, the Bruins' loss was the Flyers' gain.

A couple more things that stand out to me about that 1970–71 squad. For the first time since we overachieved as a club in our inaugural season, I could see light at the end of the tunnel in terms of the roster that was being put together.

Bob Kelly was a rookie that year, straight out of junior hockey. The Hound was like a runaway bowling ball on the ice. Just a bundle of energy, and he hit anything that moved. A total team player from day one. We all teased Hound, but that's because we all loved the guy. It never mattered to Bob whether he played two minutes or 14. He didn't care who his linemates were. Never tracked a stat in his life. All he cared about was winning, and you couldn't help but feel more energetic yourself after you saw him in action.

Hound (or Muttley) was always one of our most willing fighters. I dubbed him "Machine Gun Kelly" because Bob could throw three punches in the time it took most guys to throw one. If you never saw Bob fight, imagine a boxer hitting the heavy bag with speed-bag pace. That was Kelly.

Off the ice, Hound has become one of my oldest and dearest friends. He'll be there for you through thick and thin and remain loyal until the bitter end. Now, since Hound might read this book—or have someone read it to him—I can't be too complimentary here, so I'll stop with all the praise.

Just kidding, of course. Every team, both then and now, needs a player or two like Bob Kelly. Every person should have a few friends like him in their life, too.

That same year, Clarkie took the next step toward stardom in the NHL. He was clearly our best player and the key to our future at the age of 21. Rick MacLeish also debuted with us that year at the tender age of 20. He wasn't quite ready for prime time as an NHL player, but, holy smokes, could that kid skate like the wind and shoot the puck. Lacroix, at 25, was still one of our best playmakers.

The playoffs were a bit of a reality check as to where we really stood against the so-called Original Six. Chicago swept us with ease in four games: 5–2, 6–2, 3–2, and 6–2. I guess two was our unlucky number that spring.

Stasiuk dressed me in Game 1 of the Black Hawks series and then scratched me the remaining three games. He was fired after the season.

I can't truthfully say that I was sorry to see Vic depart Philly. I also can't honestly say that I enjoyed our coach-player relationship during our two seasons together. What I can and will say is that Vic was a hockey lifer, a good man away from the rink, and one of the more unforgettable characters I met along the way in this crazy game of ours.

On May 23, 2022, Vic Stasiuk celebrated his 93rd birthday. He passed away on May 7, 2023. He was the last living link to the original hockey operations brass of the Philadelphia Flyers. Rest in peace, Vic.

CHAPTER 8

Lifted by the Fog

My confidence in the direction of my NHL career was never lower than it was during my second season of playing under Vic Stasiuk. Vic had his mind made up that I wasn't going to be an every-game player as long as he was the Flyers' coach, and I felt like there was nothing I could do to change his mind. I'm my own biggest critic, yet there were games where I knew I'd played pretty well, and I'd still be taken out of the lineup again the next game.

In the late Jay Greenberg's book *Full Spectrum*, he told a story about how I got teary in the locker room after Bernie Parent was traded as part of the three-way trade with Boston and Toronto. I was sad to see Bernie go, but the main reason I got emotional was that I'd heard a rumor that I was about to be traded, too, and was sure it was about to come true. Keith Allen vehemently denied the rumor and said I was staying put. He was true to his word.

I just wasn't in a good frame of mind at the time. I knew by now that hockey was a business, and the chance of being traded was a fact of life in this business. But I was settled in the Philadelphia area by this point, and I wasn't feeling mentally prepared to start over again (on or off the ice) at that time.

As a matter of fact, I was seriously considering quitting hockey altogether. Thankfully, I had true friends in my Flyers roommate, Ed Van Impe, and my former Bruins roommate, Bobby Orr. They talked me off the ledge, professionally speaking.

Once I started making enough money in the NHL that I didn't need to work a summer job, I spent a few hockey offseasons playing baseball in British Columbia. I played for the Kamloops Okonots. I have a confession: While I was playing under Stasiuk for the Flyers, I began to find myself looking forward more to baseball season than to coming back in the fall for another year with Vic. Playing for the Okonots, I won the league batting championship in 1970, hitting .403. I knew I'd at least be in the lineup every game in the summer of '71 rather than watching from the stands.

As a teenager, I passed up a chance to pursue a professional baseball career with the New York Yankees organization. Baseball was my second-best sport, but I had a better chance of reaching the top level in hockey. This photo was taken while I played baseball for the Kamloops Okonots during the hockey offseason.

The Flyers fired Vic on May 27, 1971. Keith didn't hide the fact that he always felt Vic was Bud Poile's guy he'd inherited from Bill Putnam. Mr.

Putnam knew he wasn't a hockey guy and always endorsed Bud's hockey-related recommendations. As I said before, Mr. Snider got to know the hockey side, and he won an internal debate with Putnam to dismiss Poile and go in a different team-building direction. With Putnam resigning as team president and exiting ownership by selling his stake in the team, the Flyers were now fully Ed Snider's sole domain.

Bud Poile is a Hockey Hall of Fame inductee, as is Keith. Both were astute hockey men and good judges of talent. The difference was this: Keith was far less volatile and more patient but no less demanding than Bud. He gave it two seasons with Vic and kept an open mind, but he could see that our team was basically treading water even though we were starting to have younger and better talent filter up to the NHL. He could see that Vic's stubbornness, quickness to judge his players, and constant yelling of words that made sense only to him but confused his players caused many of us to tune out our coach.

Six days after the Flyers dismissed Stasiuk, they hired Fred Shero as head coach. Although I'd played against St. Paul in the Central League when Freddy was their coach, I didn't know all that much about his methods of coaching or, really, anything about him as a person. All I knew was that he'd coached five teams to championships in the minor leagues. Of course, he'd go on to win his sixth and seventh championships with us, and these were the biggest ones of all: the freakin' Stanley Cup.

Just like I never would have predicted on the day that Philly took me from the Bruins in the 1967 Expansion Draft that I'd spend most of the next 54 years with the Flyers, I never would have known on June 3, 1971, how much Fred Shero would change my career.

I certainly welcomed the change behind the bench from Stasiuk to Shero. I knew I wouldn't be long for Philly otherwise. A new coach at the helm meant a fresh start, and I certainly needed that. Holy smokes, did we get ourselves quite a new coach! Along with Harry Sinden, Freddy is the best coach I ever had. I feel very fortunate to have had the pleasure of playing for Sinden and Shero.

My career might have been in jeopardy if Stasiuk had remained the Flyers' coach. My confidence was low, and I had been reduced on the depth chart to a part-time player. I needed a change for the better. So did the Flyers.

Freddy saved my career. Along with Harry, he shaped my understanding of how a coach can bring out the best in his players and team.

It wasn't until many years later—after my playing days—that I learned more about Freddy's personal backstory and how he came to be the Flyers coach. I think a little bit of background can help clear up the hard-to-know guy who got the nickname "the Fog."

Freddy was born and raised in Winnipeg to Russian parents who fled to Canada to escape religious persecution for not being members of the Russian Orthodox Church. He always felt like an outsider growing up. He was extremely intelligent and bookish but also a good athlete. He was extremely shy, and he didn't let many people get to know him very well.

His parents did not approve of their children playing sports, but both Freddy and sister Doris ultimately had sports careers. Doris Shero played baseball for the Racine Belles in the All-American Girls Professional Baseball League. If you visit the Women in Baseball exhibit in the National Baseball Hall of Fame and Museum in Cooperstown, you'll see her name there. She's also an honorary inductee in the Canadian Baseball Hall of Fame.

Freddy served in the Royal Canadian Navy during World War II. He also boxed and played hockey as a member of HMCS Chippawa. After his military service, he considered quitting hockey and going to college but decided to go back to the New York Rangers, who had signed him to a contract at age 17 before he went into the navy. A sturdy defenseman who was much stronger and tougher physically than he looked, Freddy played three NHL seasons and then bounced around the minor leagues until 1958. That's when he took up coaching, mostly for Rangers farm teams.

In Freddy's second year as a coach, he won his first championship with the St. Paul Saints. He'd later coach the Saints, Saint Paul Rangers, Buffalo Bisons (AHL Calder Cup), and Omaha Knights to championships. Three other seasons, his teams reached the playoff finals but lost in the championship round series. All this time, the New York Rangers never seriously considered him for their NHL coaching job.

Why the hell not? I don't know for sure. I suspect it was because Freddy was never a "management guy." If a player had a dispute with the front office, he sided with the player. This was one of the things that endeared him to his players, but it didn't endear him to management. That happened everywhere with Freddy, including Philly. He butted heads a time or two with Keith and with Mr. Snider, but, over time, there was enough trust built up that Freddy usually got his way.

Freddy had a reputation as an oddball. Part of it was his social awkwardness. He was never deliberately rude to anyone, but he could walk right past you without saying hello because he was so lost in thought that he didn't even notice you. He'd sit in his office long after everyone else left, diagraming hockey plays, jotting notes, and reading books—mostly hockey, but he also enjoyed works on philosophy, theories on leadership, biographies of historical figures he found interesting, and even the law (he took correspondence courses to train himself). Freddy loved to visit the library, and he'd read anything he could get his hands on when he was away from the rink.

At night, Freddy typically went off on his own. Even when he became the first NHL coach to hire a full-time assistant coach—Mike Nykoluk in Philly, later joined by Barry Ashbee—he preferred to be by himself when he left the comfortable confines of the rink. He'd take long walks by himself. Go to bars by himself. His wife, Mariette, who was a lovely person and much more naturally sociable than Freddy, used to say that if you could climb inside her husband's head, you'd find a miniature hockey rink. He'd take long baths, thinking up drills for practice or strategizing for games.

He loved his wife and his children and was proud of them all, but he wasn't one to express it verbally. He treated us players the same way.

He didn't heap praise on us very often (he did that through the media when we'd played especially well). At the same time, he rarely yelled at the team and never embarrassed an individual in front of his teammates. That's the surest way to lose a player. He'd challenge the group but didn't single you out. If he was pleased or felt you needed a lift, you'd know it two ways: first, by your playing time and, second, physically via a literal pat on the back. He'd gently pat you between the shoulder blades. That said more than words.

Once Freddy got comfortable around you, he could actually be pretty talkative. Get him going on hockey, and he could fill reporters' notebooks

In this photo, the Flyers were going through customs at the airport during Fred Shero's first season as our coach. I'm standing behind Freddy, who is at the head of the line.

and then some. He loved to tell tall tales about his playing days, often self-deprecating ones or stories about crazy things he'd witnessed. Ask him about his love of Russian hockey and his deep admiration for Anatoli Tarasov (dubbed "the Father of Russian Hockey") as a program builder and coach, and he'd go into so much detail that you'd be almost sorry you asked.

Freddy had a gift for making every one of his players feel valued. He was a complex person and deep thinker, but he explained his expectations very simply and straightforwardly to us players. It's not hard for a coach to win over his star players: play them a lot, don't tie their hands too much in terms of feeling free to make plays, but also expect them to put team success over personal goals. The last part is the trickiest with some star-caliber talents, but we were lucky as a team in that regard. If you were selfish, you weren't a Flyer. Plain and simple.

It's harder for a coach to get equal buy-in from the stars and the role players. Freddy's genius in player management was that he accomplished just that. He'd make it clear, over and over, that Bob Kelly's eight minutes of ice time were just as important to us winning as Clarkie's 20 minutes. He got you to take pride in your role. He'd talk up Hound and Schultz, Saleski, and no-frills defensemen like me to the press all the time. The message was always that every one of us was responsible for a win, a loss, or a tie.

Here's something else about Freddy's motivation style, and this might sound contradictory, but it really was not: even with role players, he encouraged you to practice not only the things you did well but also to challenge yourself to develop other skills and become a better all-around player.

Don Saleski is a great example. In his early years, Don's role was to use his size to throw his weight around and wear down the other team. Big Bird had big penalty-minute totals early on. Over time, though, Freddy added to Don's role as Bird continued to expand on the things that he could offer the team. Not many people realize what a good penalty killer Saleski turned into. Bird had more seasons with the Flyers where he had 20 or more goals (3 of them in a row after our two Stanley Cup championships) than seasons where he had 150 or more penalty minutes (just 1).

Same thing with Hound. Freddy once famously said, "If Bob Kelly scores 20 goals, it means I'm not using him right." In other words, Bob needed as much ice time and as many scoring chances as a 40-goal scorer like Billy Barber to get half as many goals. Hound was more valuable playing limited minutes but going hell-bound for leather with his physical play. It wasn't simply that Kelly would go out on the ice, dump the puck in the corner, and go in to deliver a body check. It's that he'd do it repeatedly. Opposing players wore down. They got tired of paying that price. Then Freddy would get our most skilled players out there, and they'd find it easier to create offense.

Yup, that was Hound. But that's not the whole story. Who famously scored the Stanley Cup–winning goal for our team in 1975? It was, of course, Kelly who broke a scoreless deadlock in the opening seconds of the third period against Buffalo in Game Six. Fast-forward to the last two seasons Freddy coached the Flyers. Bob scored 22 goals and 19 goals in those seasons. When he later went to Washington, Hound had a career-high 26 goals and 62 points on a struggling team that needed all the help it could get.

That's why I will tell anyone who will listen that Bob Kelly wasn't just a guy who hit and fought. He could play the game, and Freddy was very supportive of Kelly working to bring as much as possible to the team. Kelly, who never spent a day in the minors his entire pro career, had that ability within him and a great work ethic. He also had a coach who believed in him and trusted that Bob always understood what his main role was on the team. Kelly never believed he'd magically transformed into a goal scorer, but Bob added a bit more goal-scoring production to his repertoire through what he gained from experience and working his butt off.

That, my friends, is what a great coach can do for a player.

People ask me all the time, even to this day, "What was it really like to play for Shero?" When you're living through it, you don't think about it in the terms I described for Hound and Saleski. The way I experienced it at the time was like this: Freddy was definitely different. Our coach was offbeat. Shero worked you hard and expected your best. But you knew he cared. You felt trusted. You felt treated like a man. You felt he'd go to bat for you with management or the press if you needed it. Above all, you knew that no one had the right answers for winning every night, but he'd sure as hell outthink the other coach and have you as well prepared as possible.

When Freddy told you to stop by his office, it wasn't to chit-chat or to tell you how great you were doing. But he was outstanding in how he delivered his message to you. He'd start out by pointing out something specific he'd noticed that you'd been doing right. Maybe you'd practiced well that day, or some extra skating seemed to be helping.

Then he'd quickly get to his main reason for calling you in to talk. Freddy would point out something that needed to improve and specifically what he needed to see you do to address it. He'd be very direct and blunt but speak very calmly. After the constructive criticism, he'd end it with a word of encouragement. Maybe he'd hand you something to read—a saying, an article, or whatever—that he felt applied to your situation and you might get inspirational value from.

Freddy's method of delivering personal critiques—specific but limited praise at the beginning followed by constructive criticism and then ending with encouragement at the end—was dubbed "the Shero Sandwich" by players. I know that this method is also used in the business world as an example of effective management, but to most of us hockey players in that era, it seemed unique. It was hardly touchy-feely or "soft" coaching. You knew Freddy was the boss. You knew there was an unspoken "or else" attached to the critique portion and that you'd be wise to follow his advice.

But you never felt dehumanized. You might not have liked or agreed with everything, but you also felt he had the team's interests at heart and was saying it for your betterment.

That's a tough tightrope to walk. Freddy did it better than any coach I ever saw. For all his social shyness and aloofness, he was a damn good communicator. You'd leave his office thinking, "Wow, he really knows what he's talking about. I better do what he says." We all felt that way, and our locker room leaders reinforced it. I never had a problem telling a guy if he wasn't pulling his weight, and I'd be a hell of a lot louder than Freddy about it. But it was always situational, never personal.

For all of Rick MacLeish's God-given talent, he had to be pushed to apply himself. That's part of why Shero put MacLeish on a line with Gary Dornhoefer and Ross Lonsberry. They kept Ricky in line by constantly needling him. Every once in a while, MacLeish needed an extra push. That's when Freddy would call Rick into his office.

One time, Freddy handed Rick a glass of water.

"Put your fingers in the glass," Shero said.

MacLeish obliged but was puzzled.

"Now take them out," the coach commanded after about 10 seconds.

MacLeish withdrew his hand.

"You know why I had you do that?" Shero asked.

"No."

"Because if you keep half assing like that, we'll get you out of here as fast as you took your hand out of that glass," Shero said firmly but quietly.

The message was understood, loud and clear.

OK, so I know this is coming: What about Freddy's daily chalkboard messages? Did the players take the sayings seriously? Well, some guys took 'em more seriously than others.

Some were prophetic: Most famously, Freddy wrote "Win today and we'll walk together forever" before Game 6 of the 1974 Stanley Cup Final when we won our first Cup. We certainly have walked together forever, regardless of where our lives have taken us.

Some were cryptic: "A man with a dream of pleasure can go forth and conquer a crowd. With a new song's measure, can trample a kingdom down." (Note: This was Freddy's message before Game 6 of the 1975 Stanley Cup Final—less famous than the first but not less meaningful. Freddy was telling us to keep following the dreams and ambitions that brought us to the brink of reaching an even higher summit than before.)

Some were direct and inspirational: "In hockey and life, strive to live in a world where normal is an insult."

Some were philosophical: "We know that hockey is where we live, where we can best meet and overcome pain and wrong and death. Life is just the place where we spend time between games."

Others were silly but conveyed a message: "The difference between making a contribution and making a commitment is like ham and eggs. The chicken makes a contribution. The pig makes a commitment. We need players to make a commitment."

A few were strictly comical and usually posted to alleviate pressure, such as a road game in Boston or New York: "Life in the fast lane? I live on the off-ramp."

During the second season that Freddy coached us, the Flyers acquired my old friend and previous teammate Terry Crisp. In 1977, Terry retired from playing and became one of our assistant coaches. Crispy told Freddy that he'd always been curious about where the head coach found all of the quotes he wrote on the board or gave to players. Freddy told him that they came from the tags on teabags. He'd save the tag and use the quote if he liked it.

Teabags weren't the only place where Freddy found sayings he could apply to hockey, but they were one of the most unique sources! A lot of them came from various books and periodicals. Even when he wasn't reading about hockey, Freddy found things he could use for coaching his players.

You might be surprised at which players found inspiration from Freddy's messages. For example, as much as Clarkie loved playing for Freddy, I don't think he ever found the quotes and sayings particularly useful. Then again, Bob was always a self-motivated hockey player. On the other hand, "Cowboy" Bill Flett, who joined us midway through Freddy's first season, wound up saving for the rest of his life an inspirational message that Freddy gave him.

Flett had a 40-goal season in 1972–73, but he really struggled something awful the next year. Bill was having a hard time in his personal life—his drinking was getting out of control, to the point where it was affecting him on the ice—and he was feeling pressure to start scoring again. This was long before the age of the internet and sports talk radio (where, at its worst, every fan becomes a self-proclaimed expert, every coach is an idiot, and every struggling player is a lazy, overpaid bum). Even so, Bill heard the booing when he was unable to finish scoring chances. He saw some of the newspapers wondering if the previous year had been a fluke. As physically tough as he was, Flett let the criticism get to him.

Freddy didn't call Flett into his office. Instead, he left in Flett's locker a famous excerpt of a speech by Theodore Roosevelt. The relevant portion was called "The Man in the Arena."

> *It is not the critic who counts; not the man who points out how the strong man stumbles, or where the doer of deeds could have done them better. The credit belongs to the man who is actually in the arena, whose face is marred by dust and sweat and blood; who strives valiantly; who errs, who comes short again and again, because there is no effort without error and shortcoming; but who does actually strive to do the deeds; who knows great enthusiasms, the great devotions; who spends himself in a worthy cause; who at the best knows in the end the triumph of high achievement, and who at the worst, if he fails, at least fails while daring greatly, so that his place shall never be with those cold and timid souls who neither know victory nor defeat.*

Bill didn't turn things around with the Flyers, unfortunately, on or off the ice. But he was forever grateful to Freddy. When he was in a bad place, Bill would pull out the quotation that Freddy gave him so many years before. Bill had a tough life and a lot of struggles on many fronts before he passed away at age 55 in 1999 due to liver failure. But he lived the last four or five years of his life sober. The inner strength to conquer his most torturous demon came from within Bill Flett. Nonetheless, Freddy walked with him forever on the inspirational side even though Freddy himself had passed nine years earlier and hadn't been part of his daily life in 25 years.

Freddy didn't like being called an innovator. He used to say that when the people who used to call you a kook start calling you an innovator, it means that you're not being very innovative anymore. Truth was, though, that Freddy was an innovator.

The Flyers, as I said earlier, were the first team to have a full-time assistant coach who was not employed in the dual role of player-coach. Freddy was the one who introduced the game-day morning skate to the NHL (which was a subtle way of combatting players staying out until 4:00 a.m. the night before a game without directly banning it). He was the first coach I knew of who studied video, although Roger Neilson and next-generation coaches took it further and made it a major part of their coaching instruction.

I was often amazed at how Freddy could think of things one step ahead of our opponents. During his NHL coaching career with the Flyers and Rangers, Shero went nine-for-nine in challenging an illegal stick: a penalty on the other team if a stick measurement proved there was an illegal curve to the blade but a delay-of-game penalty on the challenging team if a stick measurement showed the blade to be legal.

How did he do it? Well, back then, the Flyers practiced at the Class of 1923 rink at the University of Pennsylvania. When visiting teams came to town, many would rent ice time to practice after we did. Back in the mid-'70s, our rink attendant was a kid named Paul Stewart, who was a student at Penn and played on the Quakers hockey team. (Yes, this is the same Paul Stewart who later played as an enforcer in the NHL and then became a longtime NHL referee.)

After visiting teams practiced, there would inevitably be broken or discarded sticks left in trash cans or locker rooms. Freddy instructed Stewart and subsequent rink attendants to collect the other teams' sticks and bring them to his office. There, Freddy measured the blades, jotted down the measurements in his little notebook, and created a list for himself of which visiting players used illegal sticks. If a strategic situation arose where a stick challenge could be beneficial, Freddy would summon the referee and announce the challenge.

Shero didn't do it often, of course. But the list was ready if he needed it. To my knowledge, no opposing team caught on to his method.

Shero was among the NHL's first "systems" coaches. He stressed to us very specific methods of breakouts, forechecks, and puck support. While he was not the very first, he was perhaps the first to codify it in writing in what became known among his players as the "Shero Bible." There were 16 primary points, although they were not the full extent of the system:

- Never go offside on a 3-on-2 or a 2-on-1.
- Never go backward in our end except on a power play. Passing backward in our end to a teammate to elude opposition is OK.
- Never throw a puck out blindly from behind their net.
- Never pass diagonally in our zone unless 100 percent certain.
- Wings on wings between bluelines except when able to intercept a stray pass.
- Second man should go all the way for a rebound.
- Defense: with the puck at opponent's blueline, look four places before shooting.
- Wing in front of opponent's net must face the puck and lean on stick.
- Puck carrier over center with no one to pass to and no skating room must shoot in (Power Play also).
- No forward must ever turn his back to the puck at any time. Know where the puck is at all times. Only defensemen are allowed to turn their back for a fraction of a second on a swing to the corner in our end.
- No player allowed to position himself more than two zones away from puck.
- Never allow the men in our defensive zone to be outnumbered.
- Delayed penalty, puck carrier looks for extra man at center ice. Extra man responsible for covering opponent's goalie. (Let each other know goalie's responsibility.)
- Opponent's penalty almost up—whose [communication] responsibility? Goaltender.

- Backchecking (2 on 2) or 1 on 1 even on power play, pick up trailer. No trailer come in behind defense.
- Two men in forechecking, responsibilities of third man [play higher to help defensively].

Every player on his team received two copies of the Shero Bible; a larger one for his locker and a wallet-sized one to carry around for reference. One key strategic goal that Freddy emphasized as an every-game key to wings was this: control the four corners and the two net-front areas, and you'll control the game.

Himself a former defenseman, Freddy preached some other principles to the team's blueliners when it came to coverages. While it was OK to leave to rotate over to assist in preventing an outnumbered situation, he wanted our defensemen to be aware of their surroundings at all times.

"Generally speaking, when both defensemen end up on the same side, bad things are going to happen. Be aware of who the dangerous man really is," Shero said over and over until we knew it by heart.

To this day, when I watch a game where a defenseman runs himself out of position and leaves the back door open for a trailer to score a weak-side goal, I can't help but think of Freddy. That sort of play drove him nuts. Likewise, while he encouraged us to play physical and take the body, we had to make sure that if you were stepping up to deliver a hit, the puck did not get past you. That's how many two on ones begin. Don't get caught up-ice or way out of position.

There's nothing revolutionary about these principles. But Freddy communicated them clearly and had us commit them to mental memory and practice them into muscle memory. Shero was a firm believer in what he called the P-and-R principle: patience and repetition. That's how he transformed us into one of the best 200-foot teams of all time during his tenure. We gave our goalies a chance to give us a chance, and we soon had the scoring firepower to go along with it, too.

Freddy used to say that pro hockey is a child's game played by grown men. We were treated like men, not like children. At the same time, Freddy used to make it fun to come to the rink. Along with the meat-and-potatoes work we did daily, Freddy would work in offbeat drills or things to keep us on our toes. Famously, he had us do a drill he learned during a coaches' clinic in Russia where we'd pass around multiple pucks at a time. He was also the first coach I ever saw who would, once in a blue moon, work in a drill where defenders would do a rep or two apiece with our sticks held upside down: knob side on the ice, blade side in our hands. Sometimes, he had us do things that had no purpose whatsoever but were put in to see whether someone would question why we were doing it.

"Oh, I just wanted to see if any of you numbskulls would ask," he'd tease.

That broke us up laughing.

So did Freddy's little challenge of having skaters win a battle drill behind the net, step out, and try to score. The prize was this: a five dollar bill. After Hound scored the Cup-winning goal in Game 6 in Buffalo in 1975, he skated back to the bench and told Freddy, "You owe me five bucks, Freddy."

There wasn't very much that Freddy didn't think about when it came to keeping us focused on hockey or emphasizing our team culture. There was a letter that he sent to rookies before their first training camp. It went like this:

> *The only way to play in the kingdom of the Flyers is to submit to the discipline; it is very near to heaven. The players have their rules, and I have my ruler. We are careful not to tread on each other's toes.*
>
> *I have only two rules:*
>
> *1) The coach is always right.*
>
> *2) If you think the coach is wrong, refer back to rule No. 1.*

That was a great example of Freddy introducing young players to his offbeat and dry sense of humor, but it also delivered a message that there's an expected way of doing things. Most young players understood the intention. The few that didn't weren't going to be in Philadelphia for long regardless of their God-given raw ability.

Not every missive Freddy sent out went over that smoothly. You may have heard about Freddy's infamous letter to the players' wives. It was tongue in cheek and well intentioned, but it went over like a lead balloon with the gals. There was no such phrase as "politically incorrect" back then, but it pushed the envelope even by '70s standards.

> *How to keep a husband?*
>
> *Be to your husband all of these things:*
>
> *A Chinese cook in the kitchen.*
>
> *A Japanese wife in the bath.*
>
> *A French mistress in the bedroom.*
>
> *An English hostess in the living room.*
>
> *Do that and your husband will be true to you all your life: Maybe he'll look at another woman now and then, but only with his left eye. He'll keep the right one on you all the time.*
>
> *Compliments of,*
>
> *Fred Shero*
>
> *P.S. The next message will be your husband's on how to keep a wife.*

Boy, oh boy, did that one fall flat. The wives *hated* it, although a few found it kind of funny. By the way, Freddy never did send out the husbands' version!

Freddy was not a chauvinist, though, at least as far as hockey was concerned. In 1976, he contacted a female coach he'd met during a coach's clinic in Russia—a Swedish coach by the name of Pia Grengman (later Pia Sterner after marrying Ulf Sterner, the first Swedish player to suit up in the NHL). She was a fellow devotee of Tarasov, and Freddy found her to be extremely bright, forward thinking, and well organized. He asked Pia if she'd be interested in joining the Flyers as an assistant coach. She turned the offer down because she wasn't prepared to move to the United States.

Freddy was a candidate to coach Team Canada at the 1976 Canada Cup series. He was overwhelmingly qualified, coming off back-to-back Stanley Cup championships and three straight trips to the Cup Finals. He also knew the Soviet national team and other European national team systems better than anyone in North America. Had he been hired, Grengman would have been one of his assistants during the tournament. Once again, though, Freddy's maverick style worked against him. There was no way

Hockey Canada was going to hire Shero—the coach of the dreaded Broad Street Bullies and the guy who bucked management and came up with all sorts of ideas they considered off the wall.

Now that it's the 2020s, those ideas hardly sound crazy. I thought about this in 2021 when the Flyers had a female coach, Princeton's Cara Morey, come along as a guest instructor during Development Camp. There have been female skating coaches in the NHL, including a full-timer (Dawn Braid of the Arizona Coyotes). The day isn't far off when there will be a female coach behind an NHL bench. It seems inevitable. It's yet another example of how far ahead of his time Fred Shero was.

I will talk in a subsequent chapter about our convincing 4–1 win over the Red Army team at the Spectrum in January of 1976. But I'll lay the groundwork, hockey-wise, for that right now: no one in North America understood Russian hockey as thoroughly as Fred Shero.

For well over a decade leading up to the game against CSKA, Shero absorbed all he could read, observe, and discuss about Russian-style hockey. In back-to-back summers, he traveled behind the Iron Curtain to attend international coaching symposiums in Moscow that were run by Tarasov. He got to trade hockey-related ideas and observations with Viktor Tikhonov, Konstantin Loktev, and other top Soviet hockey coaches and instructors. Not one other NHL coach was present, but Freddy also got to know coaches from Czechoslovakia, Sweden, and Finland.

One of the greatest thrills of Freddy's life was meeting and even striking up an unlikely friendship with Tarasov, who was seven years his senior. In a private audience between the Stanley Cup–winning coach and the initial creator of the global hockey superpower, the two men developed great respect for each other.

As Freddy later told the tale, the intended courtesy meeting became a full night of sharing bottles of vodka and comparing notes on their respective hockey philosophies. Even though neither man could speak more than a few words of the other's language, their drawings of ice diagrams and physical gestures bridged the barrier.

The running joke became this: They both spoke hockey. They both spoke vodka. And neither spoke English.

Some of the methods and drills that Freddy picked up in Russia were incorporated into our systems. Freddy pondered, quite often in fact, how he would strategize for beating the Russians if he got the chance to coach against them in international competition. In other words, our strategy for playing against Red Army was multiple years in the making: Don't play chase. Let them circle and weave all they want. Keep puck support strong. Dominate them in the corners and control the slots and net-front areas in the defensive zone and attack zone. They could whirl and twirl all they wanted anywhere else.

Shero never made any secret of his deep admiration for European hockey in general and Soviet hockey in particular. As recounted in Jack Chevalier's book, *The Broad Street Bullies*, which was written in 1974, Shero was an ardent supporter of NHL teams becoming far more active in scouting and signing European talents. That, of course, included the Flyers.

"We should have more Europeans and Russians in the league," Shero told Chevalier. "But management [around the NHL] can't get it into their fat heads they're good enough to play. They always say, 'They lack this or they lack that.' What do they lack? Nothing, not even guts."

At Shero's insistence, the Flyers became one of the first NHL teams to employ a European scout (Adolph "Augie" Kukulowicz). It was also the Philadelphia organization that was the first NHL club to draft a Soviet-trained player—gifted but troubled and ill-fated Viktor Khatulev from Dinamo Riga—in the NHL Draft in 1975.

These off-ice measures did not bear on-ice fruit for the Flyers organization during Freddy's career but showed his foresight. Shero's early influence in laying groundwork for NHL acceptance of Europeans is a truer indicator of his legacy than the mistaken belief that Shero instructed "Flyers goons" to try and physically intimidate and taunt Börje Salming and other early European players in the league. While these incidents did take place, I can tell you as someone who played for Freddy, it was never done at Freddy's demand. We played against every opponent the same way.

In the latter stages of his coaching career, Shero had the opportunity to coach Swedish stars Anders Hedberg and Ulf Nilsson during his stint with the New York Rangers. In 1978–1979, Hedberg led the team in scoring with 79 points in 80 games, and Nilsson contributed 66 points in 59 games for a club that reached the Stanley Cup Finals for just the second time in a span of 29 years.

"I really enjoyed the speed and skill of the Swedish players I had with the Rangers," Shero told Hockey Digest in 1989. "I have been happy to see more European players come over and do well. I think it's good for the game."

Shero read extensively on European coaching and motivational methods, both in the sporting realm and out.

"The Russians have dry-land drills where they stickhandle on grass," Shero told Chevalier. "I've seen them skate while carrying a man on their backs."

Shero also learned from the way Russian trainers had their athletes run and skate obstacle courses, realizing that hockey players had to deke, twist, turn, and tumble. He believed these exercises to be more valuable than running long distances in a straight line.

In light of these facts, it's kind of ironic that our 1974 and 1975 teams were the last all-Canadian rosters to win the Stanley Cup. That never registered with us back in those days, but it's strange to think about it now because Freddy was such a believer in finding hockey talent wherever it was to be found.

I'll say it again: While I was living through these times as a Flyers player, I didn't try to dig deep into Freddy's hockey philosophies. My job was to follow his systems and do what I was told. But after the passage of more than 40 years since I played my last game for him, I've never seen his equal as a coach. Not Scotty Bowman. Not Al Arbour. Not Barry Trotz. Not anyone. Freddy was the most thorough hockey coach I ever had the pleasure to witness in action, and I got to see it all up close.

When it came to self-care, Shero was a bundle of contradictions. He chain-smoked and, during portions of his life, sometimes drank excessively and usually alone. As far as Freddy's drinking goes, we players didn't see it or ever think much about it. When we left the rink, we went our way as a big group, and Freddy went off by himself. Whatever he was doing, it didn't affect his coaching. We had the same standards among ourselves as players. As long as you were able to come to the rink, ready to work and ready to compete, the rest was no one else's business.

Freddy gave the players leeway to make our own judgments on the road. However, he also firmly recognized the importance of our players being in good physical condition. That was pretty rare. It's all relative, though. The mid-1970s was an era when a significant minority of hockey players were in similar shape to baseball players or even bowlers. Go off the ice and have a cigarette in the locker room. Crack open a babalooey in the locker room after practice, before heading out for lunch, and another brew or two at Rexy's. Back to Rexy's again after the game. Nevertheless, our team was better conditioned than most in that era. Freddy expected it, and Clarke led by example. He was in good shape and always showed up at camp right at his playing weight.

Here's a funny story: In 1974, the Flyers purchased a full array of Apollo exercise equipment for our training use. These were designed for weight-resistance exercises. We discovered a shortcut, though, or at least we thought we had. The harder you exerted pulling pressure on the equipment, the more resistance you'd get. Your muscle would soon start to burn. But if you applied only light pressure, you got minimal resistance. Once the boys figured that out, we'd grunt and wince and feign like we were really going all out.

Then Freddy walked by. He spoke aloud to our trainer, Frank Lewis.

"Once they are done screwing around, have them do it for 10 extra minutes," he said.

I don't know why we thought we could get away with it. We also used to do a thing during practices where, if you screwed up a drill, you had to go off to the other side and do pushups on the ice. Somehow, Freddy always knew when someone was half-assing the pushups. They'd have to do extras, too. We'd all get a laugh, even the offending party.

Hopefully by now you have a good sense of why I said at the start of this chapter that Fred Shero saved my career. But, as the saying goes, Rome wasn't built in a day, and neither were Freddy's Flyers.

During Shero's first season behind our bench, 1971–72, we still weren't ready to win or even to make the playoffs. We finished 26-38-14, in fifth place in the Western Division. With two games left, we needed only one win or two ties to beat out the Penguins for the final playoff spot. Both of the final two games were at the Spectrum, where we had a 19-12-6 record with two left to play. It was on the road where we couldn't win (7-25-7) to save our lives.

In our next-to-last game, we clung to a 4–3 lead over the Penguins. Pittsburgh pulled goalie Jim Rutherford for an extra skater. With 46 seconds left, Greg Polis scored to force a tie.

That was disappointing. But we still only needed a tie against Buffalo in the final game of the regular season.

We seemed to have that mission accomplished as the final seconds ticked off the clock with the score deadlocked. Then Buffalo's Gerry Meehan launched a shot from about 60 feet away. Doug Favell waved and missed. Four seconds remained in the game. We were out of the playoffs, quite literally, on a tiebreaker. By virtue of losing the season series to Pittsburgh, the Flyers were out and the Penguins were in, although the clubs had identical 26-38-14 final records.

I felt numb, and then I felt sick about it. These kinds of things happened to us way too often.

On an individual basis, though, the 1971–72 season was the start of better things for me once I healed from a knee injury. Freddy gained trust in me and started to play me again as a lineup regular. I received my share of ice time and regained some of the confidence I'd lost over the previous two years. I was never a stats guy, as you know. The only numbers that mattered to me were our team's record and my number of games played. The season was far from a big leap for me, but I felt things beginning to come together again in my game regardless of how the stats looked.

Keith Allen must have agreed. After the season, he signed me to a two-year contract extension. The money was just so-so, but I understood that I was still in the process of reproving myself.

We had a lot of changeover on the roster over the course of the season. Faces came and went as Keith and Freddy were still trying to find the right mix. At the start of the season, for example, we had right winger Larry Mickey on our team after acquiring him from LA in the offseason for Larry Hillman.

Mickey was a good guy and an honest, hardworking player. He was appointed as one of our alternate captains. He liked to break up some of the monotony on plane trips. Larry's specialty was the dollar-bill-on-a-string prank. He'd loop thin and nearly invisible string or fishing line around the edge of the bill and lay the dollar bill on the floor. When someone inevitably tried to pick it up, he'd yank away the dollar bill just out of his reach. If he tried again, Larry would yank it further away. He'd do it until the victim either caught on to the prank (the guys' laughter usually gave it away) or the other person gave up.

Mickey only played 14 games with us before we traded him to Buffalo for Larry Keenan. There was nothing wrong with the way he played, but the truth of the matter was that we had several other players in the lineup who had very similar styles. We needed more skill.

One guy who'd been with us since our first season in 1967–68 who left in-season during Freddy's first year coaching the Flyers was Jimmy Johnson. He'd been a teammate and a pretty reliable two-way player. Midway through the season, on January 28, 1972, to be exact, Jim was part of what was at the time the largest exchange of players in a single trade in NHL history (a record that's since been broken). The Flyers sent Johnson, Serge Bernier, Larry Brown, and Bill Lesuk to the Los Angeles Kings. In return, we received Bill Flett, Eddie Joyal, Ross Lonsberry (whom I knew from our time in the Bruins system), and defenseman Jean Potvin. A year later, Potvin went to the Islanders in exchange for Terry Crisp.

On February 8, 1972, we had a game in Vancouver against the Canucks. Bruce Gamble, who had gone from Dougie's backup to splitting time in goal, was our starter that night. Gamble played the entire game but, at one point, inexplicably fell down without contact. After the game, he felt increasingly worse. Nevertheless, the goalie accompanied our team on a trip to Oakland to prepare for a game against the Seals.

By this point, Gamble had full-fledged chest pains. He was admitted to a hospital in Oakland. It was later announced that the Flyers' goaltender had suffered a heart attack during the game in Vancouver but finished the game before telling anyone.

The heart attack forced the 34-year-old to retire as an active player. We were stunned. Bruce became a Flyers' scout after the heart attack. Tragically, 10 years later he suffered another heart attack; this one was fatal. He took ill shortly after practicing for an old-timers' game in which he was slated to play in net.

One other memory stands out in my mind from that season. We were starting to establish more of the team culture that we'd carry through our Stanley Cup years. If a player went through the motions or put himself in front of the team, the issue was usually taken care of inside the dressing room. Clarke, Ashbee, Dornhoefer, Van Impe, and I made sure that everyone understood loud and clear that the team always came first. No exceptions.

For example, Barry Ashbee detested defenseman Rick Foley (whom we'd just acquired from Chicago at the cost of Andre Lacroix, our most skilled playmaker before Clarke). I didn't have a big problem with Rick personally. I thought he was OK. Ashcan, however, felt that Foley was not a good teammate: he was in poor physical condition, took foolish offensive risks that hurt the team, and took selfish penalties to settle scores rather than battling mostly on behalf of teammates.

Was that fair? Well, there was probably at least some truth to it, especially the conditioning part and the excessive risk-taking. I'd seen worse, personally. As the season went along, it became clear that Freddy and Keith had come to similar conclusions about Rick. He was out of our lineup for a prolonged stretch (despite 11 goals and 36 points in just 58 games). Keith wasted little time after the season trading Foley to Detroit for Serge Lajeunesse.

All in all, Freddy's first year with the Flyers was more eventful in terms of the transitions that were starting to take place than for anything we accomplished on the ice. The progress still seemed glacial to me (and probably to most of the fans). I knew, though, that we now had a very bright coach at the helm, and we weren't going to keep around players who weren't truly committed to being part of the solution. Our biggest problem was that the roster itself still wasn't quite good enough.

How soon would it be the Flyers' turn to blossom? Sooner than I realized. It started the very next season.

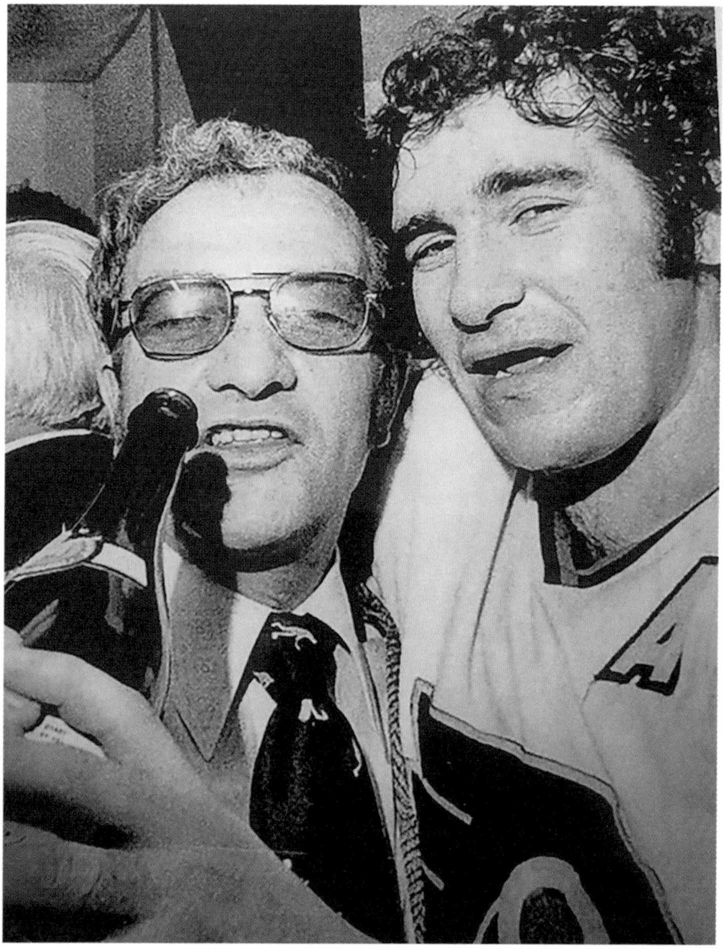

Along with Harry Sinden in the Boston organization, Fred Shero was the best coach I played for during my professional hockey career. He hated being called an "innovator," but that's what Freddy was. This photo is of our happiest moment as player and coach: celebrating the Stanley Cup championship with champagne in the locker room.

CHAPTER 9

Taking Care of Business

I want to talk a little bit about the business side of hockey back when I played. Maybe I was just a northern BC kid who left school after tenth grade to play hockey. I certainly was no financial genius or aspiring tycoon. But I was no fool. I just wanted to feel like I was being treated fairly—no more and no less.

My experience of being taken advantage of by Alan Eagleson taught me a valuable lesson. I went back to representing myself for the rest of my career. I can't say that I drove an especially hard bargain, but I did stand my ground on what I thought was fair.

In 1972, the Flyers had one of the best NHL Amateur Draft crops in franchise history. Billy Barber in the first round. Tom Bladon in the second. My brother Jimmy in the third. Al MacAdam in the fourth. Keith Allen knew what he was doing, eh?

I negotiated Jim's first contract on his behalf. I knew the drill, and I wanted to make sure that my brother got a fair shake. I don't recall the exact numbers, but I think it came out, with salary and signing bonuses, to about $30,000. He got a three-year contract.

Jimmy was thrilled. I was happy for him. Then I realized something: I'd negotiated a better contract for my kid brother than I did for myself! I was an NHL veteran at that point, and my own contract paid $28,000. Shrewd, eh?

The World Hockey Association was founded in 1972 as a rival circuit to the NHL. People have asked me over the years what I thought about the WHA. My opinion was like that of most NHL players: the competition was a good thing because it meant an opportunity to make more money if WHA teams were competing with your NHL team to get you under contract.

As a matter of fact, the WHA's Cincinnati Stingers later offered contracts to Jimmy and me. I told my brother, "I don't want to go to the WHA. I think we can win the Stanley Cup with the Flyers."

He agreed. We didn't pursue it. However, the WHA interest probably helped us get higher salaries from the Flyers. Bob Kelly also came close at one point to leaving the Flyers for a WHA offer, but he also decided to stay.

Meanwhile, although the Edmonton Oil Kings claimed Bobby Clarke's WHA rights in their 1972 General Player Draft, he declined to listen to an offer. The Philadelphia Blazers also tried, too. Clarkie was flying to Philly to sign a big extension with the Flyers.

As the story goes, someone representing the Blazers—his last name was Johnston, but I don't know his first name—approached Clarkie in a bar. The guy introduced himself and asked, "Did you sign with the Flyers yet?"

"No, I'm doing that tomorrow," Clarke said.

"Don't sign anything," the guy said. "[Blazers co-owners Bernard] Brown and [James] Cooper are prepared to offer you much more than anything the Flyers will pay you. Wait right here," Johnston said.

Ten minutes later, after the guy called the Blazers ownership, Johnston returned.

"The Blazers are prepared to offer you $1,000,000 over a five-year contract," he said. "Let us know tomorrow."

That was crazy money by 1972 standards. Clarkie told Flyers' publicist John Brogan about the encounter, and Brogan told Ed Snider. Mr. Snider then called Clarkie at home to ask what was going on.

"Don't worry about it. I'm committed to the Flyers and the NHL," Clarke said. "I'm signing with the Flyers for what we discussed."

Snider replied, "Thank you. I will never forget this."

I don't know if I have all the details of the Clarkie story right, but that's the gist of it. Ultimately, Ed Snider made sure that none of the Flyers players left for the WHA pastures.

However, there were former Flyers who went to the WHA, with mixed results. Bernie Parent was in a contract dispute with the Maple Leafs and signed with the Blazers. The Blazers also landed Andre Lacroix.

Bernie had a bad experience with the Blazers, who ran out of money amid growing financial losses and eventually stopped paying. The 1972–73 season, which started with the ice cracking at the Philadelphia Civic Center and the postponement of the opening game, turned out to be the only one the Blazers would play.

Andre, meanwhile, spent most of the rest of his career in the WHA except for an NHL return with the Hartford Whalers at the end (after the NHL and WHA merged in 1979). He was the league's all-time leading scorer.

The Blazers most famously also signed Derek Sanderson away from the Bruins on a five-year deal for $2.6 million, making him the highest-paid professional athlete in North American team sports. The Blazers got more than they bargained for with "Turk." He was a real wild child in those days.

The WHA experience turned out to be good for some players—it revived Gordie Howe's playing career after a short retirement and gave him the chance to play with sons Mark and Marty, for example—and not so good for others.

Personally, I never regretted staying put with the Flyers.

This was taken at a 1972 preseason exhibition game: Flyers vs. the Richmond Robins. This was one of only three times I ever played in a professional game against Jimmy. My brother spent most of his first pro season in the American Hockey League with our farm team in Richmond.

We opened the 1972–73 season on the road against the St. Louis Blues. The game ended in a 4–4 tie. Three things stand out for me when I look back at that game.

First, we scored three power-play goals: Bill Flett, Rick MacLeish, and Bobby Clarke. Clarke set up Flett and the doorstep, and the Cowboy knocked the puck into the net and landed on top of goalie Jacques Caron in the process. MacLeish scored on a wrist shot from the circle, something that would become a huge weapon for him. Clarke's goal was scored on a second-effort play on a scramble around the net.

Talk about tone-setting goals. When you think about a "typical" Flett, MacLeish, or Clarke tally, these three goals were it. Add in Clarke's setup pass on the first one, and these were like factory prototypes ready to start rolling down the assembly line.

Second, I remember thinking before the game—and telling Bill Fleishman of the *Daily News* afterward—that suddenly, I was the smallest player on our team. We had a lot of big, strong, and tough guys when I looked down the bench.

We'd had a lot of nasty, physical games against the Blues over the years. Now, our team was built to handle such a game and had the types of personalities that weren't going to be intimidated. Barclay Plager tried to stir things up twice during the game, and both times, we had players who could handle it. One of our holdover guys who was never afraid of the rough stuff, Gary Dornhoefer, was the first to meet Plager's challenge, but we had several others who were every bit as willing and able. In fact, there were no full-blown fights in the game. Once the Blues saw they weren't going to outmuscle or intimidate the Flyers, they settled down.

It was a good hockey game. We took a 4–3 lead midway through the third period. Unfortunately, we gave up a goal to Jack Egers with 5:25 left in the game. With 1:24 left, referee Dave Newell called me for a very marginal tripping penalty where my skates simply got tangled with a St. Louis player. Both of us went down. They got a power play with a chance to win the game.

I let Newell hear about it. Then Newell tagged me for a 10-minute misconduct. The game ended in a tie as Doug Favell and the penalty killers did a good job.

My third and final recollection is this: As a team, we were angry at the outcome. We felt like it was a game we should have won. A tie, even one of the so-called hard-fought-point-on-the-road variety, no longer felt OK to us.

We were cursing and angry at the end. We were mad at ourselves for not nailing down a win that was within our grasp. We were mad at Newell, too, for a couple of bad calls, but none of us were going to use officiating as an excuse.

To put it another way, we were starting to develop the mindset of a winning team.

When we came home to the Spectrum for our second game, the stands were filled to capacity, even in the brand-new third deck. So much for the fears that fans would desert the Flyers in favor of the WHA's Blazers. The battle for the affections of Philadelphia hockey fans soon turned out to be a TKO. The Flyers fans stayed loyal to us. Again, I had no beef with any player who went to the WHA, but I was grateful to our fanbase, which would only continue to grow after those earliest days back in '67, when none of us felt too sure there'd even be an NHL team in Philly for the long haul, let alone where our individual career paths might lead us.

We trounced the Vancouver Canucks, 7–3, that night. Our fans went nuts for every goal—ex-Flyers farmhand Dunc Wilson absorbed all seven for the Canucks—and every hit and especially a third-period fight. Fans booed loudly when Favell got an extra penalty for leaving the crease during the altercation. I mean, our fans were really into the game.

Beyond the first two games, the start to the 1972–73 season was not our best hockey. We got off to a 3-4-2 start. Freddy and assistant Mike Nykoluk (the NHL's first full-time assistant) put us through a long practice the day after a 4–1 loss to the Seals, but it wasn't something they did to be punitive. Rather, I remember that it was corrective and helpful.

Shortly after that, we rattled off six wins in eight games. Our fourth win of that stretch was a 5–3 win over Chicago. Having been dismantled by the Black Hawks in the playoffs in the spring of 1971—barely 18 months earlier chronologically but which already felt like a long time ago—it felt gratifying. Schultz beat the stuffing out of Keith Magnusen in a second-period fight. MacLeish scored a hat trick in flawless fashion: three shots on goal, three tallies. Clarke walked in and scored a put-away goal.

I earned an assist on Clarke's marker. Afterward, I was asked about the play.

"Easy. I just passed him the puck and stayed the hell out of the way," I said. "He's persistent."

One thing about hockey, though, is this: this game will keep you humble. After winning six of eight, we lost five of the next seven games, including a 6–3 game to the Rangers at Madison Square Garden on November 15, a 6–5 decision to the Canadiens in Montreal, and then a 3–2 loss to the Flames in Atlanta.

Freddy warned us to take Atlanta, a first-year expansion team, as seriously as would any other opponent. He even hand-wrote a little prescout of sorts, which was published in *Philadelphia Flyers Magazine* before our rematch with the Flames on November 30 at the Spectrum.

"Atlanta isn't playing very aggressive hockey. They're just sending one man in and waiting for their breaks. If the goaltending is good, and they get that break, they win. It's as simple as that," Shero wrote, and then discussed how Atlanta had some talent at center but was a rather undersized team that could get worn down.

"Talking about the Flames isn't going to beat them, though. Getting out on the ice and doing what we're supposed to do is. When we went down to Atlanta last week, I think we took them too lightly. Well, we got beat, 3–2. That just goes to show what can happen when you're not up for a game."

Shero, as usual, was right. I saved Freddy's short article, which is preserved in one of my scrapbooks. That game was a lesson that, if we didn't come ready to outwork the other club, we weren't even half as good as we'd started to think we were.

When the calendar flipped to December, we went on another hot streak: five wins in the month's first seven games. Leaguewide, we were starting to get more notice for the number of fights in our games than for the influx of young talent that was coming into its own. Honestly, that annoyed me a little bit. We got no respect around the league, especially our defense corps.

A 5–2 win over the Canadiens on December 5 felt especially good. The legendary Jack Chevalier of the *Philadelphia Inquirer* wrote a great article.

"Burned by public criticism and prodded consistently by coach Fred Shero, the Flyers defense put it all together last night and repelled the mighty Montreal Canadiens with a textbook demonstration before 16,600 at the Spectrum," he wrote.

Chevalier went on to mention various plays, both big and small, that our defensemen made in the game, both on the offensive and defensive sides of the puck. He also discussed how we collectively did a good job in front of rookie goalie Michel Belhumeur, who earned his first NHL win.

Freddy summed it up like this, "I was worried. Usually, the defense comes in and plays tighter in front of a new goalie."

Both Shero and Clarke also emphasized another point: the Canadiens seemed to think we'd roll over for them. They rested Ken Dryden that night and started AHL callup Wayne Thomas. Freddy noted their arrogance in throwing pucks at the net all night from ridiculous angles, as if Belhumeur or our D were bound to misplay a few for easy goals. Clarke added, "They must not think much of our hockey club."

These were old-fashioned locker room motivation tactics, yes. But it worked. To a man, every Flyers player was determined to make the Canadiens fight for every inch of the ice. We hit. We blocked shots. We outworked them in the trenches. We won, 5–2.

A couple weeks later, Chevalier wrote another article that lifted my spirits. The article, entitled "New System for Flyers Aids Watson," talked about how the Flyers defensemen in general, and I, in particular, had figured out how to move the puck up-ice efficiently within the highly structured systems Freddy preached. We had more talent on the team than we did before, so Freddy and Mike tweaked things just a little to enable our team to dial up the offense. Defensemen had a role in this, too.

"The coaches have been stressing offense for all the defensemen, and I've been carrying the puck more. It must be our new system. That's the only explanation I have for it," I told Jack.

"Four of the five skaters are attacking now. If the opportunity arises, Freddy wants us to go. Eddie Van Impe and I have been playing together for so long that we know each other's moves. He's more of a defensive defenseman, so I've been the one going up ice more."

Up to that point, my season high in points in the NHL was 19 during my first year in Philadelphia. In both 1970–71 and 1971–72, I had three goals, seven assists, and 10 points. Now, in 1972–73, I went to post 26 points (2g, 24a). That ended up being the second-best offensive season in my career (the most was 30 points in 1976–77).

Let's face it, though: there really wasn't much to say about me as an offensive-minded defenseman. I chuckled when Jack asked me about my uptick in points. I didn't think anyone would notice that. Even so, it's also nice to be recognized for contributing in different ways. That year, it just worked out that I started to have more chances to jump into the attack.

Speaking of Van Impe and me knowing each other's moves, this was the season when speedy but pint-sized (five-foot-five, 155 pounds) Vancouver Canucks rookie Bobby Lalonde twice dangled right around Eddie. After the second time, Eddie decided there wouldn't be a third.

"All I want you to do, Beave, is this: if he attacks on your side, make him go over the middle, and I'll take care of the rest," Van Impe said, referring to my old nickname, Beaver.

I did as Ed instructed. As Lalonde moved across the middle, Eddie had leverage with his stick and sent Lalonde quite literally flying. We still got a chuckle out of that one even years after our respective retirements.

No one was chuckling about our flight home from Chicago after a 4–1 loss on December 20. Here was our full traveloge of what turned out to be one of the longest days and evenings of any of our playing careers.

7:15 a.m. CST: Wake-up call at our hotel in Chicago.

8:00 a.m.: Team bus departs the hotel.

8:30 a.m.: Bus arrives at a very foggy Midway Airport.

9:30 a.m.: The pilot gets on the intercom, and we sit at our departure gate. He tells us we're going to be delayed. Then he says he's not sure if it is a good idea to be carrying 32 people and 1,750 pounds of equipment in the F-27 aircraft given the conditions. Yikes!

11:30 a.m.: The plane finally departs, roughly two hours behind schedule.

12:30 p.m. EST: They do not have hot lunches for us on the flight, as it was slated to be a morning departure. They serve us a late breakfast.

1:30 p.m.: We make a refueling stop in Cleveland.

3:00 p.m.: The captain delivers some more bad news. We are in a holding pattern over Philadelphia. We must fly to Harrisburg to get more fuel.

3:30 p.m.: We land safely in Harrisburg. Assistant coach Mike Nykoluk announces that he's going to go home to Hershey for supper and asks if anyone wants to join him and then ride to Philadelphia.

4:00 p.m.: Many of our players call their wives and tell them to simply meet us at the rink.

4:30 p.m.: We're still waiting on word that we'd be OK to land in Philly. If not, we could go to Richmond. Instead, Ed Snider hires a bus to take us from Harrisburg to Philadelphia.

5:00 p.m.: Our driver, a kindly Pennsylvania Dutch man, departs. He informs us that he does not drive on expressways or the turnpike. We'd go via King of Prussia, PA. There, a police escort arranged by John Brogan would assist us.

6:30 p.m.: After traffic had come to a lengthy standstill due to an accident involving an 18-wheel truck, a fireman in Avondale, PA, gets aboard to guide our bus around the accident.

7:30 p.m.: We arrive at the Spectrum. See, I saved the best part for last. We had a home game that night against the LA Kings. We won, 6–3. I don't remember a damn thing else except that we were all exhausted. A photo of me, half-awake at my locker postgame, ran in the newspapers the next morning.

We were all exhausted after our hellish return trip to Philadelphia from our December 20, 1972, road game in Chicago. We made it back to Philly with little time to spare before our December 21 home game against the LA Kings (a 6–3 win).

Experiences like these are excruciating when they happen, but they can also have a bonding effect on a team. We had a so-so spell after Christmas to shortly after New Year's but then went on one of the best teamwide runs I'd experienced to that point of my NHL career. From January 13 to February 4, we won or tied 9 of 11 games. Even the two losses—on the road against the Rangers and Canadiens—were competitive games most of the way.

By now, it was clear that our group of young players—led by Clarke, MacLeish, and rookie Bill Barber—were already becoming upper-tier NHL talents, the likes of which we'd never had before on our team. We had the toughest and hardest-working team I'd ever been part of up to that point in my pro career. Other teams knew by now not to mess with Dave Schultz, Bob Kelly, or Don Saleski.

We had strong coaching. We also had more young talent, including my brother Jimmy, in the pipeline. The one thing I wasn't sure about was whether we had the goaltending. Dougie Favell still ran hot and cold, and neither Bobby Taylor nor Belhumeur were ready to be NHL starters.

On January 17, 1973, the Flyers named Clarke the team's new captain. Ed Van Impe had been our captain since our second season, and he'd been a damn good one, too. But the decision was the right one at the right time. We were creating a new era and a strong identity. There's no two ways about it. We had a lot of good leaders on our team, but Clarke wasn't just our best player on the ice; he set an example with his work ethic.

Bob was far from the most vocal guy in the room, but when he had something to say, everyone paid attention. I want to reiterate a crucial point here about leadership—italicized for emphasis. *Leadership isn't about style of communication. A leader is someone who knows the way, goes the way, and shows the way.*

That was Clarkie. He was a winner, through and through. Everything he did as a player, and everything we did as a team, put the good of the team first. It was impossible to outwork Bob or play with a higher pain threshold or be mentally tougher, but we all competed to model those same traits. As a team in that era, we had no cliques. We hung out as a group. Came to the building together and left together. Socialized together. Razzed one another constantly but wouldn't stand for outsiders (especially opposing players) doing it.

A very hard-fought 2–2 tie against the Bruins on February 4 saw Barber score his 19th of the season (on the way to 30). Clarke played an outstanding all-around game, continuing to build his case for the Hart Trophy as league MVP, and scored his 23rd goal of the season. Barber and Clarke assisted on each other's goals, something that would become very commonplace for the rest of the decade and into the early 1980s.

To add a little muscle and toughness to our blueline, Keith Allen had recently acquired Ande "Moose" Dupont in a trade: one of my all-time favorite teammates. The Boston game saw Moose drop the gloves with Orr in the third period.

Jimmy got his first call-up to the Flyers that season. I remember the pride I felt when he told me. But my brother, who eventually got his feet wet with four games at the NHL level in 1972–73, also witnessed one of the biggest scares I had in my career.

We had a game against Atlanta at the Spectrum. He'd just settled into his seat in the press box when Atlanta's Ray Comeau and I got tangled and went down to the ice. My teammates signaled urgently for the trainers. They assisted me off the ice with a towel pressed near my left eye and blood on the ice.

Someone in the press box told Jimmy, "Maybe you'd better go down [to the locker room]."

What happened was this: Comeau's skate cut me dangerously close to my left eye. Thank God my eye itself wasn't sliced. Thirty stitches later (administered by our team's oral surgeon, Dr. Borghesani, because he was the closest medical professional on hand, and our trainer, Frank Lewis, was in the hospital with pneumonia), and I was OK— still a little shaken because it was so close to something way more serious, but otherwise OK.

I was less lucky in our 7–2 home loss to Chicago on February 11. I wrenched my shoulder and missed the next 13 games. In hockey, one player's misfortune is another's opportunity. During my absence, Jimmy made his NHL debut in our 5–3 road win over St. Louis on February 20. He'd also dress in each of the next three games and handled himself well. It was obvious that he'd be knocking on the door of becoming a regular in our NHL lineup by the next season.

When I returned to play, there were eight games left in the regular season. We finished strong, including a 9–0 blowout over Vancouver at the Spectrum, a 5–2 win at home over the Blues, and a 10–2 shellacking of the visiting New York Islanders in our final home game. The regular season ended with a 5–4 road loss in Pittsburgh.

Clarke (37 goals, 67 assists, 104 points) and MacLeish (50 goals, 50 assists, 100 points) became the first two players in our team's history to achieve a 100-point season.

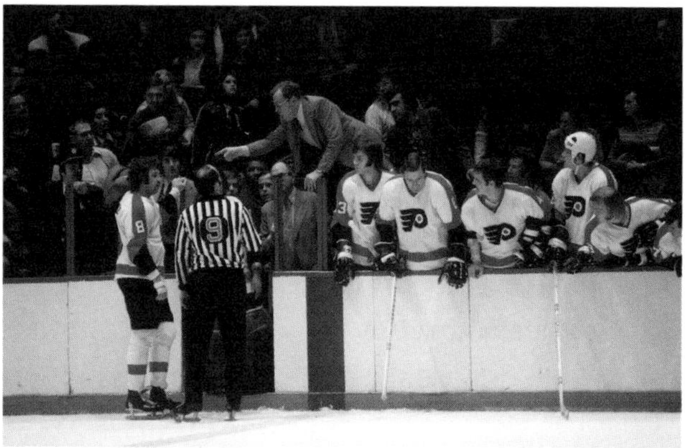

Fred Shero rarely showed much outward emotion. It was unusual for him to raise his voice to his players, although he let us know in no uncertain terms about our play if it was subpar. Not much broke his calm demeanor. Here, however, Freddy was furious at the officials when Dave Schultz got the only penalty in a scrum with the Minnesota North Stars in this February 18, 1973, game at the Spectrum. We went on to win the game, 5–1.

Clarke also became the first player from an expansion team to win the Hart Trophy. Barber (30 goals, 64 points in 69 games) was the runner-up to Steve Vickers for the Calder Trophy as the NHL's Rookie of the Year.

However, few outside of Philly were willing to credit all the skill we now had in the lineup or the strong work ethic and leadership group we had. Not a word on Shero's coaching genius. Nope, but there was a whole lot of self-righteous complaining about all the fights and penalty minutes we accumulated. The same people who couldn't have cared less when Noel Picard sucker punched a defenseless Claude LaForge or when the Blues in general brutalized our undersized and not particularly feisty team now were suddenly gravely concerned about the integrity of the game being compromised.

Schultz led the NHL with 259 penalty minutes. My buddy, the Hound, was second with 238. Moose was fourth with 215 combined PIMs between the Blues and Flyers. Don "Big Bird" Saleski was fifth (205) and Dorny was tenth (168th).

What the knuckleheads missed was the fact that our undeniable team toughness and the intimidation factor we now had working in our favor for the first time in our team history were only two aspects of our club. We were still underestimated for all the other things that were starting to define our club.

The history books show that we defeated the Minnesota North Stars in the 1973 Stanley Cup Quarterfinals, four games to two. For many years, a statue representing Gary Dornhoefer's overtime winning goal in Game 5 stood outside the arena complex. "Dorny's Dash" is perhaps the most famous pre-Cup goal in Flyers' history—so much so that many people mistakenly believe that it was the series-clinching play. We wrapped up the series two nights later with a 4–1 win in Minnesota.

I'd won minor-league championships while I was a Bruins prospect, but this was the first Stanley Cup series win of my NHL career, and it came when I was a few months shy of my thirtieth birthday. It was a long time coming between Boston and Philly, and it's a special memory to this day.

In the Stanley Cup Semifinal, we played Montreal. In Game 1 on the road, we pulled off a 5–4 upset win in overtime. MacLeish netted the game-winner. Game 2 also went to OT, but the Canadiens won this one, 4–3. I've always felt deep in my heart that if we'd pulled that one out to come back to Philadelphia with two road wins at the Forum to our credit, the rest of the series might have turned out differently.

In Game 3 at the Spectrum, the Canadiens edged us out, 2–1. Subsequently, they beat us at home in Game 4, 4–1, and then ended the series back at the Forum in Game 5 by a 5–3 score.

You win as a team or you lose as a team. I reiterate that here because I don't want what I'm about to say to be misunderstood. Doug Favell served our team well for many years. He and I went back to the Boston system together. I liked and respected Dougie. But the truth of the matter is that goaltending was our weakest link in that series against Montreal and the biggest upgrade our management needed to compete with teams like the Canadiens, Bruins, or Rangers for the Stanley Cup. Dougie just wasn't of the same caliber as Ken Dryden, Tony Esposito, or Eddie Giacomin, and that's not a slight to Favy. We're talking about a comparison to Hall of Fame goalies.

Overall, though, we came away from that Montreal series feeling upbeat about our future.

We gave the Montreal Canadiens a tough battle in the 1973 Stanley Cup Semifinal, but we weren't quite ready—yet—to win the Cup. This playoff year was the first of six in a row when the Flyers reached at least the Semis.

We knew that beating the best teams in the league—even the mighty Canadiens—was within our reach. The message was sent even before we left the dressing room after Game 5.

Clarkie spoke up. "Boys, we need to get in the best shape of our lives this summer. If every one of us does that, we'll win the Stanley Cup next season."

Those words always stuck with me. Deep in my heart, I knew Bob was right. I felt the same way he did. We were closer to reaching the top than anyone in the NHL seemed to understand or be willing to admit.

Our fans sensed what we sensed. When our flight arrived back from Montreal, an estimated 1,000 fans waited for us at the airport. They cheered as soon as they saw us. We weren't expecting so many people. It was gratifying, even in defeat.

The magic of our next three seasons—back-to-back Stanley Cup championships, our win over Red Army, and another Cup Finals run—tends to dwarf what we accomplished in 1972–73. But as someone who lived it firsthand, the 1972–73 season is when we started to understand that we were onto something special.

The Flyers fans believed in us. We believed in ourselves. If no one else believed, well, screw 'em.

CHAPTER 10

A Dream Dressed in Work Clothes

There's been a lot said and written about our Stanley Cup championship seasons of 1973–74 and 1974–75. Let's face it. If it weren't for those two magical seasons, this book probably wouldn't even exist. I'm a realist. What defined my career as a hockey player wasn't what I did. It was all about what the team accomplished. Everyone had a part to play.

In chapter 11, I'll retrace the seasons themselves. First, though, I'll try to answer the two questions that I get asked the most often about those years. *What was it like to be part of those teams on and off the ice? What set the Flyers apart beyond the "Broad Street Bullies" reputation?*

To have a hockey team that wins multiple championships and stays in contention for a long period of time after that, you must start at the top. We had the strongest ownership under Ed Snider. Take away Mr. Snider, and we'd either have folded within a year of NHL expansion or, at best, have been just another also-ran club.

Ed Snider, as a boss, often said that the key to success is to hire good people and let them do their jobs. I could tell both during my playing days and my later years of working for the organization on the business/sales side that Ed practiced what he preached. It's something worth emulating. I'll also add here that Joe Scott was a wonderful man, who really helped build a fan base and connected the organization to the community.

Our hockey operations staff was second to none. Bud Poile was a Hockey Hall of Fame general manager in his own right, but somehow Keith Allen was even better. Easier to get along with on a day-to-day basis but someone who was very much in charge. An incredible judge of talent both on the player personnel and staffing sides. A shrewd negotiator who drove a hard bargain. Keith was a good, solid coach, but he was a once-in-a-generation GM. He was rarely wrong, but when he was, he didn't double down on a mistake. He corrected it ASAP.

Quick anecdote here: One time after a game in Toronto, I went to the Brass Rail. The bartender, Owen McManus, was a friend of mine. At the bar was a man with a walking cane. The cane was filled with booze. Owen introduced me to him. The man was famous daredevil Bob "Evel" Knievel.

We struck up a conversation. Knievel told me he used to play hockey in Butte, Montana. Later, he tried out for a minor league team, the Seattle Totems. I told him our general manager in Philadelphia used to coach the Totems.

"Who is your general manager?" Knievel asked.

"Keith Allen," I replied.

"That's the guy!"

I later asked Keith if he remembered Knievel. He did. Apparently, Knievel wasn't a very good hockey player. There was never serious thought given to signing him.

I digress. Anyway, so strong was the trust between Allen and Mr. Snider that, when they had a disagreement, Ed usually deferred in the end. Ed Snider was used to getting his way when push came to shove, but in hockey matters, what Keith Allen thought was best for the team was the most important factor.

Bud Poile built a very good scouting staff, and Marcel Pelletier was one of the best around as a player personnel advisor for the NHL roster. Keith Allen then refined, added to, and further improved those functions.

This is all infrastructure stuff: not very entertaining, perhaps, but absolutely vital to building a first-rate hockey organization. As a player, I really didn't think about it much. But I came to realize after I retired that our team's glory years would never have been possible had the organization not been so well assembled from ownership to behind-the-scenes hockey operations right on down. We're not even up to the players yet.

Next stop is the coach's office. Could we have won one championship, let alone two, without Fred Shero as our coach? I doubt it. He wasn't just a great coach; he was the right coach for our group of players. We didn't always understand his eccentricities, but he understood us, and that was more important.

It's not that Freddy treated everyone as equals. He defined your role clearly, and the expectations were nonnegotiable. In fact, if someone truly needed a reality check, Shero reminded the person that no one is irreplaceable, but some are more readily replaced than others. If a player felt the game was doing him wrong, well, the world needs farmers and factory workers and painters, too.

Thankfully, we didn't have such attitudes on our team, at least not among anyone who found a spot. Bad apples were identified and removed very quickly. Of course, there were sometimes disagreements in the room and isolated times when someone needed to be called out, but that's the nature of hockey or any team environment.

Freddy let our dressing room be self-policing. We were as vigilant as our coach in holding every player accountable, but we did it at a much higher volume and expressed it in ways that were much less cerebral. Because we were self-policed, "the Fog" stayed out of the way.

As Shero himself was fond of saying and writing, "The players have their rules, and I have my ruler. We're careful not to tread upon each other." He believed that.

What Freddy did best, apart from communicating his systems was this: he defined very clearly what he expected from each player and made each of us take equal pride in doing whatever our defined role was on the team.

Other teams like Boston or Montreal or the Rangers had more great players—meaning Hall of Fame caliber—than we did. Bernie Parent, Bobby Clarke, and Bill Barber are Hall of Famers, and Rick MacLeish and, later, Reggie Leach were All-Star caliber guys. But we had more good players than other teams had great ones.

Another way to put it is this: we had the best team. The notion of the whole being greater than the sum of the parts doesn't exist in math or science, right? But it absolutely does exist in team sports. We have the Stanley Cup rings to prove it.

I'm not a "jewelry person" ordinarily, but this is special: my Stanley Cup rings mean the world to me, and I still wear them to this day. I often allow hockey fans I meet to try on a Cup ring, and it makes me happy to see their faces light up. The rings are my proudest material possession.

There was no magic involved. There was a whole lot of hard work and a lot of trust in each other and our coach. Simple as that, yet something that is hard to capture and hold onto unless you've got the right pieces in place.

The biggest piece of the puzzle was goaltending. When the Flyers reacquired Bernie Parent in the summer of 1973, that's when we truly had everything that we needed to win the Stanley Cup.

In our first Cup-winning season, Bernie bailed us out more times than I could count, both in the regular season and the playoffs. He won the Vezina Trophy and the Conn Smythe Trophy. He'd win them again the second year, too, and was still clearly the best goalie in the NHL.

To me, the difference was this. In the second Cup year (and even in 1975–76), we had a better overall team in front of Parent. There were a lot of nights when we helped other teams to about 15 or 18 shots on goal. Bernie took care of the rest. There's no way in hell we could have won the 1973–74 Stanley Cup without Bernie being at the peak of his game. In 1974–75, it would have been harder with a lesser goalie but still possible.

Bobby "Chief" Taylor, Bernie's backup, was a great team player and a great guy in general. He was never sour about going very long stretches—in a time before there were goalie coaches and the only way to stay even somewhat sharp was to take as many reps in practice as he could get. During the next season, we acquired Wayne Stephenson from St. Louis.

"Fort Wayne" was, in all honesty, a better NHL goaltender than "Chief." There were a lot of teams for whom he'd have been the number-one goalie. When Bernie was injured, Wayne filled in capably for him. He wasn't of Parent's caliber, though, nor was he on par with the other elite goalies like Dryden or Esposito.

Wayne struggled with accepting the number-two role, even though he performed it well. It was only after his playing days that he came to grips with it, saying that it was simply a matter of "growing up" and facing reality.

Although Stephenson struggled privately with not playing as often as he felt he deserved, he didn't make it a distraction to the team. Actually, most of us never got to know Wayne very closely. He kept to himself most of the time. He was one of the few who didn't hang out with the other guys very often.

Wayne was a very intelligent man with a mind for business. We'd be reading the sports section of the newspaper or *The Hockey News*. He'd have his face in the *Wall Street Journal*. He was also a good family man.

After his hockey career, Stephenson became a banking executive. That came as no surprise to his old teammates. I was sad when Wayne passed away in 2010 at age 65 after a battle with brain cancer. We weren't close friends, but I respected him both as a hockey player and as someone who clearly had a game plan for life after hockey.

Goaltending is hockey's lone solitary position. For that reason, it's a little less vital that the goalie be one of the guys off the ice, so long as he stops the puck. Stephenson did that as well as any number-two goalie in the league. He didn't have to be the social butterfly or fun-loving sort that Bernie was (and still is).

Bobby Taylor, meanwhile, was destined for a long and successful hockey broadcasting career after his playing days. Chief had to study the game to be ready to step in when he was called to play, which wasn't very often. He's always been charismatic and likeable—just fun to have around as a teammate and someone who understood and accepted his role.

Having players who embraced their roles and worked like hell to be the best at whatever their duties were was key to how Shero sustained his coaching success in Philadelphia for as long as he did. The Stephenson case was an outlier, but you can work around the goalie being a bit of a loner off the ice.

Among his position players, Shero made sure that Hound understood that his five to eight minutes of ice time were just as important to winning as Ross Lonsberry's 14 minutes. The penalties that Terry Crisp or Barry Ashbee or I helped to kill were as important as a Rick MacLeish or Bill Barber power-play goal.

Clarke's skill and tenacity set the tone in obvious ways. But the supporting players like Orest Kindrachuk anchoring the third line or the toughness of Dave Schultz or Moose Dupont, the size of Don Saleski, or the speed of Bill Clement also sent a message in their own way.

The message was this: whatever way you try to play against us, we've got the weapons to deal with it. That started with Freddy getting every player on the roster to believe that, and our leadership group in the dressing room reinforced it, day in and day out.

No one was ever "forced" to do things he wasn't good at. I was a vocal and emotional guy by nature, and I wasn't afraid to get on someone if he wasn't pulling his weight. Barry Ashbee did the same thing in a quieter and more stoic way, leading by example and playing through pain. Ed Van Impe was a true "Steady Eddie," and he had more of a mean streak on the ice than I did.

Whatever your personality type and skills on the ice, it was all blended into the mix. My brother Jimmy was our fastest-skating defenseman, and you could see he was going to be a team leader when older guys like Eddie and Ashcan—or, hell, Joe Watson—were no longer around. Jimmy was enthusiastic, emotional, and driven to win.

I mentioned this back in chapter 1: Jimmy has said that when he was a kid growing up in Smithers, I was his hero. As adults, quite honestly, we switched roles to a large degree.

I'd have loved to be as good of an NHL player as Jimmy was: a five-time All-Star who did it without big offensive numbers. I'd have given anything to be able to skate as well as he did and be as practical and mechanically inclined as my younger brother. He's such a good man. I admire him as much as a person as I did as a fellow hockey player and teammate.

Our hardest-shooting and most offensive-minded defenseman was one of our club's young guys: Tom Bladon. So that was his role. We called him "Bomber" for obvious reasons. At the same time, Tommy was a very quiet and laid-back type of guy. His other nickname around the club—we all had at least one nickname, and some of us had several—was "Sparky." That was a tongue-in-cheek type of nickname because you didn't get much emotion out of him.

The nicknames weren't just a "Flyers" thing. They've been around hockey forever and are still around today. Nowadays, to be honest, I think there's a lot less creativity—most are just variations of someone's last name—because there's a lot more political correctness these days.

For example, on our mid-'70s teams, Billy Barber was often called "Arnie" or "Piggy" because some of the boys teased him about resembling Arnold, the pig on the old *Green Acres* television show. My brother Jimmy was "Chan," as in the Charlie Chan movie character, because they had a similar cleft in their chins.

Here's the thing, though: we could internally call Barber "Piggy," but we wouldn't stand for some opponent or other outsiders doing it. It was our thing, and ours alone, to have permission to refer to him by that name.

The boundary lines were known but not verbalized. To this day, I could be out in public somewhere or at a hockey clinic and call over to my brother, "Hey, Chan! Come over here for a second, willya?" It also wouldn't feel strange if Hound or Bernie or Gary Dornhoefer said it. But I'd have never, for example, tolerated my son Ryan calling Jim his "Uncle Chan."

My own "original" nicknames, "Beaver" (Beave, for short) and "Whispers," predated my arrival on the Flyers. "Thundermouth," which legendary Flyers announcer Gene Hart coined, was the one that took off during the Broad Street Bullies years. That's fine. I don't mind it. I do speak in a loud, booming voice. I can't help it.

Some nicknames on our club were, of course, name based. "Crispy" was too natural not to use for Terry Crisp and had always been his nickname at every stop of his career. We called Bernie Parent "Bennie." Bob Clarke also went by "Whitey," but the straightforward "Clarkie" is what has stuck for the ages. Gary Dornhoefer was, and still is, "Dorny." No explanations are needed for those.

Bobby Taylor, like virtually every player of Canadian First Nation tribal heritage, was "Chief." Meanwhile, a lot of us still had young kids at home in those years, and we often used Sesame Street characters as nickname inspirations: "Big Bird" (or Bird, for short) was the very tall Don Saleski. We had "Ernie," "Grouch," and when acquired from Vancouver a few years later, Bob Dailey became "the Count" because his Canucks nickname was "Moose," and we already had one of those. It was Dupont himself who rechristened Dailey because of how he slung a dark jacket over his shoulder, and it looked like a cape.

The guy with the most nicknames was Orest Kindrachuk. He had a bunch. I can't remember them all. "Ernie" (thick mop of dark hair like the Sesame Street character, long gone nowadays!) and "O" (or "Little O" or "Oscar," which were puns on basketball superstar Oscar Robertson being "Big O") were the ones that had the most staying power.

Orest also was sometimes called "Chuck" or "Chuckles" (a pun on Kindrachuk). Early on, some guys called him "Doc," because he studied to become an optometrist before pursuing his hockey career. Some guys tested out "Russ" (as in Walrus, because he had a thick mustache) or "Chico" (due to having a slight physical resemblance to the character played by actor Freddy Prinze on the *Chico and the Man* television show).

Dave Schultz was and always will be "The Hammer." Among the boys, he also went by "Zeus" (big and strong). Schultzy was also our resident

"Grouch." MacLeish went by "Hawk" (for his nose), "Beauty," or "Bedrock."

Apart from being "Hound" or "Hound Dog," Bob Kelly answered to "Mutt" or "Muttley." I called him "Machine Gun" (as in gangster George "Machine Gun" Kelly) because, when he fought, Bob could throw three punches in the time other players needed to punch one.

To this day, Bob Kelly is one of my best friends. We roast one another constantly, just as we did when we played, but it's all in good fun. I know he always has my back and would be there at the drop of a hat if I—or any of our Flyers Alumni—needed someone there for them. He has a heart of gold. As much as I tease him (and vice versa), I consider him like I had another brother on the team in addition to the one I'm related to by blood.

There's a lot of down time and travel in hockey, and you need things to pass the time. Nowadays, players stick their faces in their electronic devices. We didn't have those things back then. In fact, I still don't. I don't use a cell phone. I barely use email. I have a computer at home and had one at my desk when I worked for the Flyers, but I did the bare minimum.

Back when I was playing, we spent most of our time away from the rink with our teammates: at the bar, in the airport terminal, aboard the plane, riding on the bus, or bullshitting in the locker room. To make the time pass, we tried to one-up each other with putdowns or pulling practical jokes. It broke up the boredom.

The best verbal battles were between Hound and Gene Hart. The broadcasters traveled with the team. To us, Gene in particular, was one of the boys.

For years, Kelly endlessly teased the rotund Hart about his weight, and Hart countered by ragging on Kelly's receding hairline and (greatly exaggerated, but I'll deny it if you ask me in front of Bob) lack of hockey talent and intelligence.

Kelly's trump card was inventing nicknames for Hart, including "Gene the Dancing Machine," (a nod to *The Gong Show*), "The Round Mound of Sound," and "the Great Pumpkin" (for the orange blazer Hart wore on the air).

Jack Chevalier, in *Broad Street Bullies*, recorded the following debate on a Saturday bus trip in October 1973. Dornhoefer and MacLeish served as the "official judges," awarding points as Hart and Kelly traded barbs.

Kelly fired the first salvo. "No airplane today, Gene. You don't need an extension for your seat belt."

"Kelly, are you still with the club?" fired back Hart.

Hound went right back on the offensive. "So will they have a TV lens wide enough for you this time, fat boy?"

"I've got a better chance of getting on camera than you," replied Hart.

Dornhoefer interceded. "That's 2–2. Your turn, Mutt!"

"Hey, Gene, what's wrong with your slacks? It looks like they're flared at the wrong end!"

Hart didn't miss a beat. "I'd rather be fat than ugly like you. I can always lose weight."

Kelly then scored what MacLeish deemed a two-pointer. "Gene, you're nothing but an educated derelict."

Hart fired back, "Those are big words, Kelly, for a guy whose IQ matches his uniform number [9]!"

Kelly paused. Then he broke up everyone and won the contest.

"What's an IQ?" he asked in feigned confusion.

Dornhoefer—who loved to pose the riddle, "What do Harvard and the Hockey Hall of Fame have in common?" (Answer: "Bob Kelly can't get into either one")—promptly declared Hound the winner because he came up with a better Bob Kelly putdown than any of Hart's.

Some of the guys liked wagering, whether it was card games, the horse races, or sports events. That has never been my thing. I don't gamble because, as someone who grew up without a lot of money, where everyone I knew had to work hard for every dollar, the idea of casually throwing money away on bets never appealed to me. To this day, I'm not a casino-goer. While I'm definitely a sports junkie and will watch and admire just about any major sport on TV, I couldn't care less about betting on the games.

What was a typical day like for me when I played? Let's say the Flyers were at home. I'd go to our training rink at the Class of 1923 Arena on the University of Pennsylvania campus. I'd get there early. After practice, although I lived in Delaware County, I'd drive over the bridge and go to Rexy's for lunch and a babalooey or two.

I was a big fan of naps. I still am. On game day, I'd try to get in some shuteye before heading to the Spectrum. After the game, we usually went back to Rexy's.

Many Flyers fans have asked me over the years, "What was it really like at Rexy's? Was it as wild and crazy as the stories?" Honestly, it depended on the night.

In general, it got loud and boisterous at Rexy's. We did a lot of laughing. The food was good. We made friends with the people who worked there and with other regular customers, and some of these folks remained friends for years. We were just regular people ourselves, so it was hardly out of the ordinary for us to mix and mingle with as many nonhockey people as we did with teammates. Friends are friends, regardless of their walk of life.

It wasn't all that different when we were on the road. We had a couple regular places that we went to in various cities, certain people we'd meet up with to hang out. Here's one story I remember.

During a road trip in Vancouver, Flyers team attorney Gil Stein joined us at our favorite bar. We ordered a round of beers. One round became two as we shot the breeze. The guys who were smokers—much of the team in those days—dragged on a couple of cigarettes or had a cigar.

Two rounds became three. Barry Ashbee lit a match. He then reached across the table and casually put it to "Cowboy" Bill Flett's bushy beard, which caught fire.

Flett didn't skip a beat. He dunked his beard in his beer mug, withdrew it to check that the flame was out, and then took a long swig of beer from the glass. It was so ridiculous that all the boys laughed.

Gil, however, was horrified. "You guys are crazy!" he shouted.

We laughed harder. Stein wasn't wrong.

I don't want to glorify drinking or smoking, but I want to be honest about what hockey culture was like back then.

The Flyers drank like typical 1970s hockey players: in other words, it would be considered excessive by today's standards, but it didn't feel outrageous to us back then on an average night (the Stanley Cup victory celebrations were a different story).

We differentiated between beer consumption and hard alcohol. The basic attitude was this: drink all the beer you want, but go easy on the heavy stuff.

It was the guys who guzzled whiskey or gin who we worried about whether they could get home safely or get to the rink in time for the morning skate. Beer was nearly "free rein."

I'm not saying these attitudes were right. We know a lot more nowadays. So many of our hockey brethren battled alcoholism in the late stages of—and especially after—their playing days. So it's not all just happy memories of good times with no consequences.

Flett was one of the first casualties. Even by mid-'70s standards, it became clear that he had a drinking problem while still in his athletic prime. He was gone after our first Cup-winning season and never again had a season like he did for us in 1972–73.

Bill was a good man at heart. He'd give you the shirt off his back. He really would. As a means of trying to prevent others from his fate, he publicly admitted to his struggles both before and after his playing days.

Flett was sober the last four years of his life before his death due to liver failure. His wife, Doreen, and sons, Cody, Dean, and Shane, are good people, too. That's how I choose to remember Bill: an honest, kind, generous man who struggled with a fight that took a fatal toll on him.

I didn't mean for this chapter to take a dark turn. My point is that I know quite well that the hockey lifestyle of that era wasn't a never-ending party. The party eventually ends, and you must deal with real life. A lot of the guys ultimately suffered in their personal lives or paid the price in terms of their long-term health.

I consider myself blessed to have been able to play hockey for a living. The game has given me much more than I could ever pay back or even pay forward. For every negative, even the bigger ones, there are five positives. Besides, we're all responsible for our own actions. To blame hockey or blame hockey culture for personal issues or postcareer physical impairments has always felt like excuse-making to me. The game owes us nothing.

Let's move this discussion back to a happier train of thought: *What was the best part of winning the Stanley Cup?*

Part of it was internal: accomplishing the biggest dream that any of us had as hockey players. We won our sport's ultimate prize, twice. When Freddy talked about "walking together forever" when you win the Stanley

Cup, he was exactly right. The bond with your teammates is permanent and unshakeable no matter where your lives take you thereafter.

I had so many great teammates in Philly, Boston, and even Colorado, but the closest and most special relationships with the group came with the Stanley Cup teams. Hell, even winning the Adams Cup winner in Oklahoma City was like nothing else I experienced in the minor leagues. Championships have that bonding effect.

Winning the Stanley Cup changed all our lives permanently. For a few years, every time we went out in public, people recognized us. You somehow become a local celebrity. In fact, even many years later, it's not unusual to still be recognized. People tell you where they were when you won and how much your team's success meant to them.

It's very gratifying and humbling. Fans still thank me for being part of two Stanley Cup teams that brought joy to their lives. My attitude is this: we should be thanking the fans instead.

Winning the Stanley Cup opened so many off-ice friendship doors me. I've gotten to meet famous athletes from many sports, even playing golf with the likes of Tom Watson and Gary Player.

I met Muhammad Ali twice. Actually, there's a funny story around the first chance meeting, which was in St. Louis. Bernie Parent and I introduced ourselves to the legendary boxer, who was with promoter Don King.

"You're with the Broad Street Bullies?" he asked.

"Yup," I said.

"Well, Broad Street Bullies, this is for you [he held up his right fist toward Bernie], and this is for you [left fist held up toward me]," he said.

Ali then smiled warmly, and we chatted for a while. He was a nice man. He was living in Cherry Hill, New Jersey, at the time. We'd meet again years later.

I was a Detroit Tigers fan growing up, and I also liked the Big Red Machine-era Cincinnati Reds. But living and playing in Philly made me a Phillies fan, too. I've made friends with members of the Phillies' glory-year teams of the late 1970s to early 1980. I counted Larry Bowa, Tug McGraw, Mike Schmidt, and broadcaster Harry Kalas among my friends.

One time, I was cutting the grass outside my house. Tug pulled up to the house and called over to me. He had an open beer on his lap while he drove to Veterans Stadium.

"It's fine. I'll have one more, get a massage and a nap at the park, and be ready for the game," McGraw said.

Elsewhere in the local sports world, I made friends with longtime Philadelphia 76ers basketball player, NBA coach, and broadcaster Doug Collins. We were both in the hospital recuperating from surgeries. From the world of football, I became good friends with legendary Philadelphia Eagles linebacker Bill Bergey. Years later, I brought Bergey to visit Smithers. I was also friends with Eagles broadcaster Charlie Swift. Tragically, Swift suffered from depression and took his own life at age 43 on December 8, 1977.

Through our Cup-era fame, I made friends in the world of entertainment. Philadelphia native Bobby Rydell is one that immediately comes to mind because he was a diehard Flyers fan and used to come around the Spectrum to say hi.

My association with the Flyers opened many doors in my life and sparked countless wonderful friendships with people I'd never have otherwise met. Here, during a postgame visit to the Flyers locker room, Bobby Rydell introduces me to his son. The late singer and actor—a Philadelphia native—became a fan of our team and a frequent attendee at the Spectrum.

My Stanley Cup experience was the ice breaker for many business relationships while I did advertising sales for the Flyers. To this day, I still get together with some of my old clients as well as friends who worked for the Flyers.

I can't even count how many friends from all corners of the earth and all stations in life I've met. People whose faces light up when they try on my Stanley Cup ring and take a photo. It's not about me. It's all about the allure of the Stanley Cup and the enduring Flyers crest, whether you're in Philly, Canada, Italy, or even Moscow.

Some of my happiest and most enduring memories of my family members, especially my now-deceased parents, center around our Stanley Cup years.

My dad didn't own a suitcase, nor would he accept luggage as a gift. He traveled with a cardboard box with a rope tied around it, like a vagabond. During the 1974 playoffs, he traveled all the way—by train and by bus—from Smithers to Philadelphia to surprise Jimmy and me.

We were at the practice rink, and I was told there was a phone call. My father was on the other end of the line. I assumed at first that it was a long-distance call to wish Jimmy and me luck in the postseason.

"Dad!" I said. "That's really nice of you to call."

"Joey, I'm here!" Dad said.

"Where's *here*?" I asked.

"Philadelphia. At the airport. Can you come get me?"

"For Chrissakes, Dad, Jimmy and I can't leave here yet," I said. "Can you take a taxi to the rink?"

"I don't have any money on me," my father replied.

"See if you can get a ride here," I said. "I'll pay the driver."

Instead, my father charmed a cabby into giving him a ride for free by telling him that he was here to surprise his sons who played for the Flyers.

The first time my father met most of my Flyers teammates was quite an experience for everyone. Throughout the trip, Dad wore the same overalls and makinow (even with summertime fast approaching). His boots were caked with dried manure. He reeked.

"Dad, you need a shower!" I said for his own good.

My father nodded. Then he proceeded to get undressed and walk into the shower room with my teammates, most of whom had no idea who this burly naked man was and why he was allowed in the team shower room.

At a more opportune moment, I went to introduce my teammates to my dad. But he'd already made the rounds.

"Pleasure to meet ya! Joe Watson Sr. here. Joe and Jimmy Watson are my boys," he said.

During our 1974 Stanley Cup Semifinal series, we won all four games in Philadelphia but lost all three games in New York. I'll discuss the games themselves in the next chapter. For now, I'll share this memory. The Rangers tied up the series at two games apiece by beating us in overtime, 2–1, in Game 4.

Our postgame locker room was quiet. We still believed we had what it took to win the series, but there's a big difference mentally between going up, three games to one, versus being deadlocked at 2–2.

Suddenly, my father walked in the room. He surveyed the group and then exclaimed, "Who's down?! We're not down!"

Jimmy and I exchanged horrified looks.

"Dad!" I hollered. "Get the hell out of here!"

Clarkie took our dad's side.

"You don't speak that way to your father," he scolded.

During my dad's stay—and then every Philadelphia visit to come—he became something of a local celebrity. Gene Hart interviewed him on the radio. My dad being the beauty he was, loved every minute of it. At the games, he'd stand up and holler to anyone in hearing distance, "Those are my boys! Joe and Jimmy Watson!"

When we won the 1974 Stanley Cup against the Bruins in Game 6 at the Spectrum, my dad was there. He didn't have tickets, and there were none available, but Mr. Snider invited him to sit in the owner's box, next to Kate Smith and Mayor Frank Rizzo.

During the postgame celebration, Jimmy and I posed for pictures with Dad in the locker room. He also drank champagne from the Stanley Cup. Jimmy and I had him do so before we did, and it was one of the best moments of his entire life (ours, too).

Dad came back for the 1975 Cup Final against Buffalo and was part of that locker room celebration and trip back to Philly, too. But the two funniest memories from that visit were away from the rink when my father was staying at the house with me and my first wife.

Late one night, there was a big commotion. Our neighbor's outside lights were on, and their dogs were barking their heads off. Now everyone was wide awake. The police were called. Fortunately, neighbor Frank Pelico recognized my dad and sorted out the mess.

What happened? Well, Joe Watson Sr. saw the neighbors' pool, figured no one was using it and the owners wouldn't mind if he took a dip in it.

My dad was an early bird by nature. He liked to wake up early in the morning and take a long walk. One morning, I got a phone call from someone who lived a couple miles away.

To make a long story short, while my dad was walking, he saw that the resident had a bench on his lawn. He took a seat to rest.

"Can I help you with something?" the gentleman asked, a little uneasy about the random stranger who was casually sitting on the property.

To my dad, though, there was no such thing as a stranger. This was the same guy who once took out a harmonica at the train station and entertained commuters. An audience formed around him.

"That would be great!" my father said. "I'm Joe Watson Sr. My two sons play for the Flyers. I'm staying with my son, Joe."

"Oh, OK," the man said. "He lives not too far from here."

"Yeah, but they didn't fix me any breakfast today," he said.

Taking pity on my dad, the homeowner's wife made him breakfast.

They must have thought I was a horrible son, refusing to feed my father after he traveled across North America!

Another time, one of the local television stations scheduled an interview with my dad at the Spectrum. However, at the last moment, my father decided to go across the street to Veterans Stadium instead. The Phillies were playing a doubleheader, and the idea of seeing two baseball games for the price of one was irresistible.

My parents were long since permanently separated by that point. But my mom also made several trips to Philadelphia while Jimmy and I played for the Flyers—actually, the whole family came along at one point. She was at the second Stanley Cup parade.

This was when streaking was in vogue. There were numerous streakers along the parade route and especially at JFK Stadium. When one ran past, Jimmy said, "Mom! Don't look! Cover your eyes!"

Even all these years later, these are stories that still make me grin and chuckle to recall. Those two Cup celebrations, the parades, and the team parties hosted by Ed Snider were wild beyond belief. In our first parade, we rode on the backs of convertibles. The police hadn't anticipated such large crowds—an estimated two million people came out both years. The first parade was a little scary because the crowds could literally come right up to you. Most folks just wanted a handshake or to snap a photo, but some people got overexuberant, like a guy who tugged at Don Saleski's shirt and tore the sleeve clean off.

In the second parade, we rode on flatbed trucks, and there were secure barriers with ample security. The funniest memory from this one was Bernie Parent and Reggie Leach stopping the procession to go take a leak.

Ed Snider's first Cup party for the team was held on the waterfront with a big boat. Guys were jumping into the water or pushing in fellow partygoers. As someone who can't swim and once nearly drowned during an offseason, I avoided putting myself into that situation.

The second year's celebration was a pool party and outdoor celebration. We all wore T-shirts that said, "Do it again...and again...and again...and again." That second year, even Fred Shero was smiling and laughing.

Ever since then, both for the duration of my playing days and every year since, it's been one of my fondest wishes for the Flyers—the players, their families, the coaches, management, and especially the fans—to experience everything that goes along with a Stanley Cup championship.

One of these years, it will happen again. When, I don't know. What does winning a Stanley Cup mean? It means everything, and it changes your life on and off the ice.

Remember the story of the so-called Welcome the Flyers Parade on Broad Street back in 1967? The one where the mayor no-showed the city hall ceremony, where there were more players than fans in the parade, where we got heckled and some guy and his kid even flipped us off before we'd ever played a home game that would raise their ire? The exact opposite of that experience were the two Cup parades, with all the outpouring of love and jubilation.

Among my Cup-era teammates, only Bernie Parent, Ed Van Impe, Gary Dornhoefer, and I had previously been part of that 1967 embarrassment. But it made each one of us truly realize and appreciate how far our hockey organization had come in seven short years.

This photo from the Flyers Archives collection was taken on the plane ride back from Buffalo to Philadelphia after we won our second Stanley Cup championship.

CHAPTER 11

The Magic Years

In 1973, the Flyers relocated training camp—for the first time in our history—from Canada to the Philadelphia area. We'd been in Ottawa previously and, before that, in Quebec City. Freddy sent an offseason letter to each of the players, informing us of the change of camp venue and urging everyone to report as close to our playing weights as possible. He wrote the following:

> *We made good strides as a team last season, but we did not attain our ultimate goal of defeating Montreal to play for the Stanley Cup. The objective is within our reach, I believe.*
>
> *The first order of business is to make the most productive use of training camp that we can. The better the physical condition that everyone reports, the more time we can devote to our preparations on the ice. Plan accordingly.*
>
> *Success is 10 percent inspiration and 90 percent perspiration. To be ahead of the competition, we much outwork our competitors.*

Apart from changing training camp venues—and adding Apollo isometric exercise equipment to our training routines—we had a couple additions to the roster. The most famous one was the reacquisition of Bernie Parent.

Bernie had a contract dispute with the Maple Leafs and spent the 1972–73 season in the WHA with the Philadelphia Blazers. Still at odds with Toronto's crusty and penny-pinching owner, Harold Ballard, Parent asked for a trade. Keith Allen pounced, bringing Bernie back to the Flyers in a deal that sent old pal Doug Favell to the Maple Leafs.

With Wayne Hillman leaving the Flyers to sign a WHA contract with the Cleveland Crusaders, there was an NHL roster spot available for a defenseman to win out of training camp. My brother ran away with the competition, beating out George Pesut and Serge Lajeunesse (whom the Flyers acquired in a trade with Detroit for the underachieving Rick Foley). I was very happy for Jimmy but not surprised. He earned his spot.

Shero's practices took some getting used to. Most of the session was 30 minutes of highly structured drills done daily. Everyone learned these drills by heart.

However, there were also the occasional offbeat one-off drills I mentioned earlier that existed mostly to keep the boys alert. To this day, I chuckle at the memory of Freddy introducing the upside stick in the passing lane drill until Crispy and Clarkie asked why the hell we were doing this since no one would ever do that in a game. At the end of practice, we routinely did a drill that started from behind the net, with players competing to be the first to step out in front and score. A small cash prize rode on the outcome.

Actually, when Hound scored what proved to be the Stanley Cup–winning goal in the opening seconds of Game 6 of the 1975 final in Buffalo, it was on a play very much like the one Shero had us practice. He got the puck behind the net, came out in front, and scored. Skating by the bench, Bob announced. "Freddy! You owe me five bucks!"

During our two Cup-winning seasons plus the 1975–76 campaign, winning home games became virtually automatic. The so-called "Philly flu" was absolutely a real thing. We took huge pride in making the Spectrum a place even the top opponents in the NHL dreaded to set foot in. So did our rabid fans.

In 1973–74, we were 28-6-5 on home ice during the regular season. In 1974–75, we went 32-6-2. Then, in 1975–76, we were 36-2-2. That's a combined 96-14-9! In the Stanley Cup playoffs, we were undefeated on home ice in 1974: 10–0. During our second championship season, we were 8–1. In 1976, before Montreal won two in our building in the Cup Final to dethrone us as champions, we were 6–1 at the Spectrum over the quarterfinals and semifinals.

I've always associated good times with winning. These were the best times of my playing career. It's not even close. Every day, every game, all of us Flyers drove to the Spectrum not just hoping to win but fully expecting to win. As hard as we played on (and off) the ice and as much as we hated losing, we were simply having a blast. We were a decent road team, too, but we were on a whole other level when we played at home.

The destination—the two Stanley Cup parades—is what everyone remembers. But the journey to get there was what makes the memories so special to me from a hockey standpoint. I never before—and never again—got to be part of such a team. It all came together perfectly for a few years.

This is strange to recall in hindsight, but Bernie's first preseason home game of his second stint with the Flyers could hardly have gone worse. The visiting Rangers lit him up for seven goals in just 22 minutes before Michel Belhumeur or Bobby Taylor (I don't recall which one) came in. The Spectrum crowd booed the hell out of Bernie. That was the last time Bernie got booed at home, though!

Shortly before opening night, Ed Snider hosted a formal team dinner where the players all came dressed in tuxedos and the wives in evening gowns. That became an annual team event, along with the family Christmas party. Other teams had similar get-togethers, but Ed Snider always went all out to have ours be first-class, and his first wife, Myrna, made sure the wives and kids were included.

At any rate, as I write this, I am looking at the group photo we took at our 1973 preseason dinner. I'm chuckling because, for some reason, Hound, Schultzy, and I are wearing the exact same powder-blue tux with velvet lapels and dark-blue bow ties. I guess we went together to purchase them and decided to get the same ones. Jimmy and many others sported classic black tuxes. Since goalies are wired to be different, Bernie had a blue-gray tux, and Belhumeur had a golden one. Side note: Taylor ultimately beat out Belhumeur for the backup job to Bernie.

We opened our 1973–74 season at home against the Toronto Maple Leafs. Dougie was in net for Toronto. Kate Smith sang "God Bless America" in person before the opening faceoff (by the way, the decision many years later by Comcast to basically erase her from team history was wrong).

Favell and Crisp, both products of the Niagara Falls Flyers, Oklahoma City, and Boston, were old friends. While they were together in Philly, Dougie used to take off his glove at practice and dared Crispy to shoot the puck at his bare hand. Terry's shots were "muffins" without much velocity to them. On opening night, though, Crispy had the last laugh as he scored the season's first goal. Barber added a third-period power-play goal. Parent stopped all 28 shots he faced, and we won, 2–0.

Two nights later, we had our road opener against the Islanders: another shutout for Benie as we won, 6–0. We scored two shorthanded goals (Flett, Clarke), two power-play goals (MacLeish and Saleski), and two even-strength goals (Saleski and Kindrachuk).

After that, we scored a combined 10 goals over the next two games as we cruised past Detroit, 5–2, and the Seals, 5–1. Even in magical seasons, though, there are ups and downs. We lost three in a row after starting out 4-0-0. Clarke was like a man possessed as we ended our minislump with a 6–0 blowout win over the Penguins at the Igloo: two goals, an assist, and a nasty cross-check to Bob McNamara.

I got my foot bruised pretty bad from the puck in the next game, a 2–1 win over the Seals in which a Kindrachuk shorthanded goal and a Bill Clement breakaway made the difference. The *Philadelphia Daily News* reported that I might have to miss our next game, which was at home against Chicago, our biggest challenger in the Western Division.

"Like hell I'll miss it," I said to *Daily News* beat writer Bill Fleischman. "I'll play if I possibly can."

We were already hurting on the blueline. Barry Ashbee was dealing with nerve damage in his neck, although he was playing through the pain. Dupont had been left woozy from an elbow by Montreal's Peter Mahovlich in a recent game, but Moose kept on playing. I could hardly put a skate on my right foot—I never took it off in the Seals game because our assistant trainer, Jimmy McKenzie, advised me not to until after the game—but if Ashcan and Moose could keep going, I sure wasn't going to sit with a bone bruise.

Our November 1, 1973, game at the Spectrum was a classic: a goaltending duel between Parent and Tony Esposito and a grind-it-out physical game. There were no fights in this one, by the way, just hard-nosed hockey. Again, with all due respect to Favell, this was a game we'd probably have lost during the 1972–73 season. On this night, Bernie outdueled Esposito. We made a late first-period Barber power-play goal stand up the rest of the way in a 1–0 win. In the second period, we got the Black Hawks back on their heels, but Esposito turned back 13 shots, while we held Chicago to seven. In the third period, Bernie stepped up with 11 saves as we closed out the win.

A group of Flyers players, me included, went to a Saturday night Sammy Davis Jr. show at the Latin Casino in Cherry Hill, New Jersey, on November 4, after we beat the Penguins, 7–0. Hell of a fun time. I was just glad the show hadn't been one night earlier, when we lost a 2–1 game to Atlanta. I probably just would have gone home.

I will be the first to admit it: I wasn't all that fun to be around after a loss. Losses ate me up inside, and I could get grouchy when we had a bad night at the rink. "Taking the game home with you" isn't healthy. I made New Year's resolutions and offseason promises to myself that I'd work on leaving the disappointment of a loss at the rink.

It didn't work too well, though. In 1976, I had an offseason vacation planned. After we lost to Montreal in the finals and were no longer the champions, I was in no frame of mind to enjoy a vacation. I canceled the trip.

Thankfully, though, the losses were few and far between in this time frame. We went off on another run of wins, blemished only by a 4–2 loss in Boston with Taylor in net. On November 29, we rallied for a 2–2 home tie against a very talented Rangers team. A late goal by Barber against Eddie Giacomin pulled us even.

I left the game against the Rangers in the third period with an injury that forced me to subsequently miss our road win over the Islanders (2–1) on December 1 and a 5–1 home win against the Seals the next night.

The latter game was one of the most notorious from the "Bullies" era. In the second period, Clarke clipped Seals rookie Barry Cummins with a high stick. Cummins snapped.

He took a two-handed stick swing at Clarkie's head. Our players reacted immediately, emptying the bench. Flett got there first, flinging a glove at Cummins's face and then raining down punches as other Flyers arrived to join in the battle.

Before Cummins's teammates could rescue him, our players formed a human wall. Cummins was beaten to a pulp.

Things went too far on both sides. Only one team—the Flyers—took the blame. The New York and Toronto media had a field day calling the Flyers "animals" and "barbarians."

Guess what? It wasn't the first time and wouldn't be the last. I can honestly say we didn't care what outsiders thought of it. By the way, after the game, Cummins called Clarke (who needed 20 stitches to close the wound from Cummins' baseball bat–like swing) to apologize.

As Bill Clement has said over the years, and he's right, our Flyers teams could win a penalty-free 2–0 game, possibly even with Schultz and Saleski as the goal scorers that night, just as readily as ones with a half dozen fights. When we went on the road, we felt like we had our backs to the wall. That kept us united.

We had a game in Vancouver shortly before Christmas in '73, where fans showered us with beer and rubbish at the end of the second period (again, not the first time or the last). We crushed the Canucks, 9–2, in a game where a bench-clearing brawl erupted at 13:01 of the second period when we were leading by a 5–2 score. Even backup goalies Taylor and Gary Smith squared off with one another.

Schultz became Public Enemy No. 1 in every road building in the league. Something his critics either didn't realize or refused to acknowledge was this: He could do more than just fight. He could also play hockey. On January 3, in a 4–2 win over the Rangers at the Spectrum, Schultz compiled a hat trick. On January 10, he did it again in a 7–4 road win in Minnesota.

I understand why people, to this day, think first about Dave's 348 penalty minutes in 1973–74 and 472 PIM in our second Cup year. Just realize he was also a 20-goal scorer in our first Cup season, and he went on to score a couple of huge playoff goals for us, too, in both 1974 and 1975.

The night after Schultz's second hat trick, we had a January 11 road game in Atlanta. Parent got the night off, and we started Taylor against the Flames' Phil Myre. I felt bad for the goalies that evening. A combined 13 goals were scored. Fortunately, we had seven to their six. The goals were so plentiful that I even scored one: my lone tally of the 1973–74 season.

The 1974 NHL All-Star Game was held on January 27 at Chicago Stadium. I was one of four Flyers players chosen to play for the Western Conference All-Stars, along with Clarke, Parent, and Van Impe. The West won the game, 6–5.

After the All-Star game, we came home to play Buffalo and Detroit. Both games were memorable, for different reasons. In the Buffalo game, referee Bryan Lewis called one of the worst-officiated games that I had ever seen. He missed blatant infractions and then issued makeup calls seemingly out of thin air a few minutes later. The game ended up getting out of hand with stickwork and fights because there was a lot of frustration on both sides.

During a stoppage of play in the second period, Gerry Meehan (my former Flyers teammate during the 1968–69 season) said to me, "Someone's going to get hurt out there, Joe." He was right, too.

We beat the Sabres, 4–3. Our second (Lonsberry-MacLeish-Dornhoefer) and third (Schultz-Kindrachuk-Saleski) lines led the way, including two goals by Schultzy on top of Dave getting fighting, charging, and roughing penalties at different junctures of the game.

In the same game, we got a preview of what Buffalo's fast-rising "French Connection line" (Richard Martin, Gilbert Perrault, and Rene Robert) was all about. Martin scored twice, including on a penalty shot goal against Parent after Dupont hooked Martin to impede a breakaway. The Sabres piled up 40 shots in the game—much more than we typically gave up—and a combined 15 of them were from their French Connection line.

One more note from this game: Lonsberry played one hell of a game on both sides of the puck, including scoring the game's first goal. That didn't surprise me, and I told Chevalier that after the game. Lonsberry was four years younger than me, but we'd been teammates in the Bruins' system, and I'd later played against him. I knew we'd gotten a nice addition when he came over from LA.

"Roscoe doesn't get nearly enough credit for what he brings our club," I said. "He's a good player up and down the ice for us. He saved us a goal tonight [in a scramble where I was down on the ice with a Buffalo player on top of me]."

Lonsberry was a great example of why I said that our Flyers teams had more good players throughout the lineup than supposedly more talented teams had great ones. MacLeish was the big scorer on that line with his speed and wrist shot. With all due respect to Ricky, though, the heart and soul of that line was Lonsberry and Dornhoefer. Ross was a two-way forward who scored 32 goals that season and had 13 points in 17 playoff games. Any championship team needs a couple players like that.

To this day, I don't know if even older diehard Flyers fans realize what we had for a few years in Lonsberry. He just went about his business quietly and played the same steady game night after night. Ross passed away in 2014 at age 67 after a very long battle with cancer. He was a good man as well as a good hockey player, and he's missed by the Flyers Alumni who knew him and got to play with him.

Ross got plenty of attention, for once, in our next game. That's because he scored a hat trick (hitting the 20-goal mark on the season) in our 12–2 blowout of Detroit. Simon Nolet, playing right wing with Clarke and Barber, had a three-point game (in his own right). This was a night where everyone joined in the fun offensively. I even had two points (both via assists) in the game.

I'd be remiss here if I didn't say a few words about Simon. He wasn't an NHL star but was yet another good example of the type of high-quality depth we had on the Flyers. He made a lot of important contributions to the organization first as a player and, years later, as a scout for 30-plus years.

Nolet came up to the Flyers from the Quebec Aces during our inaugural season, and we were teammates through the first Cup year. He played in an NHL All-Star Game in 1971–72 and had several hat tricks in his Flyers career and a couple 20-plus goal seasons. His role was reduced as we started to add younger talent to the roster, but he still managed 19 goals and 36 points in 56 games for our 1973–74 Cup winning team.

Nolet was always a team-first type of player. It didn't surprise me that he later served as the captain for the short-lived Kansas City scouts. That KC team was horrible, but Nolet was one player who competed no matter what. He wasn't one of our best defensive players, but he found key spots to contribute.

Simon was also surprisingly tough for a guy who rarely fought. We had a game (January 10, 1971) where he dropped the gloves with John Ferguson, for Pete's sake, and more than held his own. He also got the better of Skip Krake, Al Karlander, and, during the 1973–74 season, Hilliard Graves directly after a kneeing incident.

Many years after his retirement as a player, Nolet became a Flyers scout based in Quebec. It was Simon who recommended the team draft Simon Gagne in 1988, Patrick Sharp in 2001, and Claude Giroux in 2006. Between his playing and scouting days, I'd say Simon had two pretty damn good shifts in the organization!

As a team, we never let ourselves get too satisfied or complacent. In late February '74, we lost back-to-back road games to Chicago (3–1 after the game entered the third period in a scoreless deadlock) and the Rangers (3–2 after we led, 2–0, at the end of the first period). We didn't need Shero or Nykoluk to tell us we'd let two winnable games against top rivals slip away.

We took care of the discussion ourselves, first in the dressing room, then over postgame beers. This sounds like a myth, but it's true: Clarke and Van Impe challenged us to do whatever it'd take not to lose back-to-back games again the rest of the year. Mind you, at the time, we had 20 regular-season games remaining.

We posted a 15-2-3 record over those 20 games, including a 9-1-1 mark at the Spectrum. A run like that isn't about one player or one line shining: it takes an entire team.

"When we play this way, we can beat anybody," Shero said after we humiliated the Canadiens, 6–0, at the Spectrum on March 3.

As I've noted, Shero preached the vital importance of controlling six areas of the ice: the four corners and the two net-front areas. This was the real estate worth fighting for, and we did just that. Defensively, we took away the middle of the ice consistently and forced the other team to take shots from above and/or outside the dots. That played right into Parent's strengths because he was an excellent goalie in playing the angles.

On March 30, we had a home game against the Bruins. If we won, we'd wrap up the regular-season championship in the West. Only thing was this: we were winless against the Bruins in our last 27 head-to-head meetings (23 losses and four ties). To a man, our club was determined to put an end to that streak.

It was one hell of a hockey game. The game was tied, 2–2, after the first period as MacLeish and Lonsberry scored, only for Andre Savard and Wayne Cashman to answer. However, on the first shift of the second period, Flett stole the puck from Orr, moved in, and beat Gilles Gilbert to put us ahead, 3–2.

The Spectrum crowd went bonkers. The atmosphere was even crazier 50 seconds later when Schultz won a puck battle, and Flett powered his way around the net and fed Clarke for a goal that made it a 4–2 game. The rest of the period was evenly played, highlighted by a toe-to-toe fight between Schultz and Terry O'Reilly.

In the third period, we outworked the Bruins and established an 11–5 shot advantage. Lonsberry scored again midway through the period to open a 5–2 lead. Apart from John Buycyk scoring a late goal that only served to reduce our final margin of victory to 5–3, we staged one of our best closeouts of the entire season. The Bruins hardly had the puck.

We still had the playoffs ahead of us, but Shero allowed himself after the game to reflect on how cohesive we'd become as a team.

"This is the best team I've ever seen for discipline and desire," Shero said. "I don't think I'll ever see one better."

Freddy's quote was a big inspiration to me. To this very day, when I do public speaking engagements, I discuss the 3Ds that are my guiding principles for success in life, business, or sports: desire, discipline, and dedication.

We drew the Atlanta Flames in the Stanley Cup quarterfinals. They'd played us tough during the regular season (two wins, two losses, two ties), but the two losses came before we really started to hit our stride.

The Flames had two good goalies in Dan Bouchard and Phil Myre. They had some toughness and some skill. Even so, we felt confident of winning the series.

We won Games 1 and 2 handily at the Spectrum: 4–1 and 5–1. Kindrachuk scored twice, and Dornhoefer and Bladon (power play) tallied one apiece in the first game. In Game 2, MacLeish had a natural hat trick in the second period to turn a 1–0 lead to a 4–0 advantage. I had an assist on the first of Ricky's goals.

The scene shifted to Atlanta for Games 3 and 4. We won a fight-filled Game 3 by a 4–1 count. The game had a bench-clearing brawl in the second period. This was also the night when, long after the game, Shero got mugged in the wee hours.

Freddy had a way of getting himself into strange predicaments. He'd get lost in thought—so much that he could walk right past you without noticing you were there—and take long walks at odd hours. He tended to be a loner, so he'd go alone and eventually realize he had no idea where he'd been going or how to get back.

As I have said, it was hardly unusual for hockey people—players, coaches, scouts, etc.—to spend long nights at the bar after a game. Players hung out at one bar, coaches at another. Freddy was that way, too, but he only sporadically had company with him. Typically, he much preferred going out alone.

On this night, at some point, Freddy left the bar at our hotel and wandered out into the Atlanta streets. Around 2:00 a.m., police were called about a disturbance outside the hotel. He'd been roughed up pretty bad: his glasses had been broken, his thumb was fractured, and he had cuts and bruises on his face. He said he had no recollection of anything that had happened, apart from vaguely remembering a verbal disagreement. Shero did not know where he'd gone beforehand, who had attacked him, or any of the details of the physical altercation.

The other Flyers players and I didn't find out until the next morning what happened to Shero. We were just happy to hear that he'd be OK, but otherwise, to us, it was just Freddy being Freddy.

Nykoluk was behind the bench for us in Game 4. We trailed, 3–0, in the latter stages of the second period. At 16:35, Schultz dropped the gloves with Bryan Hextall (son of Hockey Hall of Famer Bryan Hextall Sr., brother of longtime NHLer Dennis Hextall, and father of future NHL goalie and general manager Ron Hextall). Schultz beat Hextall to a bloody pulp.

Just 13 seconds after play resumed following the Schultz vs. Hextall fight, Dupont scored to get us on the board. In the third period, power-play goals by Dornhoefer and Bladon tied the game at 3–3. The game went to overtime. At the 5:40 mark, after receiving a pass from Clarke, Schultz fired a low shot past Myre to end the game and the series with a 4–3 win.

Heading into the Cup semis against the Rangers, I knew we'd be in for a grueling series. The Rangers were filled with star power, although many of their top players were aging (Giacomin, Rod Gilbert, Jean Ratelle, Pete Stemkowski). Offensive defenseman Brad Park was still in his prime, along with Walt Tkaczuk. The guy who'd beaten out Billy Barber for the Calder Trophy the previous year, Steve Vickers, was coming off a 34-goal regular season. The Rangers also had my old buddy and roommate, Teddy Irvine.

Thank goodness for home ice advantage! We won Game 1 at the Spectrum, 4–0, and limited them to 19 shots as Parent recorded a shutout. MacLeish led us offensively with two goals and an assist. In Game 2, Parent made 28 saves, and we had five different players score a goal as we earned a 5–2 win.

So far so good. However, the series turned into a war when the scene shifted to Madison Square Garden for Games 3 and 4. The Rangers, frankly, had been meek in the Spectrum. They found their moxie when they went home to Manhattan.

We led Game 3 by scores of 2–0 (first period) and 3–1 (2nd period) but went on to lose, 5–3. There were numerous fights in the third period. We lost Hound in this game. He suffered torn knee ligaments and was out for the rest of the playoffs.

In Game 4, I scored a late first-period goal, but we were unable to add to it. A power-play goal by Bobby Rousseau tied the game in the second period. After a scoreless third, Gilbert won the game at 4:20 of sudden-death overtime.

This was the game where my dad mortified Jimmy and me by walking into the nearly silent postgame locker room and shouting, "Who's down? We're not down!"

On a much more somber note, this game also turned out to be the final one of Barry Ashbee's career. In overtime, a rising shot by New York's Dale Rolfe struck Barry in the right eye. Over time, he'd only regain about 15 percent vision in the eye and was forced to retire.

Bill Clement was injured during our next practice. He suffered torn knee ligaments. The injuries were starting to add up.

The series moved back to Philly for Game 5. We were a bit back on our heels early, but Parent kept us in the game and limited the damage to one goal. We took over thereafter. Goals by Bladon and MacLeish sent us to the second intermission with a 2–1 lead. In the third period, Nolet and MacLeish (empty net) sealed a 4–1 victory. This is a minor footnote but kind of neat since we won the game: I assisted on Nolet's goal, and Jimmy assisted on a MacLeish tally. It was the first time both of the Watson boys got points in the same game, and our dad was there to see it.

In Game 6 back at MSG, we led first on a Saleski goal. The game went to the third period in a 1–1 tie. Unfortunately, we couldn't pull it out. The Rangers scored three times to beat us, 4–1, and send the series back to Philadelphia for a seventh and deciding game.

Once again, thank goodness for home ice. Game 7 at the Spectrum is probably best remembered for Schultz putting a beatdown on Rolfe in a first-period fight, but it was a whale of a game in its own right.

Regarding the fight, it is true that the rest of the Rangers players on the ice just stood around and watched as Schultz pummeled Rolfe. At one point, Dave grabbed a fistful of Rolfe's hair. Moments later, Schultz headbutted Role as they were tied up in close quarters behind the net. Had that been a Flyers teammate, one or more of us would have jumped in (automatic game misconduct notwithstanding) to assist. Frankly, we were surprised no Rangers tried to intervene. Rolfe was a good player and a good teammate. He deserved better from the other guys in red, white, and blue, to be totally honest about it.

By the way, hair pulling and headbutting as fight tactics, along with taped fists (which various regular NHL fighters, including Schultzy, sometimes sported), would soon be outlawed in the NHL Rule Book.

The game was tied 1–1 after the period, courtesy of a MacLeish power-play goal set up by Clarke and Barber that erased an earlier Rangers lead. In the second period, tallies by Kindrachuk and Dornhoefer—once again, notice our scoring balance across different lines—put us ahead, 3–1. Dorny added extra insurance in the third period, popping in a goal from near the net. That proved to be vital because the Rangers scored twice. We won the game and the series, 4–3.

In so doing, we became the first expansion team to beat one of the NHL's Original Six in a playoff series.

The Rangers showed class in the postseries handshake line. Despite his disappointment, Giacomin threw his arm over Crisp and gave him a big hug to congratulate Crispy on reaching the Stanley Cup Final. Others such as Gilbert and Teddy Irvine were very gracious when I shook their hands. Gilbert wished me luck in the final, and Teddy smiled and gave me a couple taps on my shoulder despite feeling lousy about how the series turned out.

Moments like those show a lot about a player's character: being gracious in defeat or humble in victory. You're dying on the inside, believe me, but it's a gesture of respect for your fellow players and for the game.

Giacomin said afterward, "Every time you think you're about to gain some ground on them, they kick everything out from under you. They won because they were all over us all the time."

Almost to a man, the Rangers made similar statements. The one exception was Brad Park.

After Game 7, he told the media, "I decided that, if I have to maim someone to win the Stanley Cup, that it wasn't worth it. I'd be prouder to lose with these guys than I would be winning with the other club."

At the time, I was peeved at Park for his sour grapes comments. We later made up and became good friends.

We would not have home-ice advantage in the Stanley Cup Final against the Bruins. That meant we'd have to win at least one game at Boston Garden, where we won way back on November 12, 1967, and not even once since then.

Before the series started, I saw a newspaper article with a quote from

Shero. He said something along the lines of, "I'm not worried about the Bruins. We've already beaten a better team in the Rangers."

I was in disbelief. After Shero confirmed that the quote was real, I said to him, "Freddy, why the hell would you say something like that?" He told me that he wanted to give Boston something to think about and send a message to our own players that he believed we could beat the Bruins.

Once explained, it made a little more sense. Even so, it had the potential to backfire big time. The Bruins had the NHL's best record with 113 points (we had 112) and had won the Stanley Cup in 1969–70 and 1971–72. They had the likes of Orr, Phil Esposito, Ken Hodge, Carol Vadnais, and Wayne Cashman. It was still a very formidable club.

Here I am with Hart Trophy winner Bobby Clarke and Bruins superstars Phil Esposito and Bobby Orr. Orr once told me, "Beave, I wouldn't wish my knees on anybody." A few years ago, the Flyers Alumni Association had me talk at a Speakers' Series event. I recounted what Orr told me. A fan asked, "Would you switch knees with Orr if he'd have switched hands, too?" I had to chuckle.

In our preseries team meeting, Freddy said something else that flabbergasted me.

"Whenever we can, dump the puck in on Orr's side," he said. "Then go in to forecheck and be sure to hit him. Even if they come away with the puck, do it again the next time."

That seemed foolish to me. Why would we deliberately give the puck to Orr? There was no more dangerous defenseman—or any position player, actually—with the puck on his stick than Bobby. But Freddy was the boss, and we had faith that there was a reason for his strategy.

Shero explained that the purpose was to wear down Orr. It was risky, but nothing else had ever worked against him.

Game 1 of the Cup was at Boston Garden on May 7. In the first period, Orr set up Cashman for a power-play goal. Gregg Sheppard added to the lead, and we went to intermission trailing by a 2–0 score.

We pushed back in the second period. Kindrachuk scored on a rebound of my shot at the net. We also held even with the Bruins in shots, 12–12. At 5:32 of the third period, Clarke jammed home a loose puck at the net to tie the game at 2–2. I was credited with an assist on this goal, too.

Heading into the final minute of regulation, the game seemed destined to go to overtime. We had an odd-man rush, and Clarke set up Flett for a scoring chance, but the shot hit the post. The whistle blew for a stoppage.

Boston won the faceoff, and play swung toward our end. Cashman got away with interference on Dupont, and Hodge passed back to Orr. With assorted traffic in front of the net, Orr threaded a shot that got past Parent and into the net with 22 seconds on the clock.

We lost, 3–2. Who's down? We're not down, eh!

Our attitude after Game 1 wasn't that we'd just given our A performance and still lost to Boston. Actually, we felt we could play the Bruins to an up-for-grabs game. With a little better execution, we could win it.

Game 2 went similarly. The Bruins jumped ahead, 2–0, on goals by Cashman and Esposito. In the second period, Clarke combined with Flett and Schultz to cut the deficit to 2–1 with a deflection goal at the 1:08 mark. From there, we worked our butts off for a chance to win the game and got a combined 24 saves from Parent over the final 40 minutes of regulation.

Entering the final minute of the third period, however, we were in deep trouble. We were still down by a goal and pulled Bernie for an extra attacker. Lonsberry dumped the puck in deep and moved in, pressuring Orr on the forecheck. Orr sent the puck up the wall to Hodge, and Clarke pounced. The puck came loose to MacLeish.

Seeing a wide-open lane, Dupont skated down to the hash marks and called for the puck. MacLeish's pass was on the money, and Moose slapped the puck past Gilbert about waist high at 19:08. Moose launched into the running/dancing/arm-pumping goal celebration that came to be known as the "Moose Shuffle."

Overtime was a grind, as one would expect. Finally, Flett kept a puck alive, and Schultz made a nice pass across to Clarke on the right side. In one of the most famous plays in Stanley Cup–playoff lore—and nothing short of an iconic moment in Flyers history—Clarke was stopped on an initial shot attempt but scored on his own rebound. Clarke jumped for joy, several feet above the ice.

We now had our long-elusive win in Boston, and it couldn't have come at a better time. Going back to the Spectrum for Games 3 and 4, we felt very confident. We respected the Bruins, but we weren't scared of them.

In Game 3, we held the Bruins to a reasonable 25 shots on goal. After spotting them a Sheppard goal just 1:03 after the opening faceoff, we were the better team for the majority of the game. Bladon tied the game with a power-play goal, and then Crisp put us ahead in the latter stages of the first period.

We had the better of the play in the second period, outshooting Boston, 12–6, but could not solve Gilbert. However, in the third period, goals by Kindrachuk and Lonsberry broke the game open. We won, 4–1.

After the game, Bill Fleischman asked me why we were relatively subdued after the victory. I said, "We haven't won anything. There's a long way to go in the series. I think we played good tonight. But we have to play our best to win two more games."

The victory was a costly one. We lost Dornhoefer to a separated shoulder. The still-injured Clement volunteered to return for Game 4.

Game 4 started out the way you'd expect a must-win game between the Bullies and the Big Bad Bruins to be: feisty and physical. There were three fights in the first period: Kindrachuk vs. Savard, Jimmy Watson vs. Cashman, and Schultz vs. O'Reilly. There were also various roughing, high-sticking, and cross-checking minors back and forth. We scored early goals by MacLeish (power play) and Schultz before Esposito (power play) and

Savard (assisted by Orr) answered to tie the game.

The second period was scoreless. Bruins forward Bobby Schmautz gave me a stick to the ribs early in the period, but referee Ron Wicks let it slide. Later, at the 11:48 mark, Schmautz and I mixed it up a little and were both sent to the box on matching roughing minors. If you take someone off with you and there's no power play for the other side, that's fine.

I was back in the box again in the third period; this time for a scrum with Don Marcotte. The score remained 2–2 until the final six minutes of the game. Barber and Dupont tallied to open a 4–2 lead, and we shut it down the rest of the way to take a three-games-to-one in the series as the scene shifted back to Boston for Game 5.

There's no such thing in the Stanley Cup playoffs as "playing with house money." A lackadaisical attitude like that will have you on the loser's end of a handshake line before you know it. We had no intention of taking our foot off the gas pedal now. The truth of the matter is that we went to Boston for Game 5 determined to match or exceed our effort from Game 2.

However, the Bruins were too good for us to snap our fingers and impose our will. They hadn't won two Stanley Cup championships in the early 1970s for nothing. Boston came at us hard in Game 5, scored an early shorthanded goal and started to pull away over the latter 30 minutes of the game. We lost, 5–1. Orr had two goals and an assist.

Game 6 was at the Spectrum on the afternoon of May 19. Nearly 50 years later, I can still vividly recall the anticipation, the tension, the shift-by-shift intensity of putting ourselves in position to win, and then the explosion of joyous emotion afterward.

I was too focused on the game that day to contemplate Freddy's message on the board—"Win today and we walk together forever"—but the permanent bond with our teammates, the fans, and the City of Philadelphia certainly made Shero's words prophetic. Before the opening faceoff, as she did on opening night, Kate Smith sang a live rendition of "God Bless America."

We took a penalty in the first minute of the game (Dupont for interference), which was hardly the start we wanted. However, we killed it off, and it helped work out some of the nervous energy.

With O'Reilly in the penalty box for hooking at 13:58, we made our move on the power play. Sometimes, the simplest plays work the best—get the puck back to the point and a forward moving across the slot. At 14:48 of the first period, MacLeish deflected a Dupont point shot into the net for a 1-0 lead.

On the play, MacLeish cleanly won a faceoff against Sheppard back to Moose at the point. The puck was on its edge and rolling. Freddy often said, "Never shoot a rolling puck."

Thank goodness Dupont shot this one anyway. From in front of the net, MacLeish tipped the puck, and the rest was history.

Of course, we'd have loved to get some breathing room. With the way Parent was playing, however, even a one-goal deficit felt daunting to our opponents. In the third period, we were unable to score on a couple of power-play opportunities. However, with Schultz in the box for a midperiod holding penalty, we killed off the Bruins' man advantage.

Time ticked down below three minutes remaining on the game clock. At 17:38, Orr grabbed and spun around Clarke. Called for a holding penalty, Orr gave referee Art Skov an earful.

We played the power play cautiously. Orr exited the box with 22 seconds left in the game. In the waning seconds, Orr threw the puck down the ice and wide of the net. The noise was deafening. I touched up behind the net. Bedlam erupted.

One of the linesmen scooped up the puck from the ice, and Crisp came over and asked for it. The official obliged and handed it to him. It's still in Crispy's possession to this very day: any auction of the "authentic final puck" or a hockey memorabilia case purporting to display it is either a fake or a puck used at some other point during the game. Terry has the real one.

Everything that came afterward was like a slightly surreal dream. Fans streamed out on the ice as we celebrated. I hugged trainer Frank Lewis (the image made the cover of Chevalier's *The Broad Street Bullies* book). One T-shirt-clad fan, clutching a champagne bottle, got into the handshake line. NHL president Clarence Campbell's path to present the Cup to our captain, Clarke, was complicated by the mass of people in his way.

Schultzy, Clement, and other Flyers had to physically clear a path for our full-team victory lap because of all the people on the ice. When we

The third-period clock expired moments earlier in Game 6 of the 1974 Stanley Cup Final, and the celebration began. A photo taken a few moments later of me hugging equipment manager Bill Delaney became the cover image in the late Jack Chevalier's landmark book, *The Broad Street Bullies.*

got back to the dressing room, the scene was every bit as wild as the one on the ice. Already soaked in champagne, Ed Snider spoke to our group, and then Clarkie toasted with Snider, Keith Allen, and Marcel Pelletier. Meanwhile, I shared champagne with Shero.

The most special part of the locker room celebration was this: Jimmy and I being able to share the moment with our father. As I said in the previous chapter, my dad drank from the Stanley Cup before my brother or I did. Even then, it was something I knew would be special for the rest of my life. Now, with my father deceased, I look back at those locker room photos of Joe Sr. with my brother and me, and I realize how blessed I am that the photos exist for my and Jimmy's children and grandchildren and the people in Smithers to see.

After the game, I did get to have a few minutes of relative calm. Orr came over to a room adjacent to the two locker rooms in order to congratulate me.

My father, Joe Watson Sr., traveled from Smithers to Philadelphia to surprise Jimmy and me during our playoff runs in both 1974 and 1975. He was a handful! I'm thrilled that he got to share in our Cup victories with us.

"You guys wore me out," he said. "Every time I went back for the puck, I got hit. Every time I touched the puck, I had someone all over me."

Freddy's strategy had worked. It took until late in the series to have an effect, but it eventually did.

I didn't know what else to say to Orr at this point, except that I appreciated the hell out of him stopping by. All I could think to do was offer him a sip of champagne.

"Nah, I didn't earn it," he said. "Go celebrate with your team."

For several days thereafter, none of us on the Flyers got much sleep, if any. I couldn't even estimate how many people shook my hand, clapped me on the back, took a photo, or handed me a drink. The parade, scary as it was because of the mobs of people and inadequate security, was the biggest outpouring of love I ever saw. Even in the still-dazed state of mind I was in, I realized that this championship meant every bit as much to our fans as it did to us.

The love was mutual. I can say that not only on my own behalf but for every one of my teammates. Nothing could ever take that away. Thank you, Flyers fans!

This rare photo from the Flyers Archives shows the convertibles the Flyers players rode in shortly thereafter during the 1974 championship parade down Broad Street. What a wild day!

There's only one thing harder than winning the Stanley Cup: repeating as champions the next year. You spend all offseason hearing about how great you are, both individually and as a team. It's easy for egos to get overblown and the work ethic to tail off just a little bit. Meanwhile, every other team has you in the crosshairs.

Basically, when you win the championship, if you're not careful, you go from being the hunter to being the hunted. We did whatever we could to make sure we kept the mentality that we had something to prove to ourselves.

On a related note, Ed Snider had an idea (which he hoped would start a new NHL tradition for the defending champion) that our players would wear a Stanley Cup patch on our jerseys throughout the season. Our players hated the idea, and so the suggestion was dropped. We did, however, pose for publicity photos at training camp with the Stanley Cup patch on our sweaters.

As they did at the end of the 1972–73 season, captain Clarke and head coach Shero challenged us to arrive at camp in the best shape of our careers and use the camp for preparation instead of conditioning.

There were still plenty of skeptics, especially in the New York, Toronto, and Montreal media, who doubted the legitimacy of our 1973–74 Stanley Cup championship. *It was a fluke. They're just a goon squad with a great goalie and a couple of skilled players. They're too slow; it'll catch up with them this year. The WHA took away a few too many key players from other clubs. They're predictable, and they won't sneak up on anyone.*

You get the idea. We didn't care what our haters thought of us. As Shero once wrote on the board: lions lose no sleep over the opinions of sheep. It was, however, good motivation to work even a little harder as we prepared for training camp and then for the 1974–75 season.

We had relatively little roster turnover from 1973–74 to 1974–75. Ashbee retired due to his eye injury and joined Nykoluk as one of Shero's assistant coaches. Flett was not re-signed and joined Toronto. Nolet was claimed by Kansas City in the 1974 Expansion Draft, and we also lost Bruce Cowick (a member of our playoff roster) to Washington in the Expansion Draft.

On the flip side, we added 38-year-old veteran defenseman Ted Harris, a four-time former NHL All-Star with four Stanley Cup rings with Montreal (he'd win his fifth and final one with us). Young defense prospect Larry Goodenough was knocking on the door for an NHL promotion and would slot in by the end of the season.

Up front, we had one big addition. Allen acquired goal-scoring right wing Reggie Leach from the Seals. Leach had been Clarke's linemate in Flin Flon and was a dynamic pure shooter. He'd been an underachiever up to that point in his career and had some defensive deficiencies, but Clarke and Shero were certain they could get the most out of Leach.

"The Riverton Rifle," as Leach was nicknamed for his small Manitoba hometown and for his shooting ability, soon joined with Clarke and Barber on what became known as the LCB Line, the most prolific scoring trio in Flyers history. He'd go on to bag 45 goals and 74 points in 80 games during our second Cup season. Any way you slice it, Reggie was an upgrade on Flett.

During training camp, we upgraded our backup goalie spot, as Allen traded for netminder Wayne Stephenson from St. Louis. As I stated in the last chapter, Stephenson wasn't Bernie Parent's equal (who was?), but he was better than many other clubs' primary starting goalies.

Speaking of Bernie, while most of our players came to camp in peak condition, Parent needed that year's camp to shed some pounds he'd put on during all the summertime parties and public engagements from our first Cup and his Vezina Trophy and Conn Smythe Trophy performance. Bernie got off to a slow start in camp. I think Stephenson was acquired as an insurance policy, just in case.

Turned out there was nothing to worry about. We now had a better version of our first Cup team in front of him, and Bernie went on to have a second straight stellar season. Some of the toughest games for goalies can be when they hardly see any shots for long stretches of time and then suddenly must stop a Grade A scoring chance. Bernie made it look easy. He also could still dial up a 30-save or even 40-save performance when necessary. There were, simply, fewer nights where he was needed to do so.

During the 1974 offseason, the National Hockey League and World Hockey Association agreed to arrange a seven-game series of exhibition games between the two archrival leagues shortly before the start of their respective regular seasons.

In the first game of the series, the WHA's Houston Aeros defeated the St. Louis Blues, much to the dismay of NHL president Campbell. The second game of the series pitted the defending Stanley Cup champion Flyers against the New England Whalers on September 28, 1974.

Campbell, as was well known, was no fan of the Flyers. However, as much as he disliked our franchise's maverick and rough-and-tumble image, he despised the World Hockey Association even more. The thought of the NHL dropping a second straight game to the WHA was unpalatable to Campbell, especially when it involved the NHL's league champions.

Campbell called Ed Snider, begging him to tell our players to take the game seriously and to ask Shero to start mostly our NHL regulars.

Much to the league president's relief, the Flyers delivered a 4–2 win. Two goals by Schultzy, Campbell's least favorite player in the NHL, led the way. We grabbed a quick 2–0 lead on goals by Schultz and prospect Bob Sirois. On the opening shift of the second period, Bill Barber opened a 3–0 lead. Schultz tallied again midway through the second period to extend our lead to four goals.

The Whalers got one back late in the second period on a goal by ex-Flyer Don Blackburn and another late in the third on a power-play goal by Bob Charlebois (one goal, one assist on the night), but it was too little and too late.

I've got to be totally honest here: even though I played in this game and picked up an assist, I don't remember much (if any) internal discussion about it. We viewed it as just another preseason tune-up. Nonetheless, we received a congratulatory telegram from Campbell for our victory.

While the NHL brass cared about the outcome of the games in the series, the exhibitions failed to attract much fan interest. The games were all sparsely attended. As with other participating NHL clubs, members of our team had friends and former teammates on the WHA clubs, such as Blackburn with the Whalers. Quite simply, playing a WHA team didn't raise nearly the same emotion as playing against a team from the Soviet Union.

At any rate, the two leagues split the first four games of the series. The NHL clubs then won each of the final three. The final scores are as follows:

Houston Aeros 5 – St. Louis Blues 3
FLYERS 4 – New England Whalers 2
Atlanta Flames 3 – Winnipeg Jets 1
San Diego Mariners 4 – California Golden Seals 3
Minnesota North Stars 5 – Toronto Toros 3
Vancouver Canucks 4 – Edmonton Oilers 3
Pittsburgh Penguins 5 – Cleveland Crusaders 3

Opening night of the regular season didn't go as planned, however. We lost 5–3 to the Kings (the final goal being an empty netter) at the Spectrum. I scored a goal in the second period, which cut a 3–1 deficit to one goal, but it was ultimately meaningless because we lost. I was on the ice for two LA goals.

We won our second game in a 6–1 blowout of Buffalo at the Spectrum. But we didn't make the early-season statement we were hoping to make. We'd started the previous year at 4-3-0 through seven games. This time, we were a so-so 4-3-1 through eight games, including an embarrassing 4–1 loss to the friggin' Seals.

We were nearly shut out by the Seals. I was unable to break up a two-on-one rush by Al MacAdam (who was one of the players we traded for Leach) and Dave Gardner. It took a MacLeish goal in the final 1:49 of the third period to finally get on the board.

Afterward, I told the press, "Those guys skate harder than the Canadiens. Zing, and they're by you."

As there was the previous season in Philly, there was a bench-clearing brawl in this game. The two teams combined for 232 penalty minutes (144 for the Flyers, 88 for California).

Barry Cummins was no longer part of the Seals' organization by this point. But the bad blood lingered between their club and the Flyers. This was another game, as in the previous season against Buffalo, where referee Bryan Lewis lost control early, and things escalated as the game moved along.

All hell finally broke loose at 8:20 of the third period. Seals defenseman Mike Christie was on the receiving end of a beatdown. I felt bad for Christie afterward. All our guys were ready and willing to fight, but only a few Seals were equally willing. Christie was one who would take on anyone, and he ended up trying to fight Kindrachuk, Kelly, and Saleski all at once.

That took guts. The results, however, weren't pretty. Christie needed eight stitches to close a wound under his left eye, four stitches for a cut above his eye, and another two stitches for a cut under his right eye. He kept defiantly shouting, "Hit me again, you bastards!"

We all agreed that things went a little too far that night. None of us were proud of it. In fact, to a man, we all gained a ton of respect for Christie and would have welcomed him on our club (as compared to California teammates of his who yapped at our players but safely kept their distance). He was tough and brave. Several Flyers, Bladon for one, became close friends with Christie over the years. Saleski later played with Mike in Colorado, and they, too, formed a friendship. Such is hockey.

Like it or not, the brawl against the Seals spurred our own team to iron out some of the issues that were causing our early season problems. We were taking too many undisciplined penalties at bad times. We were giving up too much space in the areas of the ice we needed to control.

Over the next 10 games, we rattled off eight wins and two ties to improve to 12-3-3 on the season.

Among the victories were a 5–1 rout of the Rangers at the Spectrum featuring two goals apiece by Clement and Lonsberry, a 3–0 road shutout of the Canadiens behind 34 saves from Parent, a 2–0 shutout of Minnesota, and a 3–0 win in our home rematch with California (which included two more goals for Clement and one for Crisp). On November 9, a bit of history was made: Kindrachuk scored the first successful penalty shot opportunity in team history after he was tripped on a shorthanded breakaway by Washington's Dave Kryskow.

The struggling Scouts came to Philadelphia on December 1. Before the opening faceoff, Nolet said half-jokingly to Clarke, "Take it easy on us tonight, eh?"

Clarkie grinned. Simon knew that no such thing would happen. We scored five times in the first period, four in the second, and once in the third on the way to a 10–0 final. Scouts goalie Peter McDuffe was left in to absorb all 10 goals on 47 shots.

Bernie cruised to a shutout at the other end. The closest KC came to scoring was during a minute-long five-on-three in the first period. Halfway through killing a Lonsberry minor, I was penalized for closing my hand on the puck.

What happened was this: I was going to bat an aerial puck aside in our defensive zone, but one of the Scouts' forwards stepped in front of me. Noticing him, I caught the puck instead of swatting it. I tossed it aside immediately, but it was too late. That was a brain fart on my part: an automatic penalty.

It's a helpless feeling when you're sitting in the box after taking a penalty you know was a bad one. Thankfully, our penalty killers and Parent got us through unscathed.

Later in December, in the final game before our team Christmas party, we blanked Pittsburgh by a 4–0 score. That took us into a four-night break in the schedule with a 22-6-5 record.

At the team party, Jimmy volunteered to play Santa. He was still one of our youngest players and wasn't about to be mistaken by anyone for St. Nick. Thankfully, we also had "the real Santa Claus" show up at the end, as we always did. I look back today at some of photos taken during these years, including two of my son Ryan (one bawling in horror as a toddler and another calmly and curiously studying Santa's face when Ryan was slightly older). It makes me smile. Where do the years go?

This is a picture from our team Christmas party. I must say that my brother Jimmy made for an unconvincing Santa Claus. Thankfully, the real one was never far behind.

We hit a bump in the road shortly after New Year's on a road trip that started in Vancouver, went to California, and then came east, going 1-3-1 on the trip, including three straight losses at one juncture. Thereafter, we went 8-1-1 over the rest of our games in January and the first three in February.

However, the one loss we sustained in that stretch was a 5–1 butt-kicking at Boston Garden. In our minds, that performance was more aggravating than most of the wins had been enjoyable. Orr was a one-man wrecking crew, strafing us for five points (one goal, four assists).

February 1975 turned out to be a so-so month for our team. Freddy used to set team objectives for blocks of games, and we'd set a goal of being at 38 wins for the season by our final game of the month. We seemed to be in good shape when we beat Boston, 4–3, at the Spectrum on February 16 on goals by four different players (Dornhoefer, Barber, MacLeish, and Leach). That brought us to 35 wins, but then we went 0-3-1 in the next four games.

February closed out with a 3–1 home win over Vancouver led by the LCB Line. That marked the start of a torrid stretch drive, similar to the one from the previous season. We went 17-1-1 over our final 19 games of the season, including winning streaks of four games and eight games in a row.

We finished the 1974–75 campaign with 113 points (51-18-11 record), with the NHL's lowest goals against average, and in the top one-third of the 18-team league in goals scored. Clarke was a shoo-in for his second Hart Trophy as NHL MVP, and Parent won his second straight Vezina Trophy.

Still, this was not the hardware that any of us cared about. To a man, we were all focused on one thing: making it back-to-back years as Stanley Cup champions.

We drew Toronto in the quarterfinals, winning Games 1 and 2 at the Spectrum by 6–3 and 3–0 scores before traveling to Toronto and capturing a 2–0 win at Maple Leaf Gardens on a 31-save Parent shutout and goals from Dornhoefer and MacLeish.

One win away from a sweep, we twice fell behind by a goal early in Game 4. Leach evened things up with goals at five-on-five and the power play. Barber put us ahead in the second period, and we carried a 3–2 lead into the third period. Ron Ellis prolonged the game with a tying goal that forced OT. However, just 1:45 into sudden death, Dupont ended the game and series. He celebrated the series-winning goal by doing the Shuffle.

Wrapping up the first-round series so quickly resulted in a 10-day break before the second round started on April 29. That was both a blessing (because it gave some of our banged-up players, me included, time to heal) and a curse (because it's easy to lose sharpness with that much time off).

In the meantime, we saw the New York Islanders fall in a three-games-to-zero hole against Pittsburgh and then storm back to win four in a row. As a result, we played the Islanders in the Cup semis.

We wore the Islanders down in Game 1 at the Spectrum and held them to 21 shots in a 4–0 shutout win. New York threw a scare into us in Game 2 on our home ice. We led 4–2 in the middle stages of the third period, only for J. P. Parise and Denis Potvin to score twice in a span of 14 seconds. Thankfully, Clarke rescued a win for us at 2:56 of overtime.

When the scene shifted to Nassau Coliseum for Game 3, we limited the Islanders to just 14 shots on goal. We didn't get much offense, either, but a Reggie Leach goal scored just 30 seconds into the third period stood up for a 1–0 win.

Ideally, we'd have liked Game 4 to be as soon as possible after the third game. Instead, there were four nights between the games. We overcame a 3–0 deficit on a tally by Lonsberry and back-to-back goals by MacLeish scored late in the middle frame and early in the third period. However, Jude Drouin won the game for the Islanders in overtime.

In Game 5 at the Spectrum, we flat out got outworked and outskated. We trailed, 1–0, after the first period, 3–1 by the second intermission, and 4–1 by early in the third. Hound got us on the board in the final five minutes, but it was too little and too late.

This was our first home playoff game loss since Game 4 of the 1973 Cup Semifinal against Montreal. I guess it was bound to happen eventually, but it was pretty disappointing to have it happen in a game where we were a win away from a return trip to the Cup Final.

The same week, Rexy's had a fire. Our favorite restaurant/bar temporarily closed while undergoing repairs. Our guys wore black armbands at practice.

In Game 5 at Nassau Coliseum, we got off to an early lead on a Lonsberry goal. Potvin got it back for New York with a power-play goal late in the second period. The game had become a goalie duel between Parent and Chico Resch. Anything could happen, but we liked our chances. Win a period, win the series. Unfortunately, Gerry Hart put the Islanders ahead early in the third period. We were unable to score a second goal.

Now the series had to come back to Philly again for a seventh and deciding game. The Islanders needed just one more win for their second straight comeback from a 3–0 series deficit. However, we were confident—not cocky, but of strong self-belief—that we'd step up with the series back on our turf.

We needed someone to make an early statement that the Islanders comeback story was about to end. Dorny delivered the message with a goal just 19 seconds after the opening faceoff. MacLeish underlined the message with power-play goals at 5:02 and 7:11. Trailing 3–1 by the end of the first period, the Islanders drew no closer.

We held the Islanders to a meager 15 shots on goal for the entire game. MacLeish subsequently finished a hat trick in the third period to punctuate the win. Rather than having our run for a second straight Cup end with a blown 3–0 series lead, we restored order sufficiently to close out the series with a convincing win and return to the Stanley Cup Final.

Buffalo toppled Montreal in their semifinal series, strengthened by overtime wins in Games 1 and 5, before closing out the series in Game 6. As a result, we headed into a Stanley Cup Final series where the media touted it as Bernie and the LCB Line against the French Connection.

The Sabres were an excellent goal-scoring team that threw a lot of pucks at the net but were not as good as we were in the 200-foot game. We respected them but felt we were well suited to beat them in a best-of-seven series.

The Philadelphia portion of the series went to plan. In Game 1, Parent made 27 saves, and a four-goal explosion in the third period—two by Barber and one apiece by Lonsberry and Clarke—lifted us to a 4–1 victory. In Game 2, the score was tied at 1–1 early in the third period after Jerry "King Kong" Korab answered an earlier Leach goal. However, a few minutes later, Clarke cashed in a Don Luce hooking penalty to put us ahead to stay, 2–1.

Game 3 was held on May 20, 1975, and it was a very warm and muggy day. It was like a sauna inside the Aud. This turned out to be one of the weirdest and toughest-to-play games I ever experienced in my career.

A thick fog started to blanket the ice, causing various stoppages in order to have the players on both teams skate around the increasingly soft, slushy ice to try to break up the fog. Making things even stranger, a bat flew down from the rafters.

Buffalo's Jimmy Lorentz, forever known thereafter as "Batman," swatted the animal down to the ice with his stick, where it met its demise. MacLeish, meanwhile, took off his glove and went to pick it up off the ice and deliver it, barehanded, to the scorer's table.

"Ricky!" I hollered. "Don't do that! It might have rabies."

MacLeish looked at me quizzically.

"What are rabies?" he asked.

As the game progressed, the conditions further deteriorated. You could only see a few feet ahead as the puck and players swirled in and out of sight amid the fog. The softness of the ice, meanwhile, caused pucks to bounce unpredictably.

This photo from the Flyers Archives collection shows just how surreal the "Fog Game" in Buffalo was during the 1975 Stanley Cup Final. I'm partially visible in the background as Terry Crisp attempts a shot on goal.

Mind you, both teams were in the same boat. It just made the game exceptionally hard for either team to play to their standards.

The game went into overtime, tied at 4–4. Finally, French Connection line member Robert scored at 18:29 of OT to cut our series lead to two games to one. Buffalo was energized by prevailing in Game 3 and went on to tie the series at two games apiece, with a 4–2 victory at the Aud in Game 4.

The series came back to our house for Game 5. We won handily, leading 5–0 by the midway point of the game and going on to win, 5–1, as Parent flirted with a shutout for 54-plus minutes. Schultz scored twice. Dornhoefer, Kelly, and Leach tallied once apiece.

Game 6 was played at the Aud on May 27. We didn't do anything different or fancy. We just focused on checking the hell out of the Sabres and playing a smart hockey game. Through two periods, the game was scoreless.

On the first shift of the third period, our regular practice drill paid off as Kelly won the puck behind the net and came out and scored against Roger Crozier just 11 seconds after the opening faceoff. I never did find out if Shero paid Kelly the promised $5 for scoring that way.

The 1–0 score held until 17:13. Kindrachuk got pasted into the side boards, going down in a heap, but springing Clement on a breakaway. Clement beat Crozier from prime shooting range, and we had more than enough offensive support for Parent on this day. Parent recorded a 32-save shutout. We were Stanley Cup champions for the second year in a row.

The on-ice celebration was no less joyous for our players than the previous year's. It was, however, less chaotic. With the game being in Buffalo and the crowd either staying seated or starting to file out after the handshake line, we had room for a proper victory lap after Campbell presented the Cup.

Once we got back to the dressing room, the celebration started to ramp up. I brought my Polaroid camera and handed it to Flyers teammate Jack McIlhargey (who was among the extra players that year on our playoff roster). Two photos that Jack took—a photo of me with my arms raised in victory and Ed Snider in the foreground as well as a photo of most of the team after the media finally left the room—have never previously been published prior to the assembly of this book.

Ed Snider threw lavish celebration parties after we won the Stanley Cup in 1974 and 1975. Here, I'm chowing down during our '75 celebration.

Winning the second Stanley Cup was extremely thrilling in its own right but also validated our first. No one could call our 1973–74 championship a fluke anymore after we duplicated the feat the next year. Also, trust me, celebrating a Stanley Cup championship never feels repetitive or boring in any way.

The plane ride back from Buffalo was a blast. The second Cup parade was much better organized and more secure than the first. The party Mr. Snider held and our player-only celebrations were epic. Do it again…and again…and again…and again. If only we could!

CHAPTER 12

Tell It to the Czar

If the only thing in hockey that's tougher than winning the Stanley Cup is defending it successfully the next season, capturing the championship in three or more seasons takes a dadgum near miracle. It takes a dose of good luck—avoiding key injuries, peaking at just the right time, having the puck bounce your way in a pivotal game that could go either way—as well as good design.

In many ways, our 1975–76 Flyers team was the best team that we had, top to bottom, during the height of our club's success. The 118 points we posted (51-13-6 record) and our 36-2-2 record at the Spectrum that season set franchise records for overall success and home-ice success that still stand to this day. I feel safe predicting, 47 years later, that those marks will hold for many years to come.

The 1975–76 campaign was the season of our decisive win over the famous Red Army (CSKA) team at the Spectrum. It was the year that we set an NHL record with a 23-game unbeaten streak (17-0-6), broken a few years later by a 28-game run by the Montreal Canadiens in 1977–78 and then by a North American pro sports record 35-game unbeaten streak

(25-0-10) by the Flyers during the 1979–80 season.

Our team was stacked. It was the peak of the LCB line. Clarke won his third and final Hart Trophy and had 119 points. Barber scored 50 goals and posted 112 points. Leach scored 61 goals in the regular season (still a Flyers franchise record) and added 19 more in the playoffs (tied for an NHL record).

Our roster had six players, including Jimmy, represent the Flyers in the NHL All-Star Game. The game was held at the Spectrum, and Shero coached the Campbell Conference side.

Unfortunately, when all was said and done, we fell short of achieving our slogan for the season: "Hat Trick in '76." There's never a point when you feel like you've won "enough" Stanley Cups. No, the championships in 1974 and 1975 did not lessen the sting of not winning a third Cup.

We still had all the elements: the right mix on the roster, the right desire, and the right mix of talent, confidence, and work ethic.

We simply peaked just a little early, had miserable luck with vital injuries (Parent and MacLeish), and ran into a Montreal Canadiens team that had all the same elements as we did but peaked at the perfect time and got just a little better goaltending in the final from Hall of Famer Ken Dryden than we got from Wayne Stephenson. Again, just as when I stated earlier that Wayne was a darn good goalie, but he was no Bernie Parent, it's not a slight on Wayne to say that when it came down to Stephenson vs. Dryden, it was inevitably Wayne who blinked first. Against almost any other opponent, our team was good enough to win another Cup with Stephenson in net. He was the Vezina runner-up to Dryden and our goalie in the Red Army game. Those count for something.

We'll never know if we'd have won the Cup that year over the Canadiens if Parent and MacLeish had been healthy. I do know this: we wouldn't have lost in a sweep, especially in a series with three one-goal games and another that was tied within the third period before ending as a two-goal margin. We lost 4–3 and 2–1 games at the Forum and then 3–2 and 5–3 at the Spectrum. Every game had one preventable goal end up in our net, by my recollection.

Yes, such is hockey. Even so, it bugs me to this day talking about the way our reign as champions came to an end. The disappointment still lives inside my memories. You don't compete to come close. I'll repeat the mantra again: *anyone can lose, but not anyone can win.*

Listen, the Canadiens went on to win four straight Stanley Cup. That didn't happen by accident. In my head, I know they ended up being just a little bit better than we did as the mid-1970s moved into the latter decade. But as far as 1975–76 goes, I still feel in my heart of hearts that a third straight Cup was within our grasp.

Before I talk about my other hockey-related memories from that year, I had to get off my chest how rotten it still feels to this day that we didn't get a third Cup ring and another over-the-top parade. Hell, I could never have enjoyed a postplayoffs vacation. I'd have to fake it, and I've never been any good at masking how I feel about something, for good or for bad.

The post-Cup summer of 1975 was one big celebration. By that point, it felt like the Flyers could do no wrong. For example, when we played a charity softball game at Veterans Stadium in Philadelphia, the event drew 22,178 people to the ballpark.

Heading into training camp, Freddy wrote the following message on the board: "Champions don't show up to get everything they want. Champions dedicate themselves to give everything they have." I thought that was the perfect tone to set for the challenge ahead. Many of us had gotten salary bumps in our contracts. Locally, we were treated like royalty. Answering fan mail and autograph requests were much more time-consuming tasks than they once were!

Shero was basically warning us not to change our attitudes: focus on the work that goes into winning rather than the spoils that come afterward. He was right. Maintaining success requires doubling down on your work ethic, realizing how fragile success is, and never taking it for granted. Put your head down and keep skating.

Once again, we had only a few changes to our roster. Ted Harris retired after the '75 Cup, and Larry "Izzy" Goodenough became a regular starter. Bill Clement was traded shortly after we won our second Cup to the Capitals in a deal that gave the Flyers the first overall pick of the 1975 NHL Amateur Draft. We used the pick to select rugged young center Mel Bridgman.

My old pal and former defensive partner Ed Van Impe started the season with the Flyers and spent most of the year with the team. However, when Bernie was out with injury, Keith Allen traded Eddie and Bobby Taylor to Pittsburgh for netminder Gary "Inch" Inness. In the meantime, tough-guy defenseman Jack "Bucky" McIlhargey became a semiregular in the lineup.

Other than those tweaks, our 1975–76 roster was pretty much identical to the one we celebrated Stanley Cup number two with. One difference, though, was this was the highest-scoring team I ever played with during my NHL career. Our top three forward lines were stacked with players who scored 20-plus goals.

Don Saleski had the first of three straight 20-goal seasons for our club in 1975–76. The New York, Toronto, and Montreal media still called him a "goon," but Big Bird only had 68 penalty minutes that year, and he became a very good penalty killer and a threat around the net.

To this day, you'll hear about Don's 205 PIM in our breakthrough 1972–73 season brought up by our club's critics, yet they never mention that players like Saleski improved as NHL players year after year.

The bigger point is this: Freddy Shero didn't just shoehorn players into roles they couldn't expand or change. He challenged us all and gave us avenues for growth. The players who came along for the entire ride, almost to a man, kept growing as players. Jimmy, for one, became an almost perennial NHL All-Star.

I was now 33 years old. For me, the challenge was to keep up my level of play to where I could remain an every-game starter in the lineup. With the NHL continuing to expand, I fretted a little bit when there were offseason Expansion Drafts. I also knew there'd only be so many more years until some of the young kids came for my job. I focused on doing whatever was within my control—staying in good shape, playing to the best of my ability, and trying to hold teammates to the same standard that I held myself.

The 1975–76 season was one of the best and healthiest of my career. I dressed in 78 of 80 games, missing two games (March 14 and 16, 1976) due to the flu but none due to injury. I only know my personal stats for the season because I looked them up—a career-best plus-56 rating, 24 points—but I do remember feeling like I was playing some of my most consistent hockey. So was just about our entire team.

After six games, we were 5-0-1, even with Bernie unable to play due to a severely pinched nerve in his neck and, ultimately, out until late February. He never felt close to 100 percent healthy; in fact, and he'd be limited to 11 regular-season games and eight playoff games. For all intents and purposes, Stephenson became our number-one goalie for most of the season.

We kept rolling. On November 1, we had eight different goal scorers in an 8–1 blowout win over the Bruins at the Spectrum. One night later, we racked up a 10–0 win over Kansas City to improve to 9-1-2 on the season. Stephenson had a 19-save shutout (and only 11 shots faced over the final 40 minutes) while we bombarded Scouts goalie Bill McKenzie with 51 shots.

As we reached the 20-game mark of the season—the one-quarter mark of the schedule—we had a nationally televised Sunday game at the Spectrum against the Montreal Canadiens. We won the game, 3–1, and outshot Scotty Bowman's club by a 49–27 margin. Kelly, MacLeish, and Dornhoefer scored the goals, but my brother was, appropriately, named the game's First Star. Jimmy kept up with their speedy forwards, stride for stride, and helped us break out of our end zone with ease. I was a plus-one that night.

Afterward, I spoke with Bill Fleischman. I said, "I think we did as good a job checking Montreal as I've ever seen us do. Except for [a Guy Lafleur goal], we kept them to the outside. When we had the puck, they were running around and chasing us, which is something you almost never see with that team."

The win against the Canadiens came on the heels of a 3–1 road loss in Detroit. The momentum from beating Montreal carried over into five wins and one tie in the span of six games (improving us to 17-3-6) on the season. The lone tie came at Maple Leaf Gardens in Toronto, where Wayne Thomas made 42 saves against us. We had back-to-back power plays in the third period with a chance to take the lead, but Thomas made seven of the 17 saves he authored in the third period to steal a point for his side.

As November ended, Jimmy and I had relatives visiting from Smithers. We earned a 5–2 home win over the Canucks on Nov 30. I had two assists in the game, and Jimmy had one. We then beat Chicago, 5–2, at the Spectrum before our six-game unbeaten streak ended in St. Louis on December 6.

The next night, we made a brief stop at home. The LCB Line and the Lonsberry-MacLeish-Dornhoefer trio led the way in a 6–1 win over the Minnesota North Stars. I scored my first goal of the season (one of two I'd get in the regular season).

"Honestly, I don't think a lot of us were feeling great today at the start. We weren't at our best early. But we got a couple early goals, and that kind of set the tone. My goal was a shot along the ice. I thought Kindrachuk maybe got a piece of it, but it went off their guy. We felt better as the game went along," I said, referring to our 21–5 shot on goal edge in the third period.

After the win against Minnesota, our team left for a western road trip. We were a little sluggish in a 1–1 tie against the Seals on December 10 before a 6–4 victory in Los Angeles on December 13 to raise our record to 19-4-7.

In every city, we had our favorite bars that we always went to. As I noted previously, players and coaches didn't frequent the same place. Fred often separated himself even from assistant coaches Nykoluk and Ashbee to go off wandering somewhere on his own.

However, when we arrived in LA, Shero had a little surprise for us. Our bar of choice in Los Angeles was the Melody. A bus picked us up at the airport and took us to our hotel for check-in and to request taxi cabs. We agreed to meet back in the lobby in 10 minutes and hustled to our rooms to drop off our bags. From there, we scurried to the cabs and went to the Melody.

When we walked in, Shero lifted a beer mug and waved to us with his other hand. Sheepishly, we waved back and turned to leave and find another place.

"No, boys. You stay here," Shero said. "I'm leaving."

Our head coach finished his beer and bought a round of drinks for the team. Before he headed out, though, he grinned at us.

"Don't you want to know how I beat you getting here?" he asked with a twinkle in his eye.

As a matter of fact, we were curious. Out of respect, none of us had the gumption to ask how he'd gotten to the bar so fast.

"Yeah. How did you get you here so soon?"

"Oh, it was easy," Shero said. "I never got off the bus. I knew you'd be coming here after you checked in, so I just had the bus driver bring me here."

With that, he left. We next saw our head coach at practice on the twelfth. The win in LA was part of another six-game unbeaten streak (4-0-2). Heading into a minibreak from Christmas, we were 22-4-8. For our team Christmas party, the Sniders hired a professional portrait photographer to take family photos of the players with their spouses and children. It was a gesture the Flyers' wives, in particular, appreciated.

We didn't play our best hockey in the span between Christmas and the end of the 1975 calendar year. But we started rolling again on New Year's Day with a 4–2 road win in Kansas City that marked the beginning of a seven-game winning streak that lasted until January 18.

Maybe it'd be more accurate to call it an eight-game winning streak. On January 11 at the Spectrum, we played what was officially a "goodwill exhibition game" against the world-famous Soviet Red Army (CSKA) team but which was every bit as important to us—and most of all to Shero—as any Stanley Cup Final. This one was touted as a battle to determine the best hockey team in the world.

Two Soviet club teams—Red Army and the highly skilled, but slightly less formidable, Soviet Wings (Krylya Sovetov)—toured North America and played a series of four games apiece against NHL clubs.

The most anticipated matches were those pitting the Red Army against the Canadiens and Flyers. The final game of the Soviets' tour was played at the Spectrum on January 11, 1976. Entering the contest, the Red Army was undefeated. CSKA thumped the Rangers at Madison Square Garden by a 7–3 score, played to a thrilling 3–3 tie at the Forum against the Canadiens, and downed the Boston Bruins at the Garden by a 5–2 count.

Like every squad iced by CSKA, the 1975–76 version of the Red Army team was stacked with the best talent the Soviet Union had to offer. In goal, the team boasted the legendary Vladislav Tretiak in the prime of his career.

Up front, the club featured the high-scoring likes of Boris Mikhailov, Valeri Kharlamov, Vladimir Petrov, Viktor Zhluktov, Vladimir Popov, and Boris Alexandrov. The back line was equally deep, led by offensive defenseman Alexander Gusev, Vladimir Lutchenko, Gennadiy Tsygankov, Viktor Kuzkin, and Alexei Volchenkov. A 17-year-old Slava Fetisov made his debut that season as well.

Although technically enlisted men in the Russian military, the Red Army players' only job was to practice and play hockey. They were together on the ice virtually seven days a week, 12 months a year. As a result, CSKA was widely viewed as the world's most finely tuned hockey machine, executing plays with staggering precision.

I wouldn't say we were feeling pressure, but we understood this game was something different. With the Red Army still undefeated against the NHL's top teams and the Soviet Wings posting a 3–1 record in their portion of series (the only blemish was a 12–6 pasting by the Sabres), we found ourselves in the unfamiliar position of receiving support from fans in other NHL cities.

We were in Toronto for our last road game before going back to Philly for the lead-up to the Red Army game. The fans in Toronto hated us. We won that game (7–3), and we got our usual reception from the crowd. But as we left, those same fans were cheering for us to beat the Russians.

Clarence Campbell hated us, too, but he told Mr. Snider that it was up to the Flyers to win it for Canada and win it for the NHL. Truthfully, though, we didn't care about outside pressure. It was our team against Russia's team. Damn right we wanted to win, but we wanted to win for ourselves.

Shero had us thoroughly prepared for Red Army. We knew what to expect, and we knew what we had to do to win. Freddy emphasized that the way to beat them was to let them circle and weave all they wanted. Don't chase the puck. Keep 'em to the perimeter. They were human, and the usual key of controlling the net-front areas and the four corners applied in this game, too.

Freddy said to us, "We'll show them a real 'Iron Curtain!'"

Another reason for our confidence was this: Red Army had to come into our building and beat us. We'd made the Spectrum into the world's toughest arena for a visiting hockey team to come in and win a game.

A "friendly" get-together before the Flyers vs. Red Army game was awkward. There were few smiles and virtually no interaction between the two sides as we dined in the same room. Red Army coach Konstantin Loktev and Shero shook hands without speaking or making eye contact. Our players didn't mingle at all with theirs.

Mostly, the Red Army players stared at us. We stared back at them. It was gamesmanship. They were trying to figure out which one of us was Schultz, because they'd heard stories about the Hammer.

Mr. Snider wanted to win just as much as the guys who played. Gene Hart, who spoke Russian fluently, taught Mr. Snider a phrase in Russian, wishing the best for both teams in the upcoming game. But when he took to the podium, Ed spoke tersely and omitted the phrase.

Snider later said, "When I looked over at all those cold faces on their side glaring at us, I just couldn't do it."

Our passionate and rowdy Flyers fans greeted the Soviet visitors to the Spectrum with a true Philadelphia welcome: boos cascaded down on the CSKA players as they stepped on the ice surface. We received a thunderous ovation as we stepped out for warmups and then another just before the start of the game.

The house lights were dimmed for the player introductions as spotlights homed in on the players. A recording of Kate Smith's rendition of "God Bless America" played as the Spectrum crowd of 17,007 loudly joined in the singing both as an expression of patriotism and as a means of supporting our team. Finally, Stephenson and Tretiak skated to their creases, and the skaters got ready for the opening faceoff.

The Red Army controlled the opening faceoff and began to pass the puck from player to player as they circled and weaved around the perimeter. Heeding Shero's advice, we refused to give chase. Instead, we bottled up the neutral zone and did not allow the CSKA attackers to gain any speed as they attempted to penetrate the blue line.

As Clarke said, "You can have the puck between the blue lines all night long, but it won't do you any good if you can't get it in. We could let them do it all game and still beat them."

The Flyers soon took control of the puck-possession battle as we bumped the CSKA players off the puck in the corners and easily won the fore-checking battles. Clarke and Bridgman also dominated in the faceoff circles, giving our side instant puck possession.

We generated most of the good early scoring chances and outshot CSKA by a 12–1 margin over the first 10 minutes. Only the stellar goaltending of Tretiak kept the game scoreless. Midway through the period, we killed off Dupont and Ed Van Impe penalties to maintain the 0–0 score.

Our players stepped up their hitting game in the waning seconds of the Van Impe penalty. Dupont threw a big check on Mikhailov at our own blue line, and then Barber crunched a Red Army defenseman in the offensive corner. Stepping out of the bench onto the ice, Van Impe picked up a head of steam. Making a beeline in open ice for Kharlamov, Eddie leveled the scoring ace with a heavy body check at the 11:21 mark.

Kharlamov laid on the ice, motionless, trying to "buy" a penalty call from referee Lloyd Gilmour. No such luck. The CSKA bench screamed in protest, claiming that Van Impe had his elbows up as he delivered the check.

Loktev summoned his players to the bench, yelling in Russian and gesturing at Gilmour. Through an interpreter on the bench, Gilmour was given an ultimatum to either assess an elbowing penalty to Van Impe or the CSKA players would not return to the ice. The referee stood his ground and told Loktev that he would assess a delay-of-game penalty on CSKA if the coach did not send his players back out on the ice immediately.

In response, Loktev motioned for his players to follow him and the Soviet officials to the visiting locker room. The Spectrum crowd booed and taunted. Diehard Flyers fan Dave Leonardi (the famous "Sign Man") broke out a placard reading "Tell it to the Czar."

Our players stood around in confusion as the Red Army players left the ice. What the hell was happening? Were the Russians forfeiting? Would they come back? Meanwhile, Shero stood stoically behind our bench.

"They'll be back," he said. "I've seen them pull this before. It's a tactic they use sometimes when the game isn't going their way. They always come back."

Shero may have been convinced that CSKA would come back, but few others were sure.

In the bowels of the Spectrum, NHL president Campbell, Ed Snider, and NHLPA director Alan Eagleson held a heated discussion with Loktev and Soviet delegation head Viacheslav Koloskov. Snider angrily told the officials that the Soviets wouldn't get paid a cent for the tour if they didn't return to the ice.

The Soviets continued to stall. As a condition of their return to the ice, Koloskov attempted to negotiate a penalty on Van Impe or a cancellation of their own delay-of-game penalty. The NHL delegation conceded nothing.

Finally, after a 16-minute delay, CSKA returned to the ice.

In the meantime, our team knew, deep inside, "We've got 'em. We're in their heads. No need to change a thing."

It took all of 17 seconds on the ensuing power play for us to grab the lead. Reggie Leach deflected a Bill Barber shot from the point past Tretiak, as the Spectrum erupted. At the 16:37 mark, MacLeish (who fired a game-high nine shots on goal) beat Tretiak cleanly with a wrist shot to make it a 2–0 game. After the first period, we'd outshot Red Army by a 17–2 margin.

Early in the second period, Dupont returned to the box on a hooking minor. Rather than sitting back, we went on the counterattack. Saleski carried the puck into the CSKA zone. Meanwhile, I saw a wide-open path in front of me, all the way to the net. Big Bird shot the puck, and the rebound was right in front of me. From there, I just swept it home on the backhand to give us a 3–0 lead at 2:44 of the second period.

It's funny. To this very day, I still get asked about that play more than any other moment of my career. It wasn't a fancy goal, but it was a big moment for me and for the Flyers.

Shero joked after the game that I'd singlehandedly set Russian hockey back 20 years by scoring shorthanded against their best players. Gene Hart used to tell a joke that he was in Russia many years later, and he saw a chain gang hard at work. The men looked old and hunched over, but they were still doing hard labor. According to Gene, he asked their translator, "Who are those men?" The punchline: "Oh, those were our players on the ice when Joe Watson scored shorthanded!"

It wasn't artistic, but my shorthanded goal against Vladislav Tretiak in the Flyers' historic win over CSKA (Red Army) on January 11, 1976, was the most famous goal of my career.

Goal-scoring was never something I went into a game thinking about doing. If I'd have tried to be an offensive defenseman at the NHL level, I'd have had a short career. But when I did score one, it was a good feeling.

To get a goal against Red Army in a game watched by hockey fans all over the world—I was told something like 150 million people in the Soviet Union watched the game on their state-run television station—was beyond my wildest imagination. Even if the actual number of viewers was widely exaggerated, the bottom line is that a hell of a lot of people on both sides of the Atlantic Ocean witnessed our team dismantling CSKA.

Overseas, to this day, my one claim to fame is that I was "that Flyers player" who scored a big goal against Tretiak. That's always how I've been introduced. If you are only remembered for one thing, that's not a bad one!

Midway through the second period, CSKA finally broke through for a goal. Viktor Kutergin got loose to tuck the puck in the net at the 10:48 mark. But the Red Army couldn't draw any closer. We went off leading 3–1 after two periods, with a 31–10 shot advantage.

In the third period, we controlled virtually every facet of the game. The

Soviet squad rarely got much past the red line with the puck. That's because Loktev didn't adjust his team's tactics in the slightest. They were still doing the same thing, weaving and circling, they did in the first period. I don't think coach Loktev was crazy, so I'd say instead of "insanity" that the definition of futility is to keep doing something that isn't working and hoping for better results.

By contrast, Shero was not only unafraid to be bold and try unconventional tactics (such as dumping the puck to Orr's side as much as possible in the 1974 Cup Final), but he also wasn't stubborn about altering the tactic if it failed.

We had a game in Montreal the first year Freddy coached the Flyers. Employing a tactic that Tarasov wrote about in one of his books—specifically how an underdog team could keep a superior opponent off-balance and guessing through unpredictability—he had us come out with an ultra-aggressive forecheck.

The Habs weren't fooled, and it backfired spectacularly. By the first intermission, we were down 3–0 and getting outshot by a mile. It was bad, but it could have even worse.

At intermission, Fred said with a smirk, "Well, that was a stupid idea. Let's forget about that one."

We went on to lose that game, 5–1. At any rate, the point I'm making is that Freddy didn't always have the perfect game plan, but he wasn't too proud to recognize a miscalculation and then adjust the approach. Loktev either couldn't or wouldn't do it. This game turned into one of our easiest closeouts when playing with a third-period lead.

At the 4:01 mark, Goodenough converted a Clarke feed to rip a shot home and give us a 4–1 lead. The energy from the Spectrum crowd was electric: I can only compare it to the Cup clincher two years earlier.

As the third period progressed, MacLeish generated two more good scoring chances, but Tretiak—their best player by a mile in this game—made tough stops. He then robbed Leach of his second goal of the game from point-blank range.

Even with the clock ticking down, Loktev stubbornly refused to even try different line combinations, let alone tell his players to start firing from all angles and distances rather than looking for perfect scoring chances that just weren't there.

Meanwhile, our side put 18 shots on Tretiak in the third period to finish with a 49–13 edge in the category. Nobody tracked scoring chances back in those days, but I'd estimate that we had an equally lopsided advantage in scoring chances. Stephenson saw mostly routine saves and handled them, well, routinely.

When the final horn sounded, we received a standing ovation from the Spectrum faithful that continued even after we filed off the ice. After the game was over, a group of our players, myself included, went over to the Red Army locker room. They let us in, and we shook hands. There was a language barrier, of course, but in this moment, no words were needed. These were good guys at heart and, obviously, good hockey players. There was mutual respect, at least on a player-to-player basis.

In this Flyers Archives photo, I'm pictured in the postgame handshake line after our 4–1 win against Red Army at the Spectrum.

I was wearing a Flyers hat, an inexpensive souvenir. One of the Red Army players, who could not otherwise speak English, pointed to my hat and offered to trade mine for his: a genuine fur *ushanka* hat. I made the swap but felt rather guilty about it because his hat had significantly more monetary value than mine. I still own the hat to this day. I don't know which Soviet player it was, unfortunately.

The aftermath wasn't as friendly, though. The CSKA coach and managers, I guess, felt like their team had to save face. They complained that the Flyers played "animal hockey." That was a crock of shit, because the game was no more physical and no dirtier than an average NHL game.

It was disappointing when Tretiak and some of the other Red Army players subsequently started parroting the same stuff about us winning only because we played dirty. We won because we outplayed and outworked them all three periods, and Shero coached circles around Loktev. No other reason.

As Clarke said, "This was one game. It doesn't prove Canadian hockey is better than theirs. It shows the Flyers are better than their best team."

That's how I've always seen it, too. The win reflected the quality of our own team. At least at that moment in time, the Philadelphia Flyers were the best hockey team not just in the NHL, but in the entire world.

Ah, but the Hockey Gods never let you get too full of yourself. We won our next two games after beating Red Army, but then we hit our roughest patch of the regular season. Over our final seven games of January, we went 1-4-2. Our losses included a 3–0 shutout defeat in Chicago and an 8–4 blowout on the road at the hands of Atlanta.

When the calendar flipped to February, we got mixed news off the ice. On the positive side, Parent was starting to near a return to play (although it was unclear if he'd make it back close to 100 percent that season). On the negative end, in the third period of our February 5 game in Vancouver, MacLeish suffered a knee injury after getting hit from behind by Harold Snepsts. We lost Ricky for the remainder of the regular season and playoffs.

Hockey-wise, though, we shook off the post-CSKA hangover and went on our biggest roll of the entire season: the 23-game unbeaten streak I mentioned at the start of this chapter. The streak unfolded this way: 3–3 road tie against the North Stars, six straight wins, 2–2 road tie in Vancouver, back-to-back wins, back-to-back ties in Los Angeles and Washington (the latter being Parent's return game in a 5–5 game where we allowed just 19 shots), 3–2 home win over Minnesota, 2–2 road tie in St. Louis, a Leap Day 6–1 win over California to close out an undefeated February and start an eight-game winning streak that lasted through March 18.

During that latter stretch of eight straight wins, we did not allow more than two goals in any game. Parent was in goal for most of them. After his rough first game back in the lineup, he limited our opponents to a combined six goals in his next five outings.

I'd be remiss here if I didn't mention that March 9, 1976, was a tough day emotionally: the day when Van Impe and Taylor were traded to Pittsburgh. Eddie and I had been together since day one with the Flyers.

We had been through all the good times and bad times, the growth of our families, the comings and goings of teammates, all the hijinks we got into on the road (this is a family-friendly book, and some of those stories will go to the grave with me), and, most of all, two Stanley Cup championships together. If someone did me dirty on the ice or took liberties on our goalie, they'd have to deal with the wrath of Van Impe. That was a thought no one relished.

Eddie was my sounding board and the one who talked me off the ledge when I was barely playing under Stasiuk and even contemplated quitting hockey. He was welcoming of my brother and helpful to other young defensemen, even as he understood that eventually someone would take his job. In many ways, I had several brothers on the Flyers: my younger brother by blood and my brothers by friendship. Ed was like an older (by three years) brother.

Due to early season hernia surgery and then due to the continued emergence of our younger defensemen, Van Impe became a part-time starter that year. He dressed in only 40 games, which was hard on someone who was used to playing every game when healthy. I was hoping that we'd have at least one final playoff run together as teammates. Sadly, it wasn't to be.

Van Impe initially told Keith Allen he'd refuse to report to Pittsburgh. However, Keith did something right by Eddie—signing him to a contract extension through the 1976–77 season—and Van Impe changed his mind.

Hockey is a business. Time waits for nobody. I understood that Dorny, Bernie (second stint), and I were all that was left now from the Flyers' first season after the 1967 Expansion Draft.

Our 23-game unbeaten streak came to an end on March 20 with a 4–2 road loss to the Red Wings. We played OK—not great but not awful except in a 5–1 road loss to the Islanders—over the final eight games of the regular season (4-2-2). By then we were focused mainly on getting ready for the playoffs.

For the second straight year, we drew Toronto as our first-round playoff opponent. The 1975–76 version was a bit deeper and more talented than the one from the previous year. I respected their talent, but, frankly, the Maple Leafs were a team that was meek on the road and suddenly got brave in front of their home crowd.

On April 12, Game 1 was played at Spectrum. Toronto didn't put up much of a struggle in our 4–1 win. Leach, Kindrachuk, Clarke, and Dornhoefer scored, and Bridgman collected two assists. We collected two power-play goals and outshot the Leafs, 47–24. Let the record show that there were no fights and a combined five power plays (all for minor infractions).

In Game 2, we rolled out to a 3–0 lead on tallies by Schultz, Lonsberry, and Saleski. Toronto got one back on a goal by defenseman Borje Salming but drew no closer. We won, 3–1. Again there were no fights. There were, however, a combined 10 power plays in the game, of which seven went to the Flyers. Most of the Toronto infractions were frustration penalties.

I mentioned the power play and PIMs because revisionist history has it that we "gooned it up" all series. That was not true. The Maple Leafs had a case of the "Philadelphia flu" in the first two games at the Spectrum. We stuck to playing tactical hockey and quickly built up a 2–0 lead in the series.

It was when the scene shifted to Toronto that the Maple Leafs suddenly found their guts. Before I get into that, though, I want to talk first about Salming.

Intimidation was still a big factor in hockey during this era. Salming's talent was obvious, but we didn't know yet if he was a stereotypical European player from that era—in other words, highly skilled but soft. Well, Salming turned out to be one of their players who didn't back down when challenged physically. He competed hard, and he cared. We all came away with immense respect for him.

As far as hockey ability went, Salming wasn't a future Hall of Famer for nothing. He and center Darryl Sittler were elite talents. You'll never hear me saying anything negative about Salming. He was one hell of a hockey player.

Parent, by his own admission, was far from playing in peak form. He wasn't tested much in Philly, but when the Leafs started putting more pucks at the net, we started yielding leaky goals as well as earned ones. We lost Game 3 by a 5–4 score.

The final score, though, is not what anyone remembers from Game 3 (or Game 6, for that matter). The match turned vicious, and we ended up battling the Leafs on the ice, their fans in the stands, and Toronto cops who were less than helpful in providing security.

The fuse was lit when the Maple Leafs' Kurt Walker speared Schultz early in the first period, triggering the first of many brawls and earning a gross misconduct penalty.

As noted, throughout the series with the Leafs, we made a point of trying to hit Toronto's two Swedish imports, winger Inge Hammarstrom and defenseman Salming, every time they touched the puck. The pacifistic Hammarstrom (ironically, later a successful Flyers scout who discovered Peter Forsberg and Mikael Renberg, among others) did not respond. Salming did, both with his skill and his fists.

Toronto scored four power-play goals in the first period and a half of play to take a 4–1 lead. Goals by Dornhoefer and Jimmy Watson just 13 seconds apart quickly trimmed the deficit to 4–3. Right off the next faceoff, there was a spirited fight between "Bucky" McIlhargey and Dave "Tiger" Williams.

With the Toronto crowd still in a frenzy, Saleski was whistled off for tripping, barking at referee Dave Newell on the way to the penalty box. As he stood in the box, a Toronto fan behind the penalty box tossed a chunk of ice cubes at Saleski. Furious, Don whirled around and confronted the fan. A Toronto police officer raced over and grabbed Saleski's stick, who tried to wrestle it back as the scene continued to escalate.

Saleski was in danger. I came over to do whatever I could to help. From the ice, I swung my stick over the low glass with the intention of getting people to back away. Regretfully, I accidentally struck a Toronto policeman, Art Malloy, in the shoulder.

Order was restored, but only temporarily. The next shift after Toronto's fifth power-play goal of the game made the score 5–3. Bridgman nailed

Salming behind the Toronto net. A fight immediately broke out.

The next day, Ontario district attorney Roy McMurtry got involved. McMurty was an attention-seeker who had ambitions of running for higher office (which he did successfully, later becoming chief justice of Ontario). He saw a golden opportunity to make national news across Canada.

McMurty announced that he was filing criminal charges against Bridgman ("assault with intent to commit bodily harm"), Saleski, and me. We had to turn ourselves in to Toronto police and get booked and finger-printed before being released ahead of a court date.

During our war of a playoff series against the Toronto Maple Leafs in the 1976 Stanley Cup Quarterfinal, Don Saleski, Mel Bridgman, and I had to turn ourselves in to Toronto police after Game 3 of the series. After Game 6, the authorities came after Bob Kelly, too.

Forty-eight hours after the Game 3 debacle, we played Game 4. Bridgman answered for the Flyers the best way he knew how. Booed every time he touched the puck, Mel scored two goals and threw his weight around with abandon. Unfortunately, a poor second period doomed the Flyers to a 4–3 defeat, sending the series back to Philadelphia tied at two games apiece.

Bernie was having a tough time in goal, but his sense of humor remained firmly intact. We all needed a good laugh. Combing through his rapidly graying hair, he announced in that thick Quebec accent of his, "Hey, boys! Things are getting so bad I think my hair is turning black again!"

The series moved back to Philly for Game 5 on April 20. During warmups, McIlhargey yelled out a challenge to any Toronto player who wanted to fight right on the spot. He had no takers.

So that's how it was going to be? The Leafs were back in our building and left their moxie back in Toronto? Yup, that's exactly what happened. We steamrolled them, 7–1.

As with Games 1 and 2, there were no fights and only minor penalties called in Game 5. The only exception was Schultz and Williams getting matching 10-minute misconducts in the latter half of the third period with the outcome long since sealed. Leach and Saleski scored two goals apiece, while Barber and Dornhoefer had one goal apiece.

On April 22, we were back in Toronto for Game 6. Lo and behold, the Leafs got feisty again, with their crowd getting involved and minimal security to protect our players.

At one point, a Toronto fan struck Schultz as he was escorted to the locker room on a misconduct penalty. Once again, we defended our teammate. In the ensuing melee, Bob Kelly threw a glove into the stands, reportedly striking a female usher in the face. Later in the game, Bridgman had one whale of a fight with Walker. No one could ever say of Mel that he backed down from a challenge in a hostile building.

The game itself was another wild one in between the whistles and penalty assessment conversations at the scorer's table. We lost, 8–5.

The next day, DA McMurtry filed charges against Hound, too. Now there were four Flyers being brought up on criminal citations. At least I had company, eh?

Game 7 at the Spectrum was held on April 27. We outplayed Toronto in the first period but went to intermission trailing by a 2–1 score despite a Dupont power-play goal and a 12–9 shot advantage.

When we were behind early, 1–0, Dornhoefer dropped the gloves with Williams. That bout was more about our team than theirs. We were all in this fight together, so let's get at it.

Several of our leaders, including me, spoke up during intermission. The gist of the animated discussion was this: no way these SOBs are going to walk out of this building as the winners of this f-in' series.

We emptied the tank the second period and took over the game: 20–4 edge in shots on goal and five unanswered goals on the scoreboard. Two tallies by Bridgman and one apiece by Saleski, Lonsberry (power play), and Leach catapulted us to a 6–2 lead and made the third period academic.

Barber added an extra insurance goal on a midperiod power-play marker to build a 7–2 edge. Late in the game, Saleski fought Robert Neely. Toronto scored a meaningless goal in the final 1:36. The rest of the game was uneventful.

We won the game, 7–3, with a 43–24 shots-on-goal edge, and won the series, four games to three. Thank goodness, once again, for the home-ice edge in a playoff series!

In terms of the criminal charges, Flyers attorney Gil Stein worked on our behalf, and even Clarence Campbell sided with us. Campbell stated publicly that our players had merely acted either in self-defense or to assist someone in danger. In Bridgman's case, it was a routine hockey fight. I regretted that I'd made glancing contact with Officer Malloy when I swung my stick over the glass. That was not my intention.

The whole aftermath was a shitshow orchestrated by McMurtry. Fun times, eh?

In the second round, we played Boston. We lost Game 1 by a 4–2 score. Bernie was still hindered in net and simply not playing anything like the goalie who'd won back-to-back Vezina Trophies and Conn Smythe Trophies. Shero decided to switch to Stephenson in goal. Wayne went the rest of the way.

Game 2 at the Spectrum could have gone either way. The game went to overtime, knotted at 1–1. In a personally thrilling moment, my brother and I drew the assists as Leach fired a shot past veteran Gerry Cheevers at 13:38 of sudden death. We were now even in the series.

Games 3 and 4 were in Boston on May 2 and 4. We prevailed by scores of 5–2 and 4–2. I tallied my first and only goal of the '76 playoffs in Game 4: an insurance goal with 2:01 left in the third period. Even two years after the 1974 finals, road wins in Boston felt satisfying and vindicating after we'd had so much futility winning at the Garden.

With the upper hand in the series, we played an afternoon game at the Spectrum for Game 5 on May 6. This game was the one in which Leach tore the Bruins apart with five goals (numbers 11, 12, 13, 14, and 15 for him in the playoffs). We won, 6–3, to close out to series and win the Campbell Conference championship.

I know all the legends about Game 5 regarding whether Reggie was outright drunk or just severely hung over on the day of the game. There's no doubt about the latter, but I'll add that a lot of Flyers had a late night on May 5. As for the stories about Leach being passed out and revived just in time to play, if that's what actually happened, I didn't see it. I suspect that tale is exaggerated.

Whatever the case, thank goodness Leach was available to play with MacLeish sidelines. The "Rifle" kept right on scoring in the Cup Final. Think about it: between the regular season and the playoffs, Reggie scored 80 goals that year! It was for good reason that he became the first player on a team that failed to win the Stanley Cup to be awarded the Conn Smythe Trophy.

The operative phrase here, though, is "team that failed to win the Stanley Cup." I touched on the '76 finals at the start of this chapter so as not to have to relive it at the end. The way that season ended was crushing to us.

To me, the 1973–74 season was the culmination of a dream. The 1974–75 campaign was proof that we belonged on top. The 1975–76 season was another thrill ride that went off the rails before we could properly finish it. That's a gnawing feeling even all these decades later. This time around, we didn't quite have enough to push over the finish line to a third straight championship.

We'd never get this close again. Slowly but surely, our grip started to slip.

CHAPTER 13

Shattered and Rebuilt

The first Canada Cup tournament was played in September 1976. Jimmy was selected for Team Canada, the eventual gold medalist. My brother played extremely well until, on September 5 at the Montreal Forum, he was knocked out of the lineup by a slapshot from Team USA defenseman Gary Sargent that hit him flush in the face. Jimmy suffered a fractured cheekbone.

It was a very scary situation. Being the competitor that Jimmy was and still is, however, he was in the Flyers' lineup for opening night of the regular season.

My memories of my final three seasons in the NHL—1976–77 and 1977–78 with the Flyers and 1978–79 with the Colorado Rockies—are not as happy as the ones from 1972–73 through the Cup Semifinals of '76.

On the positive side, the Flyers reached the Cup semis in both 1977 and 1978, making it five straight years under Shero that we made it at least to the semifinal round. With the hindsight of decades, I realize now that this in and of itself is a good accomplishment even though we "only" won the Stanley Cup twice.

However, when you are wired to be competitive, that's not much comfort.

Starting with the 1976 Cup Final through my final season playing in Philadelphia, I felt our grip slipping with each passing year. I couldn't enjoy the ride when I felt like our one desired destination—another Stanley Cup championship—was moving further and further away from us. To be honest, it started to feel like we were gazing in a rearview mirror rather than looking at the horizon ahead.

In 1976–77, we still had the second-best record in the NHL, winning the Patrick Division with 112 points. We were still dominant on home ice, ranked second in the NHL in regular-season goals scored and third in goals against average. MacLeish was back, leading our club with 49 goals and 97 points. Parent was healthier and had a bit of a bounce-back season.

There were still some fun times that season. We had a 20-game unbeaten streak from November 16, 1976, through January 1, 1977. During that stretch, we posted a 15-0-5 record.

Keith Allen added some good talent to our roster over the course of the season. That was particularly true on defense when the club was dealing with injuries. Bob "the Count" Dailey, a huge-framed (six-foot-five, 220 pounds) right-handed defenseman with a booming slap shot, was an excellent addition in a January trade with Vancouver for Larry Goodenough and Jack McIlhargey. A few weeks later, we added Rick Lapointe in a deal with Detroit for Terry Murray, Steve Coates, Bob "Dreamboat" Richie, and Dave Kelly.

The reinforcements were needed. On December 18, 1976, Jimmy suffered a serious eye injury when he was on the receiving end of a high stick from Jerry Butler of the St. Louis Blues. A hard contact lens broke in his eye. Jimmy sustained permanent retinal damage and spent four days in Wills Eye Hospital. Eighteen days and 10 games later, he returned to the Flyers' lineup.

On an individual level, I experienced a career highlight when both Jimmy and I were named to the Campbell Conference All-Star team for the 1977 NHL All-Star Game. The game was played in Vancouver, making it relatively easy for our relatives and friends from Smithers to attend. My father posed for an on-ice photo with Jimmy and me in our All-Star uniforms.

For whatever reason—certainly not by design—the 1976–77 season ended up being the best offensive season of my NHL career. I reached the 30-point mark for the first and only time in the NHL (four goals and a

I played in my second and final NHL All-Star Game during the 1976–77 season. The game was held in Vancouver. Here, fellow Campbell Conference All-Star defenseman Jimmy Watson and I pose with our father. With the game being held in British Columbia, albeit a haul from Smithers, numerous friends and family members attended.

career-high 26 assists). I attribute that to the fact that Shero and Nykoluk opened things up a little more for defensemen beyond Bladon to attack a little more often. I wasn't deliberately trying to counterattack or jump in the play more often. That's just how it worked out in terms of opportunity.

From an outside point of view, I don't know if other people saw anything all that different about our team in the 1976–77 regular season from the ones we had the previous three seasons. From the inside, though, I was a little concerned. I didn't speak out publicly about it until after the season—even then, I didn't say everything that was on my mind—but things were changing in ways that worried me.

First and foremost, we weren't the same united front on and off the ice that we'd been before. We no longer came and left the building as an entire team. When a team has sustained success, it's almost inevitable that there's some pettiness and egos. We weren't the first or the last championship team to experience it. Hell, it happens even more nowadays.

Player A believes he deserves a bigger role. Player B starts worrying about what this guy or that guy is earning salary wise after the newspaper beat writer got wind of someone's raise. Player C is aging and resents incoming competition for his job. Player D's and E's wives had a falling out, and it eventually puts a strain on the players' once-close relationship off the ice.

These aren't specific things that happened with our team, just common examples of things that arise in all sports, including hockey. In the broader sense, we were still "walking together forever"—and we do to this day. But, for various reasons, we were no longer as team-first as we'd collectively been before.

The passage of time was one such reason. I think when you're a young player, there's a tendency to be naïve and think you'll mostly have the same teammates for many years. In your head, you know it's a business. In your heart, it's tough when your championship roster slowly but inevitably has fewer and fewer returning players each year.

Shortly before the 1976–77 season, Keith Allen traded Dave Schultz to the LA Kings. The move was unpopular with the fans and even with Mr. Snider himself.

Ed Snider was a sentimental guy, especially where the Flyers were concerned. For the next two years, the owner often pressed Allen to bring back "the Hammer."

Several family members, including our mom, paid Jimmy and me a visit in Philadelphia during the 1976–77 season. Here's mom with Jim.

It wasn't that Allen disliked Schultzy, either. But the GM believed, correctly, that the rise of young winger Paul Holmgren and young center Mel Bridgman had us more than covered in the toughness department and that both were also upgrades in overall talent. That's strictly a compliment to Homer and Mel, not a slight to Dave.

Schultzy could do more than just fight, and he was important to our two Cup teams. Schultz supplied us with courage to play the same way on the road that we did at home. He made physically strong but somewhat timid teammates feel emboldened to join the battle. He could play the game, too.

You'll never hear me say otherwise. Schultz wasn't just a "goon." He brought value that only his teammates and coaches—and opponents—fully grasped.

Even so, Holmgren (who later had an All-Star season and scored a hat trick in a Stanley Cup Final game) and Bridgman (later the Flyers' team captain and a player with six separate 20-plus goal seasons) were just a little better as all-around hockey players than Dave.

Holmgren, a Minnesota native, was our first American player. We'd briefly had Washington-born Wayne Hicks on our inaugural team, and we had a few Americans in the farm system. But "Homer" was our first long-term NHL roster regular who was raised and trained in the United States. We added another American, too, that season: center Harvey Bennett, a six-foot-four, 215-pound Rhode Island native from a well-known hockey family that included brother Curt and Canadian-born father Harvey Sr.

Nowadays, roughly one in four NHL players is an American-born player. No one bats an eye. Back before the "Miracle on Ice," though, Americans were considered a bit of a novelty.

They were "tested" a little more often, especially tough guys like Paul. It didn't take too long for Homer to fit in with our team—and it helped that he and Clarkie quickly became close friends—but Paul wasn't just immediately welcomed by everyone with open arms, especially as the guy who unseated Schultzy.

Holmgren was someone who quickly earned everyone's respect as a teammate. Tough as nails. Worked his ass off to become not just a feared fighter but a reliable all-around player. Didn't complain and didn't have an ego. One thing that not many people know about Paul is that he has one hell of a good sense of humor, too. It's just ultra-dry.

Terry Crisp unofficially retired on October 1, 1976, although he was still around the team off and on and dressed as a player for us in two games (December 27 in Vancouver and March 13 in Pittsburgh). Shero mentored Terry in becoming a coach—he'd join our staff as an assistant coach the next season and, in 1976–77, spent time behind the Springfield Indians' bench as the AHL team's interim coach. A decade-plus later, Terry coached the Calgary Flames to a Stanley Cup championship.

Meanwhile, after hanging up the skates, Terry also laid the groundwork for what later became a prolific broadcasting career after his playing and coaching careers. Crispy has always had an energetic manner, and he loves to talk and tell stories (even more than I do). As with me and my dad, there are no strangers to Terry.

Terry and I go back together to our respective days in the Boston organization. We were fast friends then and are still friends today. We also see the game in the same old-school way. We can go years without speaking, but the next time I see him, he's got me laughing so hard that my sides hurt.

One of Terry's favorite stories to tell—and I one I like quite a bit, too—is about Barry Ashbee. Whereas Terry and I wear our hearts on our sleeves, Ashcan was much quieter and more stoic. But he had a dry wit about him, too.

As fight-filled games and bench-clearing brawls started to become more commonplace, someone asked Barry about all the fighting. With a straight face he said, the way he saw it, "if the game doesn't last four hours, you're cheatin' the fans!"

He was kidding. Not everyone got the joke.

The biggest reason the 1976–77 season was a downer for our team is that we lost Barry to leukemia.

The first sign of trouble: Ashcan noticed random bruises all over his arms, legs, and hands. There was no obvious physical cause for the bruises. He hadn't recently fallen or been struck by anything. He also felt unusually fatigued. Barry and his wife, Donna, looked in a medical book they had at the house. They saw that these were potential signs of bone marrow cancer.

Barry stayed on with the Flyers at first in his assistant coach role. He told no one around the team, except Crispy, about the bruising and his concerns that it might be serious. He also spoke with our team doctor, Dr. Viner.

Dr. Viner was very concerned, telling Barry to come to his office the next morning for tests. Blood and bone marrow tests confirmed the doctor's and the Ashbee family's worst fears: Barry had leukemia. He'd immediately have to undergo chemotherapy. Bone marrow transplants were still considered experimental at this time, but efforts were made to find a match. Without it, Barry's prognosis was grim, even with chemotherapy.

If Barry had his way, the team would not have known until the end what he was dealing with. We were getting ready to prepare for the playoffs, and he didn't want to be the cause of a distraction or for our players to wallow in sympathy. However, it was getting impossible to hide the truth.

Barry participated in one additional practice and couldn't traverse the ice more than once. Afterward, Barry showed his scarlet, bruised skin to fellow assistant coach Nykoluk. Ashbee also confessed that he was slated to begin chemotherapy.

We played a first-round playoff series against Toronto, for the third straight year. This time around, we lost both Game 1 and Game 2 at the Spectrum, by scores of 3–2 and 4–1.

I don't remember much about the second game, which was played on April 13. On the morning of the game, Ashbee called Clarke and filled him in on what was going on with him. Barry told Clarkie that he was coming to the rink to level with the entire team. Dr. Viner had given a prognosis that, if Barry responded to the chemo, he could live 12 to 18 months with the form of leukemia he had. If not, the timetable was much shorter.

After all our players arrived, Barry was not there yet. It was almost time to go out on the ice for the morning skate. So Clarkie made a tough decision: he closed the door and broke the news to the rest of us. Our normally noisy room fell silent. I was stunned. So was everyone.

Barry arrived during the skate and spoke to us briefly afterward. He told us, "I don't want sympathy or 'Win one for the Gipper' stuff. I'll deal with this, and I'll beat it. I'll win. That's it."

I consider myself someone with a pretty good memory for game details. But to this day, even when I look at the box score from that night's game, it doesn't trigger much recall. We fell behind early, and we lost, 4–1. All I remember is that we all felt numb, and none of us were able to focus on hockey, even though we tried.

It was almost a relief when the series shifted to Toronto. Barry planned to watch every playoff game on TV and asked me to call him after each game. He wanted to report on my observations from the ice, and he'd share with me what he'd noticed from the broadcast. It was emotionally tough, but I was honored to be the one Ashcan wanted to dissect the game with.

The day after we arrived in Toronto, Bridgman, Saleski, Kelly, and I had a court hearing in front of Judge Hugh Locke in conjunction with the criminal charges that were filed against us during the playoff series the previous spring. Nice timing, eh?

The court in Toronto "conveniently" moved up the scheduled hearings for the four Flyers players, including me, who were criminally charged in on-ice incidents from Game 3 and Game 6 of the previous year's playoff series. The hearing was moved up to overlap with our 1977 first-round rematch with the Maple Leafs. Here, Mel Bridgman, Don Saleski, Bob Kelly (obscured), and I arrive at court. Charges were dropped against Mel and Don. Hound and I received fines.

The charges were dropped against Don and Mel. Our defense attorney, George Finlayson, recommended that Hound and I take a plea deal offered by the crown attorney. Mind you, the police officer who was struck by my stick provided testimony that it was only glancing and accidental contact. He sustained a superficial bruise that quickly healed. The female usher who had been hit by Kelly's glove suffered absolutely no injuries.

In pleading guilty to reckless endangerment, I was sentenced to a "choice" of a $750 fine or 30 days in jail. Bob was given the option of a $200 fine or five days in jail.

"Pay the fines, and be done with it," Finlayson advised. "That'll be best for everyone."

Yeah, no kidding! This one was a no-brainer. Hound and I signed the paperwork and were on our way. The Flyers paid for our fines.

In Game 3 of the series, we fell behind, 2–0, in the first period. By the end of the second period, goals by Lonsberry and Kindrachuk (power play) got us back to even on the scoreboard. We trailed again, 3–2, in the latter minutes of the third period. Fortunately, MacLeish forced overtime with a goal in the final 38 seconds of regulation. In OT, MacLeish won the game with a tally at 2:55.

Game 4 in Toronto also went to sudden death. This was a game that Clarke just would not let our team lose. We trailed in the third period, 5–2, rallied to force OT (Clarke's second goal of the game sent it to sudden death), and then came back to win in the final minute of OT on a goal by Leach. MacLeish was also a big factor in this game, collecting three assists.

Ashbee was in good spirits when I talked to him after the game. I told writer Jay Greenberg, "Ashcan gave me hell about how we played in the second period, and he talked to me about how we played a little better against [Lanny] McDonald. We were lucky to win. But we haven't played our best yet, and we're even in the series."

Game 5 was in Philly on April 19. We shut down Toronto, holding them to 21 shots, and Stephenson took care of the rest. Two goals by Leach, one in the first period and another in the third, were all the offense we needed in the 2–0 win. By the way, we held McDonald without a shot on goal after he'd been killing us all series. Lanny was out for both of our goals and took a penalty in the first period that contributed to the first Leach tally. The penalty expired, but Leach scored a couple seconds after the teams were back at full strength.

With a chance to close out the series, we went back to Toronto for Game 6. McDonald dinged us for two more goals—his 9th and 10th of the series—and we trailed in the third period by a 3–2 score on his second of the game. A couple minutes later, MacLeish tied the game. Finally, with 2:38 remaining in regulation, Lonsberry won a puck battle and sent the puck back to Dailey. "The Count" rotated the puck to Jimmy, and my brother scored what proved to be the series-winning goal.

Although our '76 series against the Maple Leafs went seven games, and this one was over in six, I believe the '77 series was the harder one mentally. It's not easy to come back when you lose the first two games at home, trail late in a couple other games, and must rally.

After playing Toronto for the third straight year, we drew Boston for the third playoff year of the last four. Every game was close, but, as with the Cup Final against Montreal the previous spring, we lost in four straight games: 4–3 and 5–4 overtime losses at the Spectrum in Games 1 and 2, followed by 2–1 (overtime) and 3–0 defeats in Boston.

During the Boston series, I continued to have my postgame report conversations with Ashbee, but I could tell Barry's condition was deteriorating. He wasn't as engaged in the discussion and got tired easily. When I'd try to ask him about how he was feeling, he didn't want to discuss it. I knew in my gut he didn't have long.

Barry died on May 12, 1977: eleven days after the end of the playoff series against Boston. As much as I rode the emotional wave of winning and losing throughout (and even after) my playing career, the untimely death of a teammate and friend put a lot of perspective on what's truly important in life and what's just a game.

Barry left behind his beloved wife, Donna. Their children, Danny and Heather, were still kids at the time. That was true tragedy. A lost playoff series was trivial by comparison. But Barry, like me, was a hockey lifer through and through. He hated the idea of causing any distractions to our team during the playoffs, and he was stoic by nature anyway.

Donna was a strong woman and a tremendous human being. She passed away a couple years ago, joining Barry in heaven. Danny and Heather grew up to be fine people, too, and I know Barry would have been as proud as Donna of their accomplishments. Danny still presents the Barry Ashbee Trophy to the winner of the Flyers' team award for the best defenseman.

His dad himself presented the award the first two years after its creation, when Moose and Jimmy won it.

All Flyers players wore this No. 4 memorial patch in 1977–78 to honor the memory of the late Barry Ashbee. The season would be my final one for the Flyers.

Overall, the 1976–77 season was a bittersweet time in my career. It was more than just the playoff loss to Boston. We had the second-best record in the NHL, but it was 20 points behind Montreal. Even if we'd found our way past Boston in the Cup semis, I don't think we'd have had enough to beat the Canadiens. Hell, even within the Patrick Division during the regular season, the fast-rising Islanders were gaining on us.

When the season was over, I spoke openly with the local media (as did Jimmy) about my concerns with the direction of our team. Despite our regular season win-loss record, of the two teams, we were no longer the harder-working team on an each-and-every-night basis. The guys in the room weren't as close as before. Selfishness and ego had crept in with some players. There were even guys who started grumbling about their usage under Shero or griping they were underpaid by management.

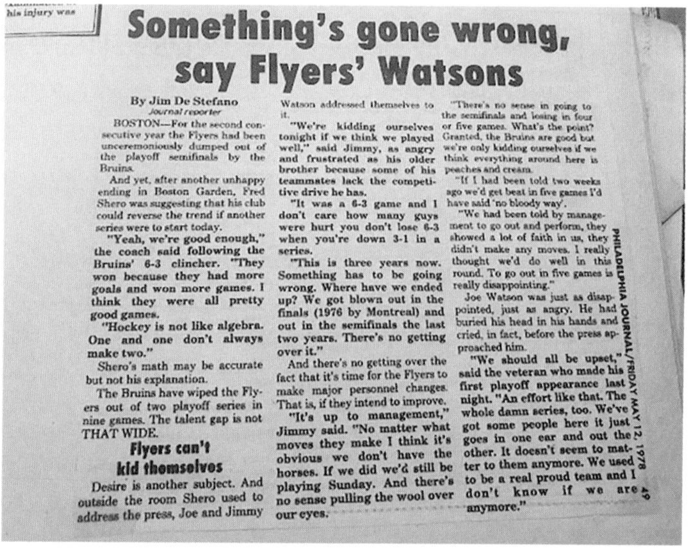

his injury was

Something's gone wrong, say Flyers' Watsons

By Jim De Stefano
Journal reporter

BOSTON—For the second consecutive year the Flyers had been unceremoniously dumped out of the playoff semifinals by the Bruins.

And yet, after another unhappy ending in Boston Garden, Fred Shero was suggesting that his club could reverse the trend if another series were to start today.

"Yeah, we're good enough," the coach said following the Bruins' 6-3 clincher. "They won because they had more goals and won more games. I think they were all pretty good games.

"Hockey is not like algebra. One and one don't always make two."

Shero's math may be accurate but not his explanation.

The Bruins have wiped the Flyers out of two playoff series in nine games. The talent gap is not THAT WIDE.

Flyers can't kid themselves

Desire is another subject. And outside the room Shero used to address the press, Joe and Jimmy Watson addressed themselves to it.

"We're kidding ourselves tonight if we think we played well," said Jimmy, as angry and frustrated as his older brother because some of his teammates lack the competitive drive he has.

"It was a 6-3 game and I don't care how many guys were hurt you don't lose 6-3 when you're down 3-1 in a series.

"This is three years now. Something has to be going wrong. Where have we ended up? We got blown out in the finals (1976 by Montreal) and out in the semifinals the last two years. There's no getting over it."

And there's no getting over the fact that it's time for the Flyers to make major personnel changes. That is, if they intend to improve.

"It's up to management," Jimmy said. "No matter what moves they make I think it's obvious we don't have the horses. If we did we'd still be playing Sunday. And there's no sense pulling the wool over our eyes.

"There's no sense in going to the semifinals and losing in four or five games. What's the point? Granted, the Bruins are good but we're only kidding ourselves if we think everything around here is peaches and cream.

"If I had been told two weeks ago we'd get beat in five games I'd have said 'no bloody way'.

"We had been told by management to go out and perform, they showed a lot of faith in us, they didn't make any moves. I really thought we'd do well in this round. To go out in five games is really disappointing."

Joe Watson was just as disappointed, just as angry. He had buried his head in his hands and cried, in fact, before the press approached him.

"We should all be upset," said the veteran who made his first playoff appearance last night. "An effort like that. The whole damn series, too. We've got some people here it just goes in one ear and out the other. It doesn't seem to matter to them anymore. We used to be a real proud team and I don't know if we are anymore."

PHILADELPHIA JOURNAL/FRIDAY MAY 12, 1978 49

The Flyers reached the Cup semifinal in both 1977 and 1978, but, as a team, we weren't as focused and united as our clubs from 1972–73 through 1975–76. Jimmy and I felt compelled to speak out publicly about it following our back-to-back series losses in Boston in '77 and '78.

None of that is good for a team. I couldn't sit back and say nothing. We weren't yet in crisis, but we needed a course correction before getting to that point.

Meanwhile, Fred himself seemed to get into spats with Ed Snider and Keith Allen every offseason, threatening to quit. It happened yearly, so I think our tendency was to just say, "That's just Freddy being Freddy." In hindsight, though, you could read between the lines and see that Shero wouldn't always be bluffing about a desire to leave. There'd come a time—and probably sooner than later—when his tenure would come to an end.

Sharp as he was, I think Keith Allen saw this even before I did. That's why the gradual breakup of the "Broad Street Bullies" started in '76 and accelerated with each passing year.

The 1977–78 campaign was my final playing season with the Flyers. It would also be Dorny's last year before he retired. Bernie would play his final full season, before a devastating eye injury prematurely ended his career the next year.

After Barry's passing, Crispy was formally named as a full-time assistant coach. Management reassigned Nykoluk from being an assistant coach to "director of player development." An old junior and pro rival turned good friend, Pat Quinn, became our other assistant coach. Quinner had just retired as a player.

As a team, we were still very good by some standards: 105 points overall and still very tough to beat at the Spectrum (29-6-5 home record, 170 goals scored, and only 80 allowed). We took our sixth straight trip to the Stanley Cup Semifinal.

Even so, the cracks were now starting to become more noticeable from the inside and perhaps even from the outside. We were now a very ordinary road club (16-14-10 record, 126 goals scored to 120 allowed). We finished second in the Patrick Division after being a perennial first-place club. Players who'd been towers of strength in our Cup years were now aging—me included—and were slowly starting to be phased out. In terms of team unity, the subtle drifting apart of our group from the previous season was getting a little more out in the open.

I'd wrenched my neck in March of '77, missing three games. I still wasn't 100 percent when I got back but felt I'd already missed too much time in the heart of the stretch drive. In 1977–78, I had various nagging physical issues—not what you want at age 34 in the NHL on an expiring contract—and periodically got sat by Shero.

Oddly enough, I nearly didn't play when we played Atlanta at home on November 20, 1977. I'd missed the previous game in Minnesota, and my skating was still hindered from a severe shin bone bruise (of course, Kelly made a wisecrack: "Who could tell?"). Jim McKenzie worked on me to enable me to play.

After watching me intently during the morning skate, Shero was still skeptical that I'd be able to go.

"Are you just hurting, Joe, or are you injured? Don't bullshit me," he said.

In hockey, that's a key distinction: A player who's hurting can suck it up and play. Someone who is injured probably shouldn't be playing. Well, I was right on the borderline. I insisted on playing, and because I was a veteran the head coach trusted, Shero said OK.

Lo and behold, I scored two goals in our 4–0 win over the Flames. It was my first and only two-goal game. Maybe a different way to put it is that I spread out my 38 career regular-season NHL goals.

On the afternoon of December 11, a Sunday, we had an afternoon home game against the lowly Cleveland Barons (the relocated California Golden Seals). We trounced them by an 11–1 score. It was the game of Tom Bladon's life. Bomber set an NHL record for a defenseman with eight points in the game: four goals and four assists.

A couple of humorous memories stand out from that day. I had a party that night at one of my favorite restaurants (both then and now): the Towne House in Media, Pennsylvania. With all the goals that were scored and a lengthy delay as penalties were sorted out after an epic fight between Bridgman and Cleveland's Randy Holt, I remember getting anxious that we might miss our reservation time at the restaurant.

Also, when Bladon scored the third of his four goals, Clarke retrieved the puck from the net for Sparky to keep as a memento of his hat trick. Tommy declined it.

"What, you think you're gonna get more?" Clarkie said.

We had a good chuckle in the locker room about it. But Bladon got the last laugh. After the game, our PR director Joe Kadlec called Tom over. Wearing his union suit after already having taken off his uniform, Bladon posed with the pucks from his fourth goal and his fourth assist. The ear-to-ear smile on his face tells the story. It was the kind of game we grow up dreaming about. In his case, it actually happened!

As the season progressed, I played decently and still managed to be +23 in 65 games. But nagging injuries felt slower to heal. Increasingly, there were times when I would have been able to play, but younger D such as Kevin "Kato" McCarthy drew into the lineup.

Late in the season, my playing time was sporadic. I only dressed in three of the final seven regular-season games, playing on the road in Colorado and Vancouver as well as the last game of the season (a 3–1 home loss to Minnesota). Overall, I played 65 of our 80 games: not terrible but also not the workload I'd gotten used to carrying under Shero.

In the playoffs, the Flyers dispatched the Rockies in two games in a best-of-three miniseries. Philly then took out the Buffalo Sabres, four games to one, in the Stanley Cup quarterfinals. Yet again, Philly drew Boston in the Stanley Cup Semifinals: fourth time in five years. Boston prevailed in five games. The lone Philadelphia win was a 3–1 victory at the Spectrum. The only playoff game that I dressed in that spring was Game 5 against the Bruins. We were eliminated as Boston sent us home in a 6–3 decision.

While he was still coaching the Flyers, Shero secretly had meetings with New York Rangers management. He was more interested in becoming a general manager (which wasn't going to happen in Philly with Allen entrenched as GM) than in continuing to coach. He struck a secret deal to fill a dual role for the Rangers as their head coach and general manager and then make a transition solely to GM duties. The Flyers discovered what was up, and it caused a huge controversy.

Philadelphia filed a tampering complaint with the NHL against the Rangers. Eventually, they settled the dispute. The Flyers allowed Shero to break the final year of his contract to leave for New York and become the Rangers' coach/GM. In return, the Rangers traded the seventh overall pick of the 1978 NHL Amateur Draft to the Flyers. Shero took Nykoluk along with him as an assistant coach.

Another major change was this: the Flyers traded Kindrachuk, Lonsberry, and Bladon to the Penguins in exchange for the sixth overall pick of the 1978 Draft. Philly landed two pretty damn good hockey players in the Draft, which took place on June 15: defenseman Behn Wilson and center Ken "the Rat" Linseman.

I had an offseason discussion with Keith Allen. He was willing to sign me to a one-year contract extension at a small raise but wanted me to know that he anticipated my role being further reduced. He asked me if I preferred to be a part-time player and stay with the Flyers or to be traded to somewhere I could get more playing time. If the latter, where might I want to go?

I told him Colorado was my first choice, because I knew I'd get playing time there and could mentor their young defensemen. Additionally, the opportunity to regularly go skiing appealed to me. But I wouldn't have minded going elsewhere if I'd get playing time, including Pittsburgh. I felt like I still had something to give as a regular player. However, the decision was ultimately up to the Flyers. If they opted to keep me, I'd stay and play whatever role they saw fit. I signed a contract extension. Weeks later, the Flyers sold my contract to the Colorado Rockies.

On September 1, Keith wrote me a letter. The correspondence touched my heart and broke it at the same time when I received it in the mail a day or two later. Even before I opened the envelope, I knew I'd get emotional reading what was inside.

Dear Joe,

Writing this letter is not easy. Saying goodbye to a friend never is.

However, I just had to drop you a note to let you know how much I appreciate all that you have done for the Flyers and for me.

As you know, we spent many great years together—years which I will never forget. What we accomplished was almost unbelievable. And I want you to know that none of it would have been possible without the contributions you made.

Joe, through the good times and the bad, you always gave it everything you had. You were a leader both on and off the ice, and you certainly can be proud of your accomplishments, even though you probably never received all the credit you deserved. I know that I am certainly proud to have worked with you.

Unfortunately, nothing lasts forever. After much soul-searching, I felt some moves had to be made with the club. I felt we just had to move some kids into the lineup. After all you had done for us, I felt it wouldn't be fair for you to sit around as the seventh defenseman. For your own sake, I feel it will be better playing regularly in Colorado than sitting around with us.

Trading a player, especially one of your stature, is the toughest part of my job—a part which I detest, but, unfortunately, one which sometimes has to be done. I just hope that you understand and that we will always remain friends.

In closing, let me thank you once again and wish you, Marianne, and Ryan all the best.

Sincerely, Keith

I got choked up reading the letter. I still get a bit emotional to this day when I think about it. Even if I hadn't come back to work for the Flyers after my playing days, there was no way that Keith Allen and I would not have remained friends. I loved the man as much as I loved Ed Snider.

Keith lived to be 90 years old, passing away in a nursing home on February 4, 2014. Until the ravages of dementia took their toll near the end of the Hockey Hall of Famer's life, his mind was sharp as a tack. I am glad I had the opportunity to visit with him. Even near the end, he still had a twinkle in his eye and was a true gentleman to those he met.

Until near the end of his life, I saw Keith at many Flyers Alumni gatherings. It was hard not to smile when he was around. He was simply a top-quality man, let alone hockey man.

Keith had a lovely family, too. His wife of 65 years, Joyce, was a gem. While I was in the process of writing this book, I attended his posthumous induction into the Philadelphia Sports Hall of Fame and had a chance to catch up with his children and other family members. Keith's son, Blake Allen, wrote a good book about him called *Keith the Thief*. It's a really good read if you want to learn more about Keith as a dad, hockey executive, and human being.

My time in Colorado was brief, as fate would have it. Even so, I am grateful for how kindly Rockies owner Arthur Imperatore treated me both during and after my stint with the hockey team. I liked Denver, and I still love the beauty of the mountains in Colorado—some of the best skiing in the world.

We had mostly young players on the team, which was coached by Pat Kelly the previous season and the early portion of 1978–79. Pat's a man who paid his dues for decades, many times over, as a minor-league player and longtime minor-league coach. He finally got his long-coveted chance in the NHL with the Rockies.

Before the season started, I was named captain of the Rockies. I wore the "C" on my sweater with pride. I hope I was able to pass along some of what had been taught to me over the years. Our team struggled, going 3-14-4 over the first 20 games and 15-53-12 overall.

I dressed in each of the first 16 games of the season. Games 13 (road) and 15 (home) were played against the Flyers. My return to Philadelphia, with Jimmy on the Philadelphia side and old friend and teammate Gary Dornhoefer (by now a television broadcaster for the Prism network) interviewing us, was almost a surreal experience. The ovation that the Flyers' fans gave me—holy smokes—had me wiping away a few tears.

The game was tied, 3–3, after two periods. The Flyers pulled away in the third period and won, 6–4. Bill Barber scored twice for Philly, while ex-Rockies forward Barry Dean had a goal and an assist.

The final NHL game that I played, start to finish, was on November 10, 1978. The Rockies hosted the Flyers at McNichols Arena. We played to a 2–2 tie (which felt like a win, given our place in the standings) with Leach and Dean scoring for the Flyers and Paul Gardner and Ralph Klassen tallying for us.

In 1978–79, I played briefly for the Colorado Rockies and served as team captain. Unfortunately, I suffered a serious leg injury that abruptly ended my career.

The next night, we had a road game in St. Louis against the Blues.

During the second period, the Blues dumped the puck in our defensive zone, and I went back to retrieve it as our goalie, Michel Plasse, stopped the puck and left it for me behind the net. Just as I was reaching for the puck, St. Louis right winger Wayne Babych pushed me in the back. To make matters worse, as I crashed into the boards, my right skate caught a rut in the ice.

For a moment, I was too stunned to realize what happened. I started to try standing up. Linesman John D'Amico, who was standing near me said, "Don't move, Joe! Don't move."

I couldn't move, anyway. D'Amico told me not to look, but I had to. My right leg was almost a 90-degree angle from my knee. My left leg, my right knee, and my right leg almost looked like three legs.

Immediately, I knew my career was over. At the hospital, I learned that, for lack of a better term, my femur shattered. There were 13 separate breaks. That's not the way anyone wants to go out.

All sorts of thoughts went through my head.

Why me? I try to be a good person, a good Catholic. I go to church. I pray. I work hard. I never cheat the game. Was this a punishment? Maybe I should have just taken a lesser role in Philly. Was I being too proud? If not, why did the good Lord let this happen to me?

Ultimately, I accepted that God works in mysterious ways. He had another plan for me. I just didn't know what it was yet. As hard as it was to accept the way my playing career ended, it ultimately strengthened my faith.

Initially, I was hospitalized in St. Louis. A doctor told me that I might never walk again if surgeries—I'd need more than one—and rehabilitation failed. I had two surgeries while in St. Louis. Four more would follow over the next 18 months alone. Doctors took bone from my hip and put it in my leg. I had electrotherapy every four hours to stimulate healing.

I was in a hard cast that went up to my chest for 10-plus months. My right leg became two-and-a-half inches shorter than the left. Yes, even once I was able to walk again, that made daily life agonizing. I'm getting ahead of myself here but, when I was subsequently able to skate again and play in Alumni hockey games, for many years I had a lift in my right skate.

While I was in the hospital in St. Louis, various Blues players stopped by to visit me. Gary Unger came. Bernie Federko came. Steve Durbano—a guy who once triggered a huge brawl with the Flyers when he hit our assistant trainer Jim McKenzie in the mouth with his stick and knocked out teeth—came by several times. He'd bring in a case of beer, and we'd down each and every can. That didn't make the nurses too happy, but I appreciated the company as well as the beers.

One Blues player who never stopped by—never even called me in my hospital room—was Babych. I few months later, he sent me a letter. He said he hoped I'd be all right but was surprised that some people seemed to think the check that injured me was a dirty hit. I wrote back saying, in my opinion, it was a cheap shot. The fact that he'd never had the decency to visit me in person or pick up the phone to call said to me that he was feeling guilty. Deep down, Wayne knew the push in the back had been reckless at best and dirty at worst even though he wasn't outright trying to injure me.

No response. Never heard from Babych again. Meanwhile, I was contacted by friends and colleagues from across the NHL: from Philadelphia, of course, but also from every other team.

A few months after the injury, I transferred to the University of Pennsylvania Hospital in Philly. I remained in traction. I received more cards, letters, and phone calls than I could count and had dozens of visitors from both the hockey realm and outside. To this day, I am greatly appreciative. It made a horrible time in my life more bearable.

The kindness I received, honestly, was humbling. *Philadelphia Daily News* society page columnist Larry Fields contacted me several times. He asked me what, if anything, I'd like to get now that I was back home in Philadelphia.

I knew immediately.

"I want a steak from Dave Shore's restaurant," I said.

There's a backstory here. During the early 1970s, the area around 12th and Camac streets used to be a great place to go for a steam bath, a massage, and then a steak at Dave Shore's. Ed Van Impe used to come along with me.

We were always treated like royalty. The funny part is these two professional hockey players from western Canada were hardly the usual clientele! Most of the regulars in those parts were old Jewish men, some of whom spoke Yiddish to one another. The steaks at Dave Shore's were my favorite in town. The restaurant is long gone, but the memories remain.

Anyway, when the restaurant's manager, Rose Linchuk, heard that I was craving one of their steaks, she delivered one personally to me in my hospital room and refused to accept any money. It was nice to be back home. To me, I have two homes: Philadelphia and Smithers.

Ed Snider told me that he'd like me to come back to work for the Flyers after I healed enough to leave the hospital. Pat Quinn suggested that I do some scouting for the team when I felt up to it.

I started to see that even though I'd never play professionally again, there was a future for me in and around the Philadelphia Flyers organization that meant so much to me. Maybe that was the greater plan for me.

I still had no idea how long it would last. As it turned out, in various and widely differing capacities, I'd work for the Flyers again from 1979 until retiring in early 2021.

By the way, I ended up having a total of nine surgeries on my right leg. Ultimately, through a final corrective procedure, both legs are now the same length. As far as my mobility goes, I felt better in my 60s and 70s than I did in my late 30s, 40s, or 50s.

CHAPTER 14

Postgame

I'm not sure who first said, "Today is the first day of the rest of your life," but it's a great inspirational saying. Throughout our lives, we have various turning points and fresh starts.

For me, one of the biggest turning points happened in 1979, when I went back to work for the Philadelphia Flyers organization. I played for the team for 11 years, but, among all the different nonplaying roles that I held before my retirement in 2021, my "second Flyers career" lasted 42 years.

When I sat down with my coauthor, Bill Meltzer, over lunch at the Towne House in Media to discuss how we should go about covering the years after my NHL career, it was Bill's idea to do it as various small chapters within a chapter rather than one long chronology. I liked that suggestion, so the final chapter is organized a little differently than the rest of the book.

Advanced scout/part-time assistant coach

From the 1979–80 to 1982–83 seasons, my main jobs with the Flyers were as a special assignments scout and as a part-time assistant coaching staff under head coach Pat Quinn.

For several years after my retirement from playing, I served as an advance scout and part-time assistant coach for the Flyers under Pat Quinn and Bob McCammon.

Sometimes, the most hated on-ice rivals end up making for some of your best friends when you get to know them off the ice and/or later go to work for the same team. For me, that was the case with Glen Sather. I hated him as an opponent in junior hockey when I was with Estevan, but then we hit it off as teammates in Oklahoma City. We're friends to this day.

It was the same with the late Pat Quinn. We never played together in junior or pro hockey, and he was someone my teams and I detested playing against. Later, as I got to know "the Big Irishman" as a person, I found it impossible to dislike Pat.

Quinner was quite the fierce competitor—we connected in that regard when we were finally on the same side—and he struck an intimidating presence with his huge frame and ever-present cigars. At the same time, he was also a kind-hearted human being away from the ice. One hell of a sense of humor. A family man who adored his lovely wife, Sandra, and two daughters. Pat was also a bright guy, who obtained a college degree in economics while still an active player and later graduated law school during the offseasons of his coaching career.

Advanced scouting of opponents—nowadays called "prescouts"—was in its infancy in 1979. Pat asked me to perform that role for the Flyers. I'd travel far and wide to watch games involving upcoming Flyers opponents to observe their systems and players. Was this a team we could aggressively forecheck into turnovers? Which of their players were hot? Who was struggling? Things of that nature, back in the days when few teams (outside of those coached by Roger Neilson) made use of video study.

During the 1979–80 season, the Flyers assembled a North American pro sports record 35-game unbeaten streak (25-0-10). They shattered not only our previous franchise record 23 games from the 1975–76 season but also the Montreal Canadiens' 28-game streak in 1977–78 that supplanted ours for the NHL all-time record. To this day, the 35-gamer stands as an unbroken and unmatched record. Now that games in the NHL can no longer end in ties, I think the record is unbreakable.

At any rate, throughout the Flyers' record streak, Quinn kept me on the road. I logged more travel miles than I could count. Honestly, it got exhausting. I wasn't happy when the Flyers' streak finally ended on January 7, 1980, but I wasn't sad either.

Actually, before the start of the season, I was also offered a chance to be a full-time assistant coach with the Washington Capitals. Their second-season head coach, the late Danny Belisle, was a friend of mine.

Danny had been the head coach of the Philadelphia Firebirds when the minor-league franchise was a Flyers' affiliate. Before leaving to take the Capitals' job, Danny was mentored as a coach by Fred Shero, along with Quinn, Terry Crisp, and Bob McCammon.

I was flattered by the chance to coach in the NHL, but the timing didn't feel right. I'd have had to move my family from the Philadelphia suburbs to Maryland or DC. Also, there wouldn't have been much, if any, job stability with the Capitals organization of that time. They were still a young, struggling franchise and had been through various head and assistant coaches in just a few years.

Turns out that I made the right decision. Danny was fired by the Caps just 16 games into the season after the club started out 4-10-2. I felt bad for him, but I'd probably have been out the door, too, almost as quickly as I'd come in.

Danny was a hockey lifer. He had a brief NHL playing career with the Rangers and the NHL head coaching stint with the Capitals but was around the game most of his life for decades at various lower levels. He was a good person and a good hockey man. He passed away on November 28, 2022, at the age of 85.

If the right opportunity had come up at the right time, I would have had interest in NHL coaching. Actually, I gained a little NHL coaching experience with the Flyers although "coach" was never listed in my job title. It was part supplement to my scouting role and part happenstance.

On Leap Day 1980—February 29—the NHL suspended Quinn for his actions in a brawl-filled 7–3 win in Vancouver the previous Friday. Pat received a three-game suspension. Since Bob Clarke was still an active player in addition to being Quinn's assistant coach, the Flyers asked me to step behind the bench as acting head coach for three games. I made my debut in a March 2 home game. Unfortunately, we lost 5–1 to Montreal.

Two nights later, the Colorado Rockies came to town. The Flyers held a special night in my honor, bringing my mom, my brothers, and my father in from Smithers. Of course, Jimmy was also there because he was still an active player on the Flyers at the time. Ed Snider and Keith Allen were on the ice for the ceremony. The Flyers and Rockies players alike stood up at their respective benches during the ceremony and tapped their sticks on the boards.

On March 4, 1980, with the Colorado Rockies visiting the Spectrum, the Flyers held a special night in my honor. Here, I am shaking hands with Ed Snider. My mom and my brothers were also on hand for the pregame ceremony.

It was very emotional and humbling to receive such an honor. Years later, I'd be inducted into the Flyers Hall of Fame in 1996 and be there for Jimmy's induction in 2016. Jimmy and I were inducted together into the British Columbia Sports Hall of Fame in 2002. Jimmy is also in the Philadelphia Sports Hall of Fame (class of 2016) for his 10 years and five All-Star Games as a Flyer, and we're both in as part of the 1974 and 1975 Stanley Cup teams' collective induction. Jimmy retired as a player after the 1981–82 season due to a severe back injury and other accumulated injuries.

The Flyers inducted me into the team's Hall of Fame in 2006. In 2018, my brother Jimmy joined me in receiving that honor. To date, we are the only brother duo in the Flyers' HOF.

Receiving accolades isn't why anyone gets into hockey. But I feel very grateful for each and every one of those honors: grateful to my teammates and coaches who helped make it possible, to the organizations that inducted us and gave us the chance to share those special nights with our family members, and, most of all, to the fans who supported us when we played and showed such caring even after our professional playing days were done.

After my brief stint as Flyers acting head coach (the games went on Pat's career NHL coaching record), I primarily went back to the scouting role for a while. But Pat had me come to training camp as an instructor in 1980, 1981, and 1982, and I later served as a part-time assistant coach in season working with the defensemen up until the 1982–83 campaign.

Pat led the Flyers to a Stanley Cup Final in the spring of 1980 and had a successful head coaching tenure overall in parts of four seasons: 141-73-48 regular season record (.630 points percentage) and 22-17 postseason record. However, things started going south in the second half of 1981–82, and the Flyers fired Pat with eight games left in the season. He was replaced by Maine Mariners head coach Bob McCammon.

Oddly enough, McCammon started the 1978–79 season as Flyers head coach while Quinn started as Maine's head coach. Midseason, they switched places. While this was going down, I was playing for Colorado and then laid up in the hospital in St. Louis and Philadelphia with my career-ending leg injury. Jimmy filled me in on some of the details, but, honestly, what went on around the Flyers during the initial McCammon-to-Quinn changeover behind the bench wasn't front and center in my focus at the time.

After the Flyers' reversal of coaching course from Quinn back to McCammon, I was more directly affected. "Cagey," as everyone called Bob, kept me on as a part-time assistant coach for the 1982–83 season, although my job title was still "special assignment scout."

I liked Cagey as a person. He was a pleasant fellow, and he'd had a lot of AHL-level success in leading the Maine Mariners to back-to-back Calder Cup championships and three runs to the finals. Away from the rink, Bob and I always got along fine.

When it came to the hockey side, though, Bob and I had differing philosophies, whereas Quinn and I had often been in lockstep. I tried not to step on Cagey's toes since he was the head coach and had a full-time staff. I was on the Class of 1923 Rink ice for practices as a part-time assistant. However, my observation was that the team lacked defensive structure. I had to be honest about what I saw and what I thought was needed to correct it.

Shortly before the 1983–84 season, I was told by McCammon, who spent that year in the dual role of head coach and general manager (Keith Allen went into semiretirement but kept an advisory role) before being dismissed from both jobs, that my services were no longer needed as an assistant.

"It wasn't working out," I said to the *Philadelphia Daily News*. "Cagey and I weren't seeing eye to eye. What the [head] coach says, goes. I understand where he was coming from. That's fine. I don't feel offended."

Pat Quinn, who was born the same year as me, passed away on November 23, 2014, at the age of 71 after a bout with cancer. Cagey died on December 23, 2021, at the age of 80, due to complications from dementia. I miss both men.

After McCammon let me go, I wasn't sure if there was a future for me in the Flyers organization. That's when fate took my hand again and I had the next "first day of the rest of my life."

Flyers sales, marketing, and executive account manager

Ticket sales and advertising revenues slumped a little bit for the Flyers around 1983–84. The "Broad Street Bullies" years were over, and the 35-game unbeaten streak was in the rearview mirror.

First-round playoff exits had become the norm for the Flyers in recent years. The Montreal Canadiens had won four straight Stanley Cup championships (the first of which came at our expense) and now the New York Islanders were in the midst of a four-year championship run (once again, the first of which was won against the Flyers).

The Flyers asked me if I'd be interested in working in the sales department, selling tickets. They told me that I still had a recognizable name to potential clients, and that I'd be a natural for the job because I enjoyed meeting and conversing with people. Also, I knew the on-ice product thoroughly.

I decided to give it a try, although I didn't know much of anything about the ins and outs of sales. After starting out selling tickets, I moved to advertising sales. This was totally foreign turf to me at first, selling ads on the dasherboards, team publications, etc.

Thankfully, the late Ivan Schlictman, the Flyers' longtime advertising sales manager, took me under his wing. Before being hired by the Flyers in June of 1972 as the organization's merchandising manager, Ivan spent 14 years as the advertising manager for wholesale tycoon Leon Levine.

Over the course of his long career with the Flyers, Schlictman moved from merchandise sales to spend more than two decades as advertising sales manager and executive account manager. As a mentor in my "second career" (or was this my third?) with the Flyers, Ivan meant as much to me as Harry Sinden and Fred Shero did in my playing days.

I went with Ivan on dozens of sales presentations. He taught me about our product from an advertising standpoint. I'm not a "technology guy"—as stated before, I barely use a personal computer, and I don't carry a cell phone—but Ivan got me comfortable with the technologies of the 1980s. He taught me the terminology that was key to making sales: the words to say and how to say them at the right time.

Beyond that, Ivan encouraged me to just be myself. I've never had trouble making friends, and I'm outgoing by nature. Schlictman told me to use those traits to my benefit. Don't rush the sale. Create a relationship first. Then, when it was time to close the deal, I'd have a sense that the time was right.

That was some of the best advice I was ever given. I could get myself in front of potential clients because they knew of me as a player. Talking Flyers, NHL, or sports in general is a passion of mine, anyway, and that was often the starting place to creating friendships and business relationships.

For much of the next 17 years, that's what I did on a day-to-day basis, selling ads and then managing clients' accounts. I absolutely loved doing it. As a matter of fact, if you'd asked me in 1979 whether I'd get more enjoyment from scouting/coaching for the Flyers or working in sales, I'd have said the former. But as it turned out, the latter was my true calling after my playing days and became my passion.

Over the years, I handled everything from multimillion dollar accounts to much, much smaller ones. Some of the smallest ones, actually, created the longest friendships.

For example, through one of our smaller advertising accounts, I became good friends with the late Kosta Hionis, the owner of the Little Inn on State Rd. in Media. He was so thrilled when Flyers players occasionally came to his restaurant as his special guests. They always got the royal treatment.

Kosta, who passed away on March 25, 2023, originally hailed from Greece and was one of six children. He emigrated to the United States in his early twenties and was a hell of a hard worker. Kosta took great pride in becoming an American and in the success of his business. He owned the Little Inn for 35 years. Just a salt-of-the-earth human being.

A couple examples of our larger accounts: one that was successful and one that we did not land.

During the 1992–93 season, when future Hockey Hall of Fame center Eric Lindros was a rookie with the Flyers, I managed the account in an Ellio's Pizza advertising campaign, "Philly's Hottest Line." The advertising package featured television commercials with Lindros, Mark Recchi, Pelle Eklund, and Bob Clarke (by then a Flyers executive on the hockey operations side). The spot ran during Flyers game broadcasts. Additionally, we also had related print ads in *Philadelphia Flyers Magazine* with Lindros, Recchi, and Eklund, and the Ellio's branding on a dashboard ad at the Spectrum.

Around the same time, while the Flyers' new arena was in development and the organization was looking to sell naming rights, I made a presentation at MBNA's headquarters in Delaware. Lindros and Recchi accompanied me on the presentation. Unfortunately, we didn't land the sale to MBNA, but I did become friendly with some of their upper executives. One later told me that they'd made a mistake not getting in on the ground floor when they had the chance. They didn't realize the Flyers had such a globally recognizable brand.

Can't win them all, but it sure would have been nice to land MBNA as the naming sponsor. It was a $45 million deal, from which I'd have received a five percent commission.

Ultimately, CoreStates Bank purchased the naming rights to the new arena, originally called Spectrum II. When the new building opened in 1996, it was called the CoreStates Center. Later, it became the First Union Center, the Wachovia Center, and, more recently, the Wells Fargo Center.

Over my years of working on the business end of the Flyers' organization, three of my closest friends were John Page, Peter Luukko, and Zack Hill. It was also great to continue to work in the same building with my buddy, the Hound.

John, the longtime president of the Wells Fargo Center, was with Comcast-Spectacor (specifically Spectra Venue Management) from 2004 to

2011. As president of Spectra, he was directly responsible for the rapid expansion of the company's footprint as it grew from 40 facilities in 2004 to more than 185 in 2020. As busy as John was, he always made himself available, and I've always loved talking to him and socializing with him. Peter was Comcast-Spectacor president and a lifelong hockey lover (and recreational player).

Zack, who worked 30 years with the Flyers starting in 1993, had the unenviable task of succeeding the legendary Joe Kadlec as manager of both media relations and public relations and as director of communications. He made a very tough job seem easy and is one of my best buddies for life. We've hung out together countless times over the years.

Every year, including since my retirement, I host a get-together to which I invite some of my longtime clients who've become good friends. We had our most recent one at The Prime Rib, located in the Live Casino in South Philadelphia near the sports stadium complex.

John Page—former president of Wells Fargo Center

It's been an honor to know Joe for 30-plus years. I'm proud to call him my friend, and he's a part of our family. Here's one of my favorite memories about Joe.

Right after he was cleared to resume full activity after having his knee replaced and leg lengthened from his career-ending fracture, we went golfing. As usual, whether or not he has honors, he stepped right up to tee off. Took a mighty swing and immediately went face down on the ground. He had some scar tissue come loose and let out quite a squeal. I was part laughing and obviously concerned and asked him if someone shot him. I helped him up, and his response was, "Geez, buddy! That wasn't good. I felt like I got shot in the leg."

We had a good chuckle and finished the round. Had a few babalooeys afterward and continued to laugh about how hard he went down.

The Flyers Alumni Association

I never actually stopped playing and teaching hockey after my career-ending injury. Once I was able to skate again, I played in a couple of Flyers' old-timers' games at the Spectrum in the early 1980s. In 1984, the Flyers Alumni Association was formed.

For the next 32 years, I was the scheduling manager of the Flyers Alumni Team and also played for the team. We barnstormed rinks both near and far, playing in benefits and raising money for various charities. We raised millions of dollars for worthy causes such as Junior Achievement, the Boys and Girls Club, police officers injured in the line of duty, etc.

During the 1980s and 1990s, the Flyers Alumni Team also traveled across the United States, Canada, and Europe to play in senior hockey tournaments, bringing the Flyers Alumni brand to Switzerland, Germany, Finland, and Norway. We also took a group vacation to Italy.

In 1996, the Flyers Alumni played a game at the Spectrum against members of the 1980 United States Olympic team's Miracle on Ice squad. The game received large-scale local coverage and even some national media attention.

On New Year's Eve 2011, the Flyers and the NHL hosted a multigenerational game at Citizens Bank Park in Philadelphia, pitting the Flyers Alumni against the New York Rangers Alumni. Roughly 45,000 fans attended the outdoor game.

Since that time, the Flyers Alumni Team played a sold-out game at the Wells Fargo Center against the Pittsburgh Penguins Alumni in January 2017 to commemorate the fiftieth anniversary of the Flyers and Penguins franchises.

In November 2021, two separate Flyers Alumni squads—Team Holmgren and Team Tocchet—played "the Hall of Fame Game" at the Wells Fargo Center as part of the celebration of the Flyers Hall of Fame inductions of Paul Holmgren and Rick Tocchet. I played in the Hall of Fame game at age 78—the only player from the inaugural 1967–68 Flyers team still participating in an Alumni game.

One of the most special and ambitious events the Flyers Alumni participated in was a goodwill hockey tour of Russia back in February 2017. We played games against Russian alumni teams in Kazan, St. Petersburg, and on the outdoor rink at Red Square in Moscow. The games in Kazan and St. Petersburg sold out the arenas. That was due to the allure of the Flyers brand itself. I only wish Mr. Snider had been alive to see it.

Given the current situation in Russia and return of Cold War–like tensions with the West, a similar type of trip may be impossible for the

Over the years, the Flyers Alumni Team (literally) traveled the world representing the Flyers name and crest as well as playing dozens of local benefit games across the Delaware Valley and throughout Pennsylvania. One of our most memorable trips was a hockey goodwill tour of Russia, playing games in Kazan, St. Petersburg, and Moscow. In this game against Team Tatarstan in Kazan, I met Rustam Minnikhanov. Mr. Minnikhanov, who is the president of the Republic of Tatarstan, played in the game.

foreseeable future. But we all had a wonderful time and great experiences on the trip. Russian media interviewed us at every stop of the tour.

The number-one question I was asked was this: tell me about the Flyers–Red Army game in 1976 and the goal you scored on the great Tretiak. Virtually all the reporters were born well after '76 and probably never saw the game, but they knew of it. Another humbling moment to realize that I'd been part of one of the most famous international games in hockey history.

For the last seven years, Brad Marsh has been the president of the Flyers Alumni Association. Early on, he took over scheduling big-venue events as well as planning signature fundraising events and community initiatives for the Flyers Alumni Association. He's done an incredible job. The Flyers Alumni Association is one of the best funded across the NHL alumni realm and does some of the most extensive and ambitious charitable work in the community.

The Alumni, for example, made a $2 million donation pledge to the Ed Snider Youth Hockey Foundation (now called Snider Hockey and

Education), reaching the $1 million mark in direct donations in 2022 and continuing to raise money to make good on the other $1 million.

One of the Flyers Alumni's signature programs is called "Every Child Deserves a Bike." This campaign, launched just before Christmas in 2019, provides special-needs children in the Delaware Valley with fully customized adaptive bicycles. The program was recognized by the *Philadelphia Business Journal* in 2023 with a Faces of Philanthropy award. Jimmy, Hound, and I came out to see Marshy accept the award.

Bottom line: I am so proud of all that our Alumni Association does and what it's grown into in the nearly 40 years since a group of us co-founded it and I was asked to manage the Alumni Team component. It's only become bigger and better since Marshy took it over.

There are so many stories from our Alumni Team games through the years that I could do an entire chapter on it. I owe a special thank you to our longtime trainer and equipment manager, Dave Culp. Having Culpy is like having an NHL-level trainer and equipment manager on hand. He's also a laugh riot to be around and one of the nicest people I know.

While many of our Alumni Team players were NHL players with the Flyers or other NHL clubs, we've also had many regulars on the team who played at other levels of the sport, such as my nephews Chase and Brett (Jimmy's sons). One of my closest friends who spent many years with the Alumni Team is Don Julich, a member of the New Jersey High School Hockey Hall of Fame. I asked Don to share some memories.

Don Julich, longtime Flyers Alumni Team member

Back in 2001, shortly before 9/11, I participated in a hockey camp in Montreal, where both the New York Rangers Alumni and the Flyers Alumni were on hand. Joe and I became fast friends, and he asked if I would be interested in playing for the Flyers Alumni. I'm a diehard Rangers fan, but this one was a no-brainer. I would up playing eight-plus years with the Flyers Alumni Team. We went everywhere: not just across Pennsylvania, New Jersey, and Delaware, but all over the US, Canada, and Europe.

I never played in the NHL, but Joe always treated me like I had. At first, I was gun shy about signing autographs. Joe confronted me about it.

He said, "As long as you've got this uniform on, you're part of our Alumni Team. We all represent the Flyers Alumni. If I hear that some kid is upset because he asked you for an autograph and you turned him down, you and I are going to have a problem."

That made it much easier to loosen up. It also made me feel like a genuine part of the team.

I remember one trip we had to Europe. Joe sat in bulkhead on the plane, and my wife and I were in the next row behind. He's the only person I've ever seen who whistles while he sleeps. He was sound asleep for hours, whistling the whole time.

I was not along on an infamous trip to Norway, but I've heard this story many times. With Joe, you'd better not be late. During the Norway trip, Al Secord and Ed Hospodar were late for the bus. Joe had the bus leave without them. That's how seriously he took the Alumni Team.

I was along when the Flyers Alumni were in Finland. At the first game, which was played against a Finnish legends team, the likes of Jari Kurri, Esa Tikkanen, and Christian Ruuttu suited up. There were 9,000 people in the stands. Joe, who was essentially our team's coach, used only two lines. We lost, 4–2, after leading 2-1 in the third period.

After the game, Joe apologized to me and told me I'd get out there next game, which was the next morning against a Russian team. We lost that one, too.

At any rate, let's just say that the referee called the game as if the vintage Broad Street Bullies were on the ice. Marginal calls galore against us. Oh man was Joe mad!

We had another game—this one was in Pennsylvania somewhere in the middle of the state—when one of the other team's players cross-checked Joe in the back. I punched the guy in the face. That was the one time Joe ever got genuinely mad at me on the ice.

It's been some years since I played with the Alumni Team, but my friendship with Joe will be lifelong. I live in Florida now, and Joe and Jamie sometimes come down to visit.

Joe is one of the most unique people I've ever met. There's nothing he won't do for a friend. We've had so many great times, on the ice and off.

Here's a quick off-ice story about what being friends with Joe is like. I came down to Philly one time to see an afternoon Flyers vs. Rangers game. Afterward, we were going to go out for dinner at the Capital Grille. We were told there were no reservations until 10:00 p.m.

I said to Jamie, "Do they know the reservation is for Joe? Call back, ask for the manager, and tell him it's for two-time Stanley Cup champion and Flyers Hall of Famer Joe Watson."

She was reluctant to do it because it's not really Joe's style to ask for celebrity treatment. But she did, and the manager got us a table for seven o'clock. The manager and Joe ended up becoming good friends.

Hollywood All-Stars

In the mid-1990s, I toured and played as part of the Hollywood All-Stars team. We played against various NHL Alumni Teams in their home buildings. I played for the Flyers Alumni side when the tour came to Philly in 1996 but suited up for the Hollywood All-Stars elsewhere. When we were in Boston, I received a nice introduction as a former Bruins player and got a warm ovation from the crowd. I doubt anyone there was old enough to have seen me play during my NHL rookie year.

The tour was a lot of fun, both on and off the ice. The best players among the bonafide celebrities: Dave Coulier, Matthew Perry, Mike Meyers (for a few games), Alex Trebek, and Alan Thicke. Famed saxophonist Clarence Clemons was one of our "coaches." The biggest party animal on the tour, by far, was Kelsey Grammer of *Cheers* and *Frasier* fame.

By his own admission, Alex Trebek may have been the worst native Canadian to ever try his hand at playing hockey. He'd never played when he was growing up. In fact, he could barely skate, but he took it all in good humor. I can truthfully say that he was one of the nicest people that I've ever met. Just a kind, gentle soul. Rest in peace.

I forged some great friendships that lasted long beyond the tour. I became particularly friendly with actor Jason Priestley, a fellow British Columbia native. I also bonded with Lochlyn Munro, a veteran of film and TV roles who also hails from BC.

My two homes: Philadelphia and Smithers

It's been more than 56 years since I first laid eyes on the city and saw the machine chopping up discarded automobiles. Fifty-six years since that "welcoming parade" down Broad Street that almost nobody attended!

Back in 1967, I wasn't very confident that the Flyers or I would still be in Philadelphia come the summer of 1968. Now it's 56 years later, and I'm still here.

I remain a Canadian citizen and carry a Canadian passport—I never applied for American citizenship, although my brother Jim obtained his US citizenship, and my son and daughter have dual citizenship as the American-born and raised offspring of two Canadian parents—but I'm a proud Philadelphian through and through.

Sometimes I think about friends I've made locally over the years from all walks of life. I'm talking about everyday people and lifelong Flyers fans, not just the "celebrity" names from the realms of sports, business, politics, and entertainment whom I've befriended. Collectively, Philadelphians have a tough outer shell, but they also wear their hearts on their sleeve. Once they embrace you as one of their own, it's forever. My kind of people!

I've always lived in Pennsylvania since joining the Flyers. I don't know why, exactly. During the 1970s especially, many of the Flyers players resided in South Jersey, but I've always lived in Pennsylvania. Early on, I lived in Upper Darby (specifically on Ridley Pike). I was there for about two or three years. During our Stanley Cup years, I lived in Lansdowne Towers, six miles from the city. Teammate Tom Bladon was a neighbor. Subsequently, I resided in Gladstone Towers near longtime Flyers physical trainer (and later successful entrepreneur) Pat Croce.

For many, many years, I lived in a house in Media, Pennsylvania, and I remain in that vicinity. In 2021, my wife, Jamie, and I bought a new house in a development in nearby Elwyn, Pennsylvania, which is an extension of Media. I love the area. Here, you're not far from the city yet also not far from the countryside of Chester County.

A few years ago, the Flyers Alumni hosted a Speaker Series event at the Flyers Training Center (then called the SkateZone) in Voorhees. I was a speaker, along with Bob Kelly, Bill Clement, Dave Schultz, Paul Holmgren, and Brad Marsh.

After I gave my talk and opened the floor for questions, the second question I received was, "What was the old Rexy's like, and do you still go there today?"

Answer: We had a lot of laughs and fun times at the original Rexy's. I've been to the remodeled version (which is under different ownership), but I'm not a regular. If I walked in there, I might not be recognized. Again, time waits for nobody.

The original Rexy's owner, the late Pasquale "Pat" Fietto, was a nice guy and a big Flyers fan as well as a Korean War veteran. His wife, Ginnie, and brother Anthony were salt of the earth people, too. The food at Rexy's was great, the atmosphere was comfortable, and the place became something of a Flyers' shrine. Yes, we really did mourn when Rexy's building was damaged in a 1975 fire. That's not just an urban legend.

The Fietto family sold the business, I think, in the 2010s. There's still a restaurant called Rexy's at that location today—the food is still good, by the way—but it looks very different inside nowadays. You'd never know it was once the Broad Street Bullies' home away from home.

Actually, in the 1980s, most of the young guys on the Flyers chose a different hangout—Kaminsky's on Brace Road in Cherry Hill—but the older generation guys who still lived in the area remained loyal to Rexy's.

Rexy's wasn't our only hangout. In the early 1970s, we enjoyed going to the old Alpine Inn in Springfield, Pennsylvania. We used to have get-togethers with members of the Flyers Fan Club. That's no longer in business, nor is the Little Inn in Media, but I carry fond memories of both places. The Towne House in Media is still open to this day, and I still go occasionally.

Veteran Flyers fans are often curious to ask me if I'm still recognized when I go out somewhere in or around the city. The answer is occasionally, but of course not as often as back in the day. That's totally fine. As Bob Kelly has said, "We're just happy anyone still remembers us."

It's still flattering to be asked for my autograph or to hear stories about where someone was when we won the Stanley Cup or beat the Red Army. It means that people still care. If I can do something to make another person happy—signing an autograph, letting the person try on my Stanley Cup ring for a photo, or whatever—it's an easy way of saying thank you for all the love and support we've received.

I never would have believed that I'd enjoy doing advertising sales for the Flyers more than I liked coaching and scouting. But that's exactly what happened! I loved the work and made a lot of lifelong friends. Here, on November 28, 2022, I got together with old friends and clients. I was retired by this point, but I still greatly looked forward to seeing each of them.

Over the years, as previously noted, I've become friends with various other former Philadelphia pro athletes, including some who played in the same era. I sent my two kids to the same school (Episcopal) as Mike Schmidt sent his children, and we forged a friendship. Larry Bowa is another longtime friend, as are Bill Bergey and Doug Collins.

Here I am visiting Smithers with Philadelphia Eagles legend Bill Bergey and my uncle Wilf. Uncle Wilf has since passed away.

One time, I did a paid signing gig at a sports collectables and memorabilia show. Afterward, I dined at a nearby restaurant with another retired local pro athlete. We were approached for autographs. I signed, but my friend declined. He told me he said his hellos, smiled for photos, and signed everything put in front of him for the contracted hours. Now, his time belonged to him.

We had a difference of opinion. My view was this: These folks were the ones who paid to see us play, helped us make a living. They celebrated or agonized with us. They welcomed us to their places of business. They were our neighbors. They treated us like family. Hell, they're still happy to see us 20, 30, or 40-plus years after our retirements as players. The least we can do in return is to show our appreciation. Without the fans, there's no pro sports.

Without pro hockey in general and the Philadelphia Flyers in particular, I'd never have been able to live out my dreams. I'd never have traveled the world, met so many interesting people, been treated like a VIP, or provided for my family.

Hockey took me out of Smithers and provided so much to me in return. The very fact that I worked for the Flyers in different capacities for 54 years before I retired is something I owe to Ed Snider, the Flyers fans, and the people of Philadelphia.

My two children and remarriage

My son, Ryan, and daughter, Heidi, grew up near Philly. I saw them go to college, become successful in their careers—Heidi in nursing, Ryan in the business world—and later give me grandchildren. How could I feel anything but lucky?

Ryan

When I was growing up, I never thought much about how it was unusual to have a father who was a National Hockey League player. I enjoyed meeting the other players and being around the Spectrum, but I didn't think it was out of the ordinary that my father was a professional athlete.

One lesson my dad taught me early in life was to appreciate the fans. He came

Here I am with my children, Ryan and Heidi, my wife, Jamie, and the Stanley Cup on November 15, 2008.

from humble beginnings in Smithers. I can't even count how many times he'd tell me, "Without the fans, I'd have nothing." He always made time for the fans. He liked the attention, but, above all, he was grateful.

My dad did not graduate high school, but he's always had street smarts. He's also someone who has been all over the world and appreciates that hockey and hard work are what made it possible. He was always very appreciative of Ed Snider giving him an opportunity to make a living back in the Flyers' organization after his playing days, but he still had to earn his keep.

When I was playing sports as a kid, my father was always very supportive of me. He'd come to my games, and he was the loudest parent on the sidelines. I appreciate that more now than I did back then. My dad has always worn his heart on his sleeve.

I think what I appreciate the most is my relationship with my dad as a grown-up. I talk to him at some point virtually every day. We do a lot of father-son things to this day: going skiing, going to a Detroit Lions football game, etc. A lot of it has nothing to do with sports.

Heidi

When I was growing up, I always enjoyed going to Flyers games as a family. For Sunday-afternoon games, we'd go out together afterward to the Towne House in Media.

My dad was always very supportive of me, especially in scholastic sports. He went to pretty much all of my tennis matches—my best sport—and my lacrosse games when I went to Episcopal. He always rooted very vocally for me and for my teams.

When I graduated college, I traveled cross-country for three months with my best friend. She was living in Boston at the time. We bought a Ford Escort wagon and drove it across the country. It was kind of an off-the-wall thing to do, but my dad was understanding and supportive of it.

Nowadays, my dad really enjoys being a grandfather. My son, Watson Riley, is almost eight years old and is starting to play hockey. It's been really cool watching them bond over the sport.

My marriage to Marianne, my children's mother, ultimately didn't work out. There were happy early times and then a lot of pain and anguish down the line. In hindsight, Marianne and I weren't compatible. But I wouldn't wish divorce on anyone. It's agonizing and leaves scars on everyone involved.

Out of it all, though, I have been blessed with wonderful children and grandchildren that I love with all my heart. I wouldn't trade those relationships for anything in the world. I spent a number of years enjoying being single after my ex and I split. In 2009, I married Jamie Comiskey. These have been happy years.

Jamie

Joe's hockey legacy is just part of what makes up the person. There is also an endearing and admirable side of Joe that he won't boast about or take credit for, but it's a side I've witnessed for more than two decades of our life together and one that is equally important to his story. It is about Joe Watson off the ice.

Bill Clement, Joe's fellow Flyers Alum and good friend, shared a story at a Flyers Alumni event about a book entitled "The Dash: Making a Difference with Your Life." The premise is this: It's not about the day you are born or the day that you leave this earth but what you do (the dash) in between those years that really counts.

As tough as Joe could be on the ice, and with all the injuries he sustained in his quest to win, Joe is, and always was, an incredibly compassionate and empathetic man. These qualities are what organically led him to find his "Dash."

Joe's "Dash" came to light when he arrived in Philadelphia in 1967. He didn't know anyone and wasn't familiar with the city. Our country was deeply immersed in the Vietnam War at that time. Less than a mile away from the Spectrum stood the Philadelphia Naval Hospital (now the site of the Nova Care practice facility on Pattison Avenue).

During those years, the Naval Hospital was overflowing with military patients, many from different parts of the US, who had returned from Southeast Asia with serious injuries, facing a long road of recovery. Monday was the Flyers' off day. Joe decided to do what his dad, Joe Sr., used to do after church every Sunday by visiting patients in the local Smithers Hospital. Joe continued the tradition, by focusing on service members who sacrificed so much and needed a warm welcome home, a heartfelt thanks for their service, and inspiration to get well.

He'd arrive at the Naval Hospital, equipped with positive energy, jokes, reading materials, and anything he could think of that might lift the patients' spirits. It wasn't a fun place to visit, but Joe gained something much more meaningful that has inspired him to continue this focus ever since. This weekly activity kept him grounded and humble. It gave him purpose beyond hockey.

As the Flyers organization became a prominent force in the community, requests came in on a regular basis for players to visit a sick child at CHOP or to cheer up a Flyers fan who was facing difficult challenges. Joe never hesitated and became one of many Flyers who would step up and help out any time they were asked.

To this day, it is one of the things that Joe will never say no to. He remembers his own career-ending injury in 1978 and the support he received from so many fans, which motivated him to get back on his feet.

It's not about money, because there is no money in giving back, and it's not always pleasant, but he recognizes that he represents an epic time in Philadelphia sports history, with fans that will never forget their favorite team and who

Bobby Orr and I were the guest instructors at this hockey clinic in Boston in late fall or early winter of 1966. I've always enjoyed teaching the game to youngsters. I've long since lost count of how many hockey clinics I've been the lead or guest instructor at over the years.

remain loyal to this day.

Nothing makes Joe happier than telling a story, sharing encouraging words or a smile with those who need it most. He often comes home wearing his heart and emotions on his sleeve, but he wouldn't trade it for anything. For Joe, it's a privilege to be in a position to turn someone's day around, give them something to smile about, and make a positive difference. As Joe always says, if it wasn't for our fans, we wouldn't be here today.

Joe continues to be involved in the Flyers Alumni that he started in 1984, which raised more than $3.5 million for charities by hosting Alumni/amateur hockey games throughout the Delaware Valley and beyond. Today, under the great leadership of Flyers alumnus Brad Marsh, the Alumni Association has expanded into a robust organization, recognized as a model of excellence by other NHL alumni organizations. Joe's passion for programs such as Every Child Deserves a Bike, Twelve Days of Christmas, and the Flyers Warriors hockey program for disabled veterans allows him to continue serving the community. He gains just as much as those with whom he interacts.

I was a teenager when I left Smithers. But my small hometown and British Columbia in general still mean a lot to me. For many years, I ran summertime hockey clinics for kids—to this day, I still periodically teach the game at some youth hockey clinics in the Philadelphia area—and those were always a joy.

You never know where some of these kids will end up in their lives. As a youngster Mark Recchi attended my clinic in Kamloops. So did someone who has become one of my dearest friends: Kent Delwisch.

Kent, who lives in Smithers, runs the annual Celebrity Golf fundraiser, which is nowadays held every two years. I always come back home for the event, which raises money for the Smithers Hospital foundation and other local worthy causes.

I still have family in Smithers, although my parents are deceased. My father predeceased my mother, who passed away on March 19, 2010 (seven days after her 87th birthday).

A few years ago, I had the opportunity to bring the Stanley Cup to Smithers. I also love to take a semiannual trip back home to go salmon fishing and visit old friends. I enlisted Kent and my brothers Glen and Jerry to talk about my bond with my hometown.

Whenever possible, I love returning to Smithers. Fishing trips are one of my favorite traditions. Some of the best fishing and hunting in the world is there. Northern British Columbia is a haven for lovers of the outdoors.

Kent Delwisch, chairman of Smithers Celebrity Golf

I was born and raised in Vancouver, but my family is from Smithers. My family moved back to Smithers when I was 13. We spent our summers with the Flockhart family, and my uncles grew up with Jimmy Watson. One of them drove all the way to Philadelphia to watch the Stanley Cup Final when the Flyers first won the Cup.

I've known Joe's younger brothers for many years: Steven, Glen, and Jerry. I got to know Joe and Jimmy later on. I participated in one of Joe's offseason minor hockey clinics. All the kids took to Joe right away.

I've been a diehard Flyers fan for as long as I can remember. Wore a sweater with Watson on the back. The Watson brothers were a huge deal in Smithers for many years. We've had other players from here, most recently Dan Hamhuis, and they've all been good guys. I think a lot of the younger kids became Canucks fans. But, for me, it's always been about the Flyers, and the Watson brothers were number one to me.

Of all of the NHL players from around this area of BC, I've never seen one who stays more involved and gives back more to this community than Joe Watson.

It was because of Joe that I first got involved in the celebrity golf event in 1991. He's been involved since the beginning, working his tail off to do his part to make it a special and successful event.

Over the years, Joe has arranged for fellow Flyers and NHL alumni—even Hall of Famers like his old roommate Bobby Orr and Maple Leafs icon Darryl Sittler, who spent a couple seasons with the Flyers late in his career—to come participate. He's brought in athletes from other sports and show business. He's arranged for some truly unique memorabilia and personal experiences to be put up for bidding at our auctions. Every time, he goes above and beyond.

One year, we had a golf event that turned out lackluster compared to previous ones. Joe was a little bit embarrassed after he'd arranged for [famed actor] Jason Priestley, who was a regular attendee, and others to attend. I felt awful for Joe, so I volunteered in 1991 to get involved, and I've been doing it ever since. I became the chairman of the event. It's a big production, so, in its more recent history, we've held it every other year rather than annually.

Over the years, we've raised several million dollars for the community, primarily for our local hospital foundation. Other local community organizations and charities also benefit.

The thing about Joe is that he doesn't believe in doing anything halfway. If he's involved, he's totally committed and goes all out. Hockey took him out of Smithers in 1959, but he always comes back.

In 2019, Joe brought the Stanley Cup to Smithers. That was an incredible experience for everyone, including me. The RCMP escorted the Stanley Cup to Smithers, and we picked up Phil Pritchard, the Hockey Hall of Fame's official keeper of the Cup.

People came out from all over the region, traveling here from hours away, to see the Cup. Joe must have signed 2,500 autographs. He also had the Cup brought to my house for a celebration. There's a photo of Joe, several of his brothers, and the Cup with the Hudson Bay Mountain behind them. I think that's a good example of how deep in Joe's heart he loves Smithers. He may not have lived here in many years, but it's always home.

My longtime friend Kent Delwisch does a heck of a job putting together the Smithers celebrity golf event, which is held every other year and raises money for the local hospital. In 2022, I brought along Flyers Hall of Fame player/coach/GM/president Paul Holmgren and Phillies alum player and general manager Ruben Amaro.

Glen Watson

My favorite story about Joe coming home was his wedding in Smithers. The streets were packed when we came out of the church. There were way more people than lived in Smithers. I asked my mother why so many people were outside to see Joe.

She said, "They're not here to see Joe. They're here to see Bobby Orr!"

Joe always laughs at that story. He's always been able to laugh at himself.

Jerry Watson

Joe and I have a 24-year difference in age. Our poor mother! Joe was well on his way in the NHL by the time I came around. But he never, ever forgets where he came from. He loves his hometown, and the town loves him.

I love this story about Joe that one of his old buddies, Andy Adema, told me. When Joe was in school, a teacher asked the students to write down a story about what they wanted to be when they grew up. Joe wrote, "I want to be a professional hockey player." He caught shit for it, because "you're not being realistic." I think that's a funny one. Joe was right, and everyone else was wrong.

Joe was a great athlete in every sport he played. He did everything well.

An old friend named Bill Kilpatrick told me this story. Joe played in a big baseball tournament. Hit the hell out of the ball. As you know, Joe had an offer from the New York Yankees but turned it down because he thought he had a better shot at a pro career in hockey. Even so, I think it's amazing that he was good enough in two different sports that he had professional scouts interested.

Speaking of old friends, I'd be remiss if I didn't a shoutout to my old baseball teammate and friend of 60-plus years Steven Rea. Steven wasn't born in Smithers but moved there in the early 1960. He was a heck of a pitcher on our baseball team and a longtime. radio DJ. I bought my first-ever insurance policy from his dad, paying $9.25 per month. When the policy matured, it yielded a real nice payoff.

In loving memory of Ed Snider and Fred Shero

As I conclude with one more thank you to everyone who has touched my life in one way or another—far more than I could list, but none are unappreciated in my heart—I want to share my final memories of Fred Shero and Ed Snider.

Freddy passed away at age 65 on November 24, 1990. I visited him in Cooper Hospital in Camden, New Jersey, one day before he died. Even to his last breath, Freddy was consumed by hockey. He diagrammed a set play and gave it to me to teach.

His late wife, Mariette, said in 1975, "My husband shows affection through hockey. The game is in his every thought."

Giving me a play to use on the ice was the final gift and lesson I received from Freddy. It was his way of saying, "I love you, Joe." I loved the man, too. So many great things and so much wisdom came into my life from him.

In 2016, not long before his death on April 11 at age 83, I visited Ed Snider at his California residence. He flew me out west in his private plane, along with Bob Clarke, Bernie Parent, Comcast-Spectacor attorney Phil Weinberg, Chief Financial Officer Sandy Lipstein, and a couple of other people with whom he was close.

We watched a Flyers game: a win. One of the last things he said to me is, "Joe, a lot of people know each other for 50 years. There's not many who can also say they worked together for 50 years."

Two longtime servers at the Spectrum, Rose and Ann, were also there. That's how loyal and caring Mr. Snider was to those who loyally worked for him. It was a two-way street to his dying day.

The years since my arrival in Philadelphia have been the happiest of my life. Without Ed Snider's generosity, passion, love, and will to succeed, none of it would have been possible. I miss him every single day.

This photo of Ed Snider, Jimmy, and me was taken on December 31, 2011, after the Winter Classic Alumni Game at Citizens Bank in Philadelphia. Roughly 45,000 people attended the game as the Flyers Alumni defeated the Rangers Alumni.

ACKNOWLEDGMENTS

This book would not have been possible without the encouragement and support of my wife, Jamie. I had never thought about writing a book before she suggested it.

Thank you to my coauthor, Bill Meltzer, for the research, dozens upon dozens of hours of interviews, photo sorting, fact-checking, and editing that went into the writing of this book. A big thank you also goes to my old friend and NHL rookie year roommate, Bobby Orr, for contributing the foreword to this book.

Special thanks go out to my son, Ryan, and my daughter, Heidi, not only for sharing stories for chapter 14 of this book but also for how proud they've made me as a father. Thank you also to longtime friends Larry Miller and Teddy Veenstra for sharing stories from Smithers and to old buddy "Stubby" McClain for his recollections of the old days. I greatly appreciate the friendship shared with—and stories shared by—Kent Delwisch, John Page, Don Julich, Phil Martin, and Bill Whitmore.

Thank you to my Oklahoma City Blazers teammate Glen Sather for his recollections of our junior hockey rivalry and lifelong friendship forged as teammates during our Adams Cup championship season.

I owe a debt of gratitude to all my coaches through the years, from the late Joe Tennant in Smithers and the late Scotty Munro in Estevan. I could never repay Harry Sinden for his coaching in the minor leagues and the

NHL with the Boston Bruins, and the lifetime friendship ever since. More than I can ever say, I appreciate Harry's generosity in sharing stories for this book. Likewise, words can't express my appreciation to the late Keith Allen and the late Fred Shero in Philadelphia.

Thank you, also, to Vic Stasiuk in Philadelphia. Vic and I had our differences on a hockey level, but he was a good man who led a long and fulfilling life in and away from our sport. I enjoyed my time with the Colorado Rockies and appreciate the trust coach Pat Kelly and team owner Arthur Imperatore had in me.

A huge thank you goes out to all of my old teammates—too many to mention all individually, but many of whom are discussed in the book—especially my Broad Street Bullies teammates with whom I won the Stanley Cup twice. Thank you to my teammates on the Bruins, the Flyers, the Flyers Alumni Team, the Hollywood All-Stars, and all our trainers and equipment managers.

Thank you to my colleagues and mentors with the Flyers organization, especially the late Ivan Schlictman. Thank you to Zack Hill, the Flyers Alumni Association, and, above all, the late Ed Snider. My appreciation goes out to all my clients, both for their business and for their lasting friendships.

Thank you to my five brothers. Jimmy, of course, was my longtime teammate on the Flyers, but there were six of us in all. The Watson boys were a handful. Thank you to our late father, Joe Watson Sr., for his pride in all of his boys' accomplishments. Thank you to my late uncles, especially my uncle Wilf, who taught me how to skate: the gift of a lifetime.

Eternal thanks to my late mother, Mary Watson: a wonderful, loving mother, my first and most devoted fan (and the number-one supporter of hockey in Smithers). This book is dedicated to her, in loving memory.

Last but not least, thank you to all the hockey fans worldwide!

ABOUT THE AUTHOR

JOE WATSON played in the NHL for fourteen seasons, winning two Stanley Cups in the 1970s with the Philadelphia Flyers as a key defenseman on their legendary Broad Street Bullies teams. As a player, he was a two-time All-Star selection and a member of the Flyers Hall of Fame. After his playing career, he served for decades as a top advertising executive with the team, closing more than $50 million in sales with major brands. In 1984, he established the Flyers Alumni Team, which has raised millions of dollars for charity and provided opportunities for former players to play exhibitions promoting hockey around the world.